D0853392

IN THE LIKENESS OF CHRIST

"LOOKING ON JESUS
THE AUTHOR AND PERFECTER OF FAITH,
WHO FOR THE JOY THAT WAS SET BEFORE HIM,
ENDURED THE CROSS,
DESPISING THE SHAME,
AND NOW HE SITTETH ON THE RIGHT HAND
OF THE THRONE OF GOD."

(Heb. xii. 2.)

IN THE LIKENESS
OF CHRIST

By
REV. EDWARD LEEN,
C.S.Sp., M.A., D.D.

But you have not so learned Christ if so be
that you have heard Him, *and have been
taught in Him,* as the truth is in Jesus.
(Eph. iv. 20–21.)

BT 205 L486 1936 glas
Leen, Edward, 1885-1944.
In the likeness of Christ / by

Computer ID: 07856

IMPRIMI POTEST: D. MURPHY, C.S.SP.
PRAEP. PROV. HIB.
NIHIL OBSTAT: ERNESTUS C. MESSENGER, PH.D.
CENSOR DEPUTATUS.
IMPRIMATUR: ✠ JOSEPH BUTT
VIC. GEN.
WESTMONASTERII, DIE 21A MARTII 1936

2238
BQT
8565
1950
CISTERCIAN ABBEY
OUR LADY OF THE GENESEE

PRINTED IN THE UNITED STATES OF AMERICA

CONTENTS

PART I

THE FORESHADOWINGS OF CONFLICT

" To them that dwelt in the region of the shadow of death light is risen."—Is. ix. 2.

PART II

THE VICTORY OF THE VANQUISHED

" Set for the fall and for the Resurrection of many in Israel."—St. Luke ii. 34.

PART III
THE HARVEST OF VICTORY

"If you be risen with Christ, seek the things that are above."— Coloss. iii. 1.

INTRODUCTION

" Be it known to you all and to all the people of Israel that by the name of our Lord Jesus Christ of Nazareth. . . . Whom God hath raised from the dead, even by Him, this man standeth here before you, whole. . . . Neither is there salvation in any other. For there is no other name under heaven given to men whereby we must be saved."—ACTS iv. 10–12.

IN a previous work, to which the present one is meant to be somewhat in the nature of a sequel, it was pointed out that it was contact with the Sacred Humanity of the Saviour that wrought the spiritual transformation of the soul. The process of transformation is a process of divinisation, as a result of which the soul becomes more and more " deiform," to borrow a very expressive term from the early ecclesiastical writers and doctors of the Church. In this change the soul sheds its " natural " [1] tendencies and habits, having them gradually replaced by those which are spiritual or heavenly. The new vitality of thought, judgment and aspiration developed in the interior reflects the intellectual and affective life of God Himself. Divine tastes take the place of earthly. It is to this objective that Jesus directed the aspirations of His hearers when He said, " Be you perfect as also your heavenly Father is perfect." [2] The contrast that St. Paul draws between the First Adam and the Second Adam perfectly expresses the contrast between the

---

[1] In the sense of perverse nature.
[2] St. Matt. v. 48.

ix

state of the soul prior to its purification and its state
after that purification has been accomplished. " The
first Adam was made into a living soul; the last Adam
into a quickening spirit. *Yet that was not first which
is spiritual, but that which is natural;* afterwards that
which is spiritual. *The first man was of the earth,
earthly; the second man, from heaven, heavenly.*" [3]
The purified soul has the qualities and characteristics
of this " second man " when it has clothed itself with
the Spirit of Jesus, as the Apostle exhorts the Ephesians
to do, when he bids them " to put off according to
former conversation the old man, who is corrupted
according to the desire of error " and " to put on the
new man, who according to God, is created in Justice
and holiness of truth ".[4]   In another place he gives
greater precision to his thought and shows his followers
what practical steps they are to take to carry out this
work of " renovation " in themselves. He points out
to them that the putting off of the old man and the
putting on of the new is nothing else than the deliberate
moulding of themselves to the spiritual form of the
God-Man, Jesus Christ. " Put ye on," he admonishes
the Romans, " the Lord Jesus and make not provision
for the flesh and its concupiscences."[5]   The whole
effort of Christian perfection lies in the endeavour to
conform oneself to the spirit of the human life of Jesus
Christ. It consists in consciously ordering the inner
movements of the soul and their translation into visible
action, with a view to assimilating oneself to Christ

[3] 1 Cor. xv. 45–47.
[4] Eph. iv. 22–24.
[5] Rom. xiii. 14.

both in one's inner life of thought, affection and decision and in one's external life of religion, right dealing and charity.

Now what the soul, eager to advance, and completely won to the ideal of " putting on Christ," desires above all else to know is, how is this to be done ? What practical co-operation is it called on, itself, to furnish in order that its lofty ambition be gratified ? In effecting divine instincts in the soul, the Holy Ghost is principal agent. Results of a divine kind can proceed only from a cause which is, itself, divine. But God deigns to make use of an instrument in carrying out this work of the sanctification of His creatures. That instrument is the Sacred Humanity of Jesus—it is Jesus, as expressed in the whole sum of His earthly experience, active, as well as passive. All know this. But there is another element in this process which is not so commonly understood. God's action, of course, is not held up by, nor is it, necessarily, gravely impeded by His creatures' want of knowledge of the way of the divine operations. But that ignorance does hamper progress to some appreciable extent and its removal can be of considerable consequence for the soul's advancement in the divine life. Efforts cannot be perfectly well directed unless there is a clear vision of the course they are to follow, the actual form they should take, and the objective they are to aim at. It does not need much experience to know that a vast deal of honest spiritual endeavour is haphazard and ineffective because ill-directed. Without exactly coming to a conclusion about it or formulating it as a principle, very many labour under the false notion that only certain elements of their daily human existence, as, for instance, their prayers, almsdeeds, reception of the Sacraments and devotions work towards the sanctification of the soul. It is only their specially religious acts that, in their half-formed thought, they associate with this work of spiritualisation. Without, of course, holding it as a theory, practically they act as if they judged that sanctifying effects in their souls were linked to a certain limited and definite number of their human experiences—to those that would be ordinarily understood as their distinctively religious ones. Few grasp the far-reaching significance of the well-known words of St. Paul: " Whether you eat or drink, or whatever else you do, do all to the glory of God." [6] This is more than a pious exhortation to the cultivation of a right intention ; it is the formulation of a profound truth—a truth too little understood. The supernatural life, as has been so often repeated in these recent years, is not something apart from, or beside, much less in opposition to, or destructive of the natural. It is the natural elevated, transmuted, penetrated through and through with a divine leaven. Grace necessarily implies the existence of what it elevates. It presupposes human life, not partially or in some scattered and isolated elements, but in its totality. It is the life of man, as man, that grace sets out to sublimate and refine unto the refinement of God. It is through man's own life, taken in all its activities and passivities, in its thoughts, views, judgments, decisions, in its deliberate emotions and reactions ; in its outward activities as guided by his rational faculties ; in all its willed contact with circumstances, with things, with men and with God ; it is

<hr>

[6] 1 Cor. x. 31.

through and by means of all this that man is to be wrought to a better, to a divine form.

The instrument of man's sanctification is, in a subordinate sense, man's own human life.[7] This conclusion is not in contradiction to but supplementary to the statement made above, namely, that the human life of Christ is the instrument of the divinity in the divinisation of the human soul. For the work of sanctification consists, precisely, in establishing vital contact between two life experiences—the life experience of Christ and the life experience of the christian. Everything is in that. There must be a species of interpenetration of these two lives in which that of Jesus moulds the other to its own spirit. There can be no compenetration in a material sense. As external individual happenings, the *facts* of the days of Jesus on earth cannot be the *facts* of the days of His followers. It is in the mental world, that is in the realm of the spirit, that men can be at one ; in the material world, that is in the realm of matter, they are divided.[8] It is therefore in thought, ideal and principles that there is to be established oneness in the lives of Christ and the christian. " Let that *mind* be in you," said St. Paul to his disciples, " which was also in the Christ Jesus." [9] When the " mind " of Jesus penetrates the doings and voluntary

---

[7] By human life is meant only that life that is made up of the sum total of what the moralists call human acts, that is, acts proceeding from the will under the control of reason. These are also called deliberate acts.

[8] " If men remain in the plane of their sensible needs and their sentimental selves, they tell their stories to one another in vain ; they cannot understand each other. . . . But once touch—*the true*, then contact is established and souls communicate. Men are only really united by the spirit ; intellectualia et rationalia congregans, et indestructibilia faciens."—Maritain : *Art et Scolastique*, Chap. V. Cf., also, *Theonas*, Chap. VIII., *Le mythe du progres*.

[9] Philipp. ii. 5.

endurings of a man's life, then is his soul open to receive the influence of the divine life of grace, perfecting in it the image of God.

Souls won by a strong impulse of grace to the divine ideal are often at a loss as to the steps they are to take to realise that ideal. They want God and they would gladly be taught how to get Him. The penetration into the world of the real interior life presents many of the features of a military adventure. For success, the operations must be rightly ordered, and directed towards a clearly seen objective or series of objectives. Serious reverses are almost certainly to be encountered if the first measures of the campaign are ill-conceived or if, what is more perilous still, the commander does not know on what point to direct his opening attack. In the spiritual campaign, what is the line of approach to be adopted by the person who is eager to advance? Grace, since it does not destroy nature, takes it into account, in its action, and makes it serve its purpose. Hero worship is an ordinary instinct in man. Those who are not born leaders (and even leaders themselves have their own idols in actual fact or in fiction or in history) instinctively look for some man whom they can look up to, admire, imitate and follow. This is the instinct that is to be turned into account in the interior life. The first step in the spiritual ways is to aim at developing and cultivating a strong personal admiration for Jesus of Nazareth—Who loves to style Himself the Son of Man. By a psychological law, admiration begets love, and love inspires imitation. He who admires the Man Jesus will feel impelled to imitate Him in His life, His principles and His actions.

It is a matter of common observation that those who
look up to and admire other characters tend, insensibly,
to shape their thoughts and conduct to the pattern of
the thoughts and conduct of such characters. The
willing and devoted follower is gradually moulded to
the form of his chief. This proceeds, at times, to an
amusing reproduction of the exterior ways, the walk
and the very mannerisms of the person who is " worshipped ". In a somewhat similar way the human
character of the Christ gradually forms to its own likeness
those who strive to cultivate an enthusiastic admiration
for Him. The acquisition of this spirit of admiration
is a matter of striving and effort. To our nature, vitiated
by the effects of original sin, what is humanly perfect,
even though it be humanly perfect, does not make a
strong appeal. Where that perfection is the perfection
of nature as wholly surrendered to the supernatural, it
makes no appeal whatsoever to the natural man. It is
extremely difficult for the fallen children of Adam, not
only to see what is right, but, also, to love what is truly
good and worthy of admiration and love. It is only
gradually and by efforts that the soul can be brought to
find in Jesus its ideal. When this point has been gained
a considerable advance has been made towards the
conquest of the divine. Much remains still to be done.

Jesus has one supreme advantage over all other
human leaders. The influence of these on their followers
is purely psychological. That of Jesus on His is
mystical as well as, and far more than, psychological.
For Jesus is not only man ; He, the same person, is
also God. His Personality is divine. The actions of
the great chiefs, that have from time to time made

their appearance in human annals, are exercised on the masses that follow them, through the senses and the imagination. They are limited to that. They can stir the emotions and sway the passions of man; they cannot directly make men other than they are. They cannot put their own spirit or their own force or their own greatness into those that swear loyalty to them. If these latter are changed, the change is due to their own deliberate decisions and actions. But Jesus can directly change His adherents and mould them to His Own Soul. He can put His Own spirit and His Own power into them. The divinity works through the Sacred Humanity and directly gaining the hearts and souls of men can work transforming effects there. Grace reinforces and gives supernatural energy to the natural psychological influence of a Great Personality on its admirers. When one has learnt to admire Jesus, and through that admiration is insensibly drawn to imitate Him, the grace of the Man-God enters into action to make that imitation real and effective, in the inner dispositions of the soul and in the outward forms of conduct.

Admiration for a man can exist even when he is known only by fame or by history; but such admiration is but bloodless and uninspiring, compared with that which is begotten by seeing and hearing him. Can we know Jesus only through hearing about Him, and is our admiration for Him to be restricted to the academic kind that is generated by mere history? In a certain true sense we can see and hear Jesus. The pages of the Gospel enable us to do so. But they do this only for those who read them with a firm faith in the divinity

as well as in the humanity of Jesus Christ. Those who
have not that faith may draw from the study of the
inspired pages a great enthusiasm for the moral beauty
of the person portrayed in these pages—but that admiration is powerless to exercise any supernaturalising
transformation. It is but the admiration that can be
extended to any historical person whose greatness stirs
the imagination and wins the approbation of the reader.
To faith, Jesus is not merely a historical person who
has lived and is no longer; He is a person Who has
lived and yet lives. Hence for faith He lives and moves
and breathes, and is seen in the pages of the Gospel.
It is the study of these pages; it is viewing in faith what
is set forth there that will transform the soul to the
likeness of Jesus and so adapt it for the inflow of the
divine life which is stored in the Sacred Humanity as
in an immense reservoir. For " in Him, dwelleth all
the fulness of the Godhead corporally ".[10] St. Paul so
tells us, and St. John corroborates his words, stating
that to Him was given the spirit without measure.[11]
A twofold effect flows from cultivating an admiration
for and practising an imitation of Jesus Christ. According as the faithful soul reproduces in its life of thought,
emotion and volition the features of the thoughtful,
emotional and volitional life of the Saviour, there is
given to it an abundant outpouring of the Holy Ghost.
The Third Divine Person dwells in the soul more fully
and more perfectly; and whilst being thus present
there in a more intimate manner than before, also
occupies Himself in fashioning the spirit in which He
dwells to an ever greater and closer resemblance to the

---

[10] Coloss. ii. 8.
[11] St. John iii. 34.

spirit of Christ. It is the active conforming oneself to Christ that paves the way for this inpouring of God, the Holy Ghost, into the soul—as was insinuated by the Saviour Himself at the last Supper, in His discourse to the apostles. He said to them : " If any one love me (and conforming oneself to Christ is but love practically expressed), he will keep My word, and My Father will love him, and We will come to him and will make Our abode with him."[12]

If, then, there is to be a serious development of the divine life in the soul, rightly conceived and success-assured procedure demands that mind and heart and imagination be " steeped " in the spirit of the earthly career of Christ, the Son of God. This " steeping " process consists in a deliberately elected, sustained and purposive study of the writings of the Evangelists. This study must be one of deliberate purpose ; if it is spasmodic, careless and haphazard on the part of the beginner the effects and results will be poor in the extreme. It is only through, and in the pages of the Gospels that contact is made with the spirit of Jesus— at least, such contact as is educative of mind and will and heart. That such contact be vital it is needful that the study of the Gospel be loving and sympathetic as well as controlled and guided by the motive of disposing the soul for union with the divine through this means. That the Gospel be effective for this purpose it must be for the reader not a mere record of what has been, but the presentation of actions, scenes, mysteries, doings and sufferings instinct with actuality and life. The incidents of the life of Jesus must be, for the aspirant after a spiritual life, as incidents which are really taking

12 St. John xiv. 23.

place before his eyes as he meditates, and as happenings in which he himself takes part. This is not a vain make-believe. In what is substantial and vitalising in the actions of the God-Man, that is, in their supernatural elements, these actions are of a perennial actuality. They are always being enacted. The divinity in Christ lifts the Sacred Humanity, serving as an instrument in the work of divinising the world, above the vicissitudes of time. That is, the human life of Christ, as sanctifying souls, transcends the conditions of time.

If the meditation on the Gospel is to prove formative, the Gospel must " live " for him that meditates. The beginner will, at first, experience an immense difficulty, if not an utter impossibility, in making it do so. In spite of all the good will he brings to his reading, he will find that it means little to him. If he knows anything of the lives of the saints, he will have learned that the inspired pages yield them up immense resources of light and inspiration. It is somewhat disheartening to find that what is so full of warmth and life for the servants of God is for him cold and lifeless. Do what he may " the Gospel does not speak to him "—that is the way in which he would express the fruitlessness of his efforts. The inspired word does not illuminate his mind, warm his heart or exercise any perceptible dynamic effect on his will. It is not that the text is difficult to understand. The main obstacle to its producing a vitalising effect seems to be the facility with which it may be understood. The sentences are so plain that they do not interest or exercise the mind ; they open up no avenues of thought, suggest no development, stir no emotions. They do not " grip " like a romance. As one turns over page after page the meaning of what one reads is almost irritatingly obvious. The simple and somewhat bald statements have all the nervelessness of a series of platitudes. The mind remains sluggish and inert under, and does not vitally react to the perusal of the story told by the Evangelists. Saints and others may speak in glowing terms of the beauty of the Sacred record and exalt the forceful simplicity of the Sacred writers' style—the average beginner feels little or nothing of all this. His experience does not corroborate that of these others, for whom the history of Jesus means so much. If the person who is all eager to make his way into the world of the interior life, but is still at the threshold, were to use a simile to express the results of his efforts to break the seal of the Gospels, he would, or could, put it in this way : the words, the phrases and the maxims of Jesus remain on the surface of his mind, like inert stones on the surface of a frozen lake. They do not penetrate and set up an agitation in the bosom of the waters. In listening to musical compositions by the great masters, a person who has no ear for, or understanding of music, experiences a pang of keen envy as he sees, in the rapt expressions and glowing eyes of those about him how they are drinking in delight and inspiration from what is to him but agreeable sound. In some such relation stands the deeply interior soul and the average one in presence of the exquisite harmonies of another world rendered to us in the words of the four Evangelists.

The Gospel is as a sealed casket in which are enclosed inexhaustible treasures of light and inspiration. The seal can be broken, but the breaking of it demands, as a rule, courageous and prolonged effort. The novice in the spiritual life must not be discouraged at gathering, in the beginning, such little fruit, in the way of suggestive thought and warm affections, from his meditations on the words and scenes set forth in the inspired pages. If he perseveres, things will gradually undergo a change. If his study be supported by a careful fulfilment of the will of God in the details of his daily life and by steady and reasonable mortification, the dry bones of the text will begin perceptibly to clothe themselves with flesh, grow warm with life, and become endowed with eloquence and persuasiveness. It is astonishing how restraint and mortification sharpen the spiritual vision and make it keenly perceptive of supernatural realities. The endeavour to shape, even in a faltering and tentative way, one's daily conduct after the manner traced for mankind by the Saviour in word and example will give insight into the admirable quality of the human life of God on earth. It is, ordinarily speaking, one who has himself tried to compose that will be able to realise the genius manifested in the composition of a Bach or a Beethoven ; it is only one who has laboured to give apt and accurate expression to his own thoughts that can properly appreciate the mastery over human language displayed in the seeming simplicity and ease of a great master of style, such as a Ruskin, a Bossuet or a Newman. The attempt to live after the principles of the Saviour will quicken, marvellously, the understanding of, and the sympathy with the life of the Saviour. The experiences that one will go through in this effort at imitation will enable one to penetrate into the inner experiences of the Perfect Pattern of human behaviour. To the man who aims at " living godly in the Christ Jesus ", the Gospel will yield up its hidden meaning. What he will have to contend with, in his relations with men

and things, will invest the oft-conned words of the
sacred text with a new and startlingly topical significance.
Like the electric signs, which are so familiar a feature of
modern life, the words and phrases which hitherto
have been dim and colourless and commonplace suddenly
burst into a vivid glow, and flash on the soul with
unexpected brilliance. Passages that have been familiar
for years at once become strange and new. The words
are the same; the meaning of the words is, of course,
unchanged; but the significance of the whole is completely different. The reason is that what was hitherto
a portion of history or a sentence in a book of moral
instruction has become an integral part of one's own
personal life experience. What has often been read
appears as if it were read now for the first time, because
it has been linked up with a reality that is actual.[13]

The *personal effort to live the Gospel gives one an
understanding of the Gospel.* Study, no matter how
able or profound, unsupported by this effort, will leave
Jesus Christ still an enigma for the student. Meditation,
divorced from a sincere attempt to grow in likeness to
the Lord, is bound to become rapidly perfunctory and
unreal—a soulless and hollow formality. But it will
happen that souls who are animated with a right purpose,
are desirous of making their mental prayer real, and
sincerely wish to become intimate with the Lord, will
nevertheless experience some difficulty in applying their
considerations on the Gospel to their own personal
everyday life. The present work has been written with

[13] What is here stated is verifiable in the case of all the Scriptures. The
Gospels are specially referred to merely because of the theme of the present
work. Besides, once the pages of the Evangelists become luminous for the
reader, they shed a revealing light on the writings of the Old Testament
and on the other books of the New Testament.

a view to meeting this difficulty. It bears to the former
one, on Mental Prayer, the relation of practice to theory.
Its aim is to instruct persons of good will how to draw
practical lessons, applicable to their own lives, from
the mysteries, from the actions, from the endurings
and from the words of Christ. The Gospel text, when
explored, analysed and made to reveal its implications,
unfolds a life experience which, whilst being unique,
is yet charged with universality. The Evangelists set
out not at all to chronicle, as ordinary annalists, interesting historical contemporary events; their purpose was
to give a vivid portrayal of a person who was ideally
human and who had power to mould all humanity to
His Own image. The Sacred writers are not silent
about Christ's miracles; these are brought forward to
prove that He was truly what He claimed to be—a
Divine envoy of Divine power, and yet—the son of
man. But their main concern was not the depicting
of a life of spectacular achievement, but a life of intense
feeling, thought, emotion and affection. They show
us the humanity of Christ in its spiritual reactions to
life's experience. Christ's life in its actual historical
aspect cannot be ours; but that life of His, in its inner
aspect—in what passed in His Heart, His imagination,
in His soul and His will, in contact with human circumstances—that, in a certain measure, can be shared by
us and therefore can, in a true sense, be ours. It is in
the principles of His inner and outward reactions to
the facts of life that there is established psychological
contact between Christ and ourselves. It is in that
contact we come to see that our individual experience
is typified in the Gospel, and that the Gospel is reproduced, in its turn, in our own experience. Once this

point has been reached, our hesitating and uncertain attempts to imitate Jesus become firmer and more assured, whilst, at the same time, the formative influence of His life on ours becomes more potent and efficacious. According as our souls manifest more definitely the traits of the spiritual physiognomy of Christ, He is enabled, more perfectly, to express Himself in and through us, and thus, in a mystical way, perpetuate throughout time the mystery of the Incarnation. That Christ should live in us and through us is the end aimed at by meditation and the mental prayer into which it naturally merges.

For the projected title, " In Habit Found as Man," was substituted the actual one, " In the Likeness of Christ." This latter more explicitly sets out the scope of the work. For these pages are a series of studies of the human character of Christ, having the practical aim of showing the reader how to grow in likeness to the Divine Model of human perfection. Each study is complete in itself, but there is to be observed throughout a certain gradation of thought. There was no progress in Christ's character but there was a progressive mani-festation of the few simple and fundamental principles on which it was based. Each mystery studied, sheds its own light on, and gives its own relief to, the features of the spiritual physiognomy of the Saviour. May He grant that those who read these pages may have a clearer idea and a greater love of the moral grandeur of Him, " who advanced in wisdom and age, and grace with God and men."

[14] St. Luke ii. 52.

PART I

THE FORESHADOWINGS OF THE CONFLICT

" To them that dwelt in the region of the shadow of death light is risen."—Is. ix. 2.

THE INCARNATION AT NAZARETH

" And the Word was made flesh."—ST. JOHN i. 14.

IT is customary in some religious communities to chant, on the eve of Christmas, the words of the Martyrology that announce the birth of Jesus Christ. These words are set to a special mode of penetrating sweetness and strange power. Under its influence the dull, tame, rather dry enumeration of the generations of men undergoes complete change. The lifeless record becomes endowed with movement and animation. By the music the listener is made to perceive that the apparently disconnected achievements and failures, triumphs and disasters, beginnings and endings of the diverse races and generations of men, were not without meaning and purpose. The haphazard movements and seemingly aimless wanderings of humanity are discerned to be an orderly progress towards an objective determined by an all-ruling power. As one listens one is, as it were, carried upwards by the strains to a height at which the tumult of the passage of the successive generations of men—discordant at close range—tones down into perfect harmony. This harmony is then borne onwards until it ends, not in a grand burst of tumultuous sound, but in a long-drawn note of ineffable calm and sweetness. Or to use another figure, the tossing and heaving waters of human destiny (a destiny of trials, labours, sorrows, and yearnings) appear, at first, as if stirred by varying tides that set towards different and unconnected points. Then one has the sense of all these cross-currents, under the direction of some hidden and overmastering force, gathering into one great tidal-wave of mighty purpose sweeping forward to break upon some ultimate and delightful shore. The listener, as the high-pitched notes succeed one another, expects to hear this mighty accumulated tidal-wave of human fortunes fall over with a crash and a roar into a mass of swirling, seething, foaming waters ; instead, it subsides into a murmur of almost unearthly sweetness, as if breaking on the edge of a new and delectable world. And, in truth, with the coming of the Son of God on earth, there began a new world and there passed away the old.

The grave words of the Roman Martyrology proclaim the manifestation to men of the event that had taken place nine months before in the quiet and secrecy of a humble homestead of Nazareth. The simple yet weighty words are vibrant with a sense of the grandeur of the event which they chronicle. As, in the dignified and majestic phrases of the Martyrology, the long series of the centuries preceding the coming of Jesus defile before the mind in ordered succession, the question will naturally suggest itself, why did God allow such a length of time to elapse before undoing the primeval disaster and committing to execution His merciful design of saving fallen humanity ?[1] Nobody, the Sacred writer tells us, can penetrate the mind of God,

---

[1] St. Thomas puts himself the question in *S. Th.* III. Q. 1, A. 5.

except the Divine Spirit Himself.[2] The reasons, there-- fore, that urged God to choose the forty-second year of the reign of Octavian Augustus for compassing His designs of mercy, it is not possible for the human spirit to penetrate. We can but know that these reasons had their source in Infinite Wisdom and Goodness and that the time chosen was that which was most apt to secure the ends aimed at by God, namely, His own glory and the liberation of mankind from the thraldom of sin. Yet though we cannot penetrate the Divine purposes, we may, using faith and reason and experience, see a great suitableness in the time as well as in the place and circumstances in which the Saviour of mankind came amongst men.

In natural things the incapacity to wonder at what is everlastingly wonderful in itself—as for instance, the night array of the stars, the glory of the rising and the setting sun, the origins of life—is a sign not of depth and penetration of mind, but of shallowness and blunt- ness of perception. Undoubtedly, as long as any vestiges of the faith remain, it is impossible that the most indifferent Christian should not feel some stirring of soul-shaking wonder when his mind is consciously brought to bear on the fact of God's becoming Man. Yet it is true that one needs a deep supernatural insight and a strong interior life to approach this fact with the never-failing, never diminishing but rather constantly growing surprise that it merits. For the Saints, their wonder grows as, year by year, the Church brings before them the mystery of the Incarnation, and as year by year their supernatural life deepens in intensity.

[2] St. Paul : 1 Cor. ii. 11.

They marvel more, not less, with the passage of years. But with the unspiritual amongst Christians, things are otherwise. Familiarised with the idea of the Incarnation from the beginnings of their intelligent life, they lose the vivid sense of its " extraordinariness " ; they take it for granted, much like other historical events ; and they regard it not quite, but almost, as something that should be, and without which the world would be unthinkable. They do not conceive it as a favour to humanity, in general, and to themselves, individually, which should be as unexpected for, as it is unmerited by, fallen man.

It is little to say of the Incarnation that it is the greatest historical event that has ever been or that ever will be, that it dwarfs into utter insignificance everything contained in human records. It is to belittle it to allow it to enter into comparison with anything that has ever affected human destinies, for it transcends comparison. Men may know this theoretically : they fail to realise it practically or else they would not assign importance to other historical happenings, except in proportion to their relation to this pivotal fact in human destinies. But though men, in their dullness where supernatural happenings are in question, fail to realise vividly the unique grandeur of the Incarnation, no such dimness can exist in the vision of God. The tremendous " Word " that came to pass on the 25th of March is ever seen by Him in its true proportion and in its proper perspective, relatively to other happenings. Before Him, it is, in the fortunes of mankind, an event, decisive, startling and sudden, like the very act of creation itself. In fact, it is a " re-creation " in grace after the first

creation in grace had been ruined by the pride of the
first Adam. In the first creation God manifested His
Goodness, His Power and His Wisdom. These attributes were, in a still more magnificent and imposing
manner, shown forth in the second creation. God
showed His goodness in constituting man in the state
of grace : He exhibited His Goodness in an incom-
parably greater manner by, Himself, espousing and
taking into the unity of His person that human nature
that had rebelled against Him. God's Infinite Power
appeared in His causing the whole ordered universe to
spring from nothingness and to emerge an ordered
thing from chaos. It was a work that in a still greater
degree manifested His power to make one and
the same Person be both God and Man, for nothing
can be greater than that God should become Man.
The Wisdom of the Almighty shone forth in the harmonies of the universe and in the way that all things,
according to their natures, were directed to their final
end and subserved God's purposes. That same divine
wisdom blazed forth more brilliantly in tracing a plan
for the restoration of humanity which should give free
play to the Divine Mercy whilst leaving intact the rights
of the Divine Justice. "To a problem of infinite
difficulty, God's wisdom found the happiest solution." [3]
God's justice was vindicated not only in this, that
through Jesus an adequate reparation was made for the
sins of fallen man, but also in this, that the devil, a
conqueror of frail man, should, in his turn, be overcome
by One who was man and not by a force exclusively
divine. It was not by violence or in a manner that

[3] *S. Th.* III. Q. 1, A. 1.

violated right order that God saved mankind from perdition.

God, from the beginning, saw and had ever distinctly before His eyes the knowledge that the fact of the Incarnation was one of transcendent importance—was a work that was worthy of God Himself. In the merciful designs of the Almighty, the assumption of created nature by a Divine Person was the culminating event in creation. It was to this event, then, that everything human should be made to converge, and from it that everything human should derive its significance. Wherefore it was eminently befitting that there should be long centuries of preparation. It belonged to the dignity of the Word Incarnate that He should not make His appearance in the world from the very beginning. St. Thomas, commenting on the text, " when came the fullness of time ",[4] writes with great appositeness : " It was eminently becoming, that, the more august the dignity of the judge that was to come, the more extended should be the line of prophets that were deputed to announce His coming."[5]   Men's minds were to be educated to have a just conception of the extraordinary mystery itself and of the Infinite Goodness and Condescension of God that made it possible.   A people had to be set apart and placed under a special Providence in order that the primitive tradition should be preserved incorrupt.   The destinies of that people were meant to typify the wanderings of humanity in search of a Saviour.   Its religion—rites and ceremonies, and the visions of its prophets set forth in outline, at

[4] Gal. iv. 4.
[5] St. Thomas, S. Th. III.   Q. 1, A. 5—quoting St. Augustine.

first obscurely, and as time went on in ever more precise details, the character, the life and the fate of the promised Redeemer. This long series of centuries was, in a manner, the orderly and dignified unfolding of some splendid ceremonial that was to prepare and lead up to the entry into this world of the " Desired of the Nations," the Son of God Himself. " God," says St. Paul, " Who at sundry times and in divers manners, spoke in times past to the fathers by the prophets, last of all, in these days, hath spoken to us by His Son, Whom He had appointed heir of all things." [6]

But there is yet another reason besides this for the tardy coming of Jesus.[7] In tasting of the tree of knowledge of Good and Evil, man had yielded to the satanic suggestion that he could himself, by his own powers, carve out for himself a high destiny and find in his own resources the elements out of which to create an ideal life and attain to complete happiness. The lapse of many centuries and the efforts of succeeding civilisations were needed to make man realise the utter hopelessness of his efforts and the folly of his endeavours. Man could not, in the course of a few centuries, try out all his experiments. It needed generations. Whole generations were required to prepare the way for those triumphs of human reason in the speculative and practical orders, which were realised in the Greek and Roman civilisations. God allowed man's reason to reach perhaps the utmost heights to which, in the actual order of things, it can, without the light of faith, attain. This was allowed to man, in order that, having exercised his

---

[6] Heb. i. 1–2. Cf. Gal. iv. 4.
[7] S. Th. III. Q. 1, A. 5.

powers to the utmost, he might experience, practically, his inability to achieve his own happiness. It was needful for the overcoming of man's pride, the source of all evil in him, that he should be made fully to sound the depths of his own wretchedness and to feel fully his own powerlessness to extricate himself from it. He had sinned through ambition; he aimed at severing himself from his dependence on God. He came to believe in his own self-sufficiency. The world seemed to him to promise all he needed. He could afford, he believed, to dispense with his Creator. He was not ignorant of the weakness that was inherent in his own nature, but trusted in the power of his own reason, in the force of the new found knowledge of good and evil, to remedy it. He was certain that he was able of himself to order his own life, without external aid. His first failures did not discourage him. The ill-success that attended his efforts in pursuit of the ideal of a human life, exempt from wrong and free from suffering, and the remorse that followed his successive relapses into sin, did not dismay or discourage him or make him diffident of his own powers. He felt sure, for a long time, that with experience and with " progress " these failures would be gradually eliminated. It was only after long centuries—when he saw that he had sunk deeper and deeper into sin and weakness and wretchedness—when he saw that he was gradually losing all rational control over his life and conduct, and approximating ever nearer and nearer to the conditions of the brute—and when he saw that his most earnest endeavours to raise himself served only, as in a morass, to sink him more hopelessly into the mire of degradation—that his pride could be brought down and that in humility he should be obliged to call on someone greater than himself to save him. St. Thomas writes : " It was with surpassing wisdom that God did not send His Son hard on the fall of man. He left man, at first, to the unimpeded exercise of his free will, in order that, under the exigencies of the natural law, he might experience what his own natural forces were capable of achieving. After failure under the law of nature, God gave to man for his guidance the Law of Moses. But under this matters grew worse, not through the fault of the law, but through the viciousness of fallen nature. God permitted all this so that man recognising his own weakness might be obliged to call aloud for a (superhuman) physician to heal his wounds and to look for grace to aid his efforts after good." [8] Had Christ immediately regenerated the world after Adam's fall, man would have attributed to himself the perfection of things to which he would, from the beginning, have been habituated. He had to experience palpably what the world would be without Christ—what man could make of it by his unaided reason.

St. Paul gives us in the first chapter of the Epistle to the Romans a fearful picture of what unregenerate society at its highest point of refinement, culture and civilisation was at the coming of Christ. The most horrible crimes were committed without compunction— unblushingly. What is more, the foulest abominations were deified and elevated to the dignity of religious worship. " For," says St. Paul, speaking of the men of that time, " professing themselves to be wise, they

[8] *S. Th.* III. Q. 1, A. 5.

became fools. And they changed the glory of the incorruptible God into the likeness of the image of a corruptible man and of birds and of four-footed beasts and of creeping things. Wherefore God gave them up to the desires of their hearts, unto uncleanness, to dishonour their own bodies amongst themselves. . . . And as they liked not to have God in their knowledge, God delivered them up to a reprobate sense, to do those things which are not convenient. Being filled with all indignity, malice, fornication, avarice, wickedness, full of envy, murder, contention, deceit, malignity; whisperers, detractors, hateful to God, contumelious, proud, haughty, inventors of evil things, disobedient to parents, foolish, dissolute, without affection, without fidelity, without mercy." [9] On reading all this we can understand to some extent why God the Son decided on the particular economy which the Redemption of Mankind assumed.

As every instructed Christian knows, the simplest act of worship on the part of the God-Man is of infinite moral value through having its source in a person who is divine, and would therefore be sufficient of itself to repair the offence offered to God's majesty by sin, and to merit the pardon of mankind. The gates of heaven would be flung open by the least of Christ's merits and man would be free to enter. But with his nature thoroughly perverted by centuries of sin, man, unless his rational instincts underwent a profound transformation, would be unable to profit by the salvation won for him. The waters of the pool might be stirred and made life-giving, but he would be powerless to

* Rom. i. 22–31.

descend therein, paralysed by ages of infirmity.[10] It
was necessary that Jesus should not only create the
means of salvation, but also as a good physician teach
invalid humanity the *régime* it was to follow in order
to make these means yield spiritual health. God's
Honour could be satisfied by a glorious Christ, man's
conversion and salvation could be accomplished only
by a suffering Christ.[11] The life of Christ, as set forth
in the Gospels, " is the way of truth which fallen man
must tread, if he is to rise from the dead and gain the
beatitude of an immortal existence ".[12] To reach the
goal of bliss man must fashion his conduct according
to a righteousness which should reflect the purity of
God's own life. The annals of fallen humanity searched
through and through revealed no model of such conduct.
The Son of God Himself alone provided a model of
the kind required : He, in His life as Son of Man, set
Himself up as the pattern of right conduct. As St.
Augustine says : " We could not follow the example
of man whom we could see : we were obliged to imitate
God Whom we could not see. In order, then, to set
before man a model of conduct whom he *should* follow
and a model whom he *could* see God became man." [13]
It was only through the example of a Christ, poor,
humble, obscure, mortified and suffering, that man could

[10] St. John v. 1–7.
[11] When speaking of the necessity of a suffering Christ for the accomplishment of the salvation of mankind there is question of a moral, not
absolute necessity. St. Thomas writes : " It was necessary (with a moral
necessity) for man's salvation that God should become man—inasmuch as
the pride of man, the chief obstacle of his union with God, might be put
to shame and cured by such humility on the part of God."—*S. Th.* III.
Q. 1, A. 2.
[12] *S. Th.*, Prologue to III.
[13] *S. Th.* III. Q. 1, A. 2 (quotation).

be nerved to brace himself to face and overcome the great obstacles to his salvation.

The work of the Incarnation was no child's play. It is difficult for us to form an adequate notion of what it involved—for, born into a world, which in spite of itself, and even in its most extreme wickedness retains some leaven of Christianity, we cannot easily picture to ourselves the fearful moral depravity of a world in which the memory of the true God had almost vanished and the influence of Jesus had not been felt. It involved an immense change in the condition of the world—not only in the interior of the hearts of men (though there can never be a great change there without external manifestation and influence on the state of things outside) but also in the state of society. Man, though fallen, began his existence with a certain knowledge of God—with an understanding of the law of nature written on his heart and a perception of the distinction between right and wrong. For a long time the primitive revelation of a Redeemer to come remained deeply impressed on the consciousness of humanity, outlawed from Eden. Even when the " plenitude of time " was reached it had not been completely obliterated, though it had undergone much perversion in the minds of the peoples who were outside the influence of Hebrew tradition. This idea of a promised Redeemer was a constant reminder to man of his own transgressions and kept alive in him the sense of sin as well as of the need of expiation and redemption. The order of the world—and the action of Providence—easily discernible by man when his intelligence was clear and vigorous and not yet corrupted by false philosophy—revealed everywhere the presence of God and His personal influence. But little by little the devil had succeeded in conquering all these defences of a moral life. Multiplied transgressions and continual flattering of the passions at the expense of reason had at length developed habits of will and intellect, to which the demarcating limits of right and wrong became obscure and blurred, and finally shifting. It was not only original sin, but the bad habits generated by continual personal sins— habits transmitted as a sad legacy from father to children and given increase by these children's own transgressions—that corrupted the mind and heart of men. The devil had to a wide extent obliterated the knowledge of the One True God in the human heart, and had placed himself on a thousand altars to be the object of an impure and degrading worship. This worship had a fearful hold, for it dignified and gilded and flattered the lowest human passions. Men were steeped in the foulest corruption and the hardest cruelty. Only in the chosen nation did God hold sway, and even there Satan had extended his kingdom over a great portion— the largest section of Israel. St. Thomas, quoting St. Augustine, writes : " Christ came just at the moment when He judged that aid should be given to man and that it would be accepted. In fact, when, because of a certain moral decline on the part of man, the knowledge of God began to fade from the minds of men, and their conduct became corrupt, God in His mercy chose Abraham to renew amongst mankind the knowledge of God and of righteous conduct. The respect for God and the moral law being on the point of disappearing once again God gave to man, through Moses, the

Written Law. The Gentiles despised this Law and would not submit themselves to it; those who had received it did not observe it. Then God, moved by His mercy, sent His Son, to give to all the remission of their sins and to present to God men robed in justice." [14]

At the moment when the Redeemer came, the world presented, to the discerning eye, the appearance of a vast temple of Satan. Its conversion involved a complete change in the whole framework of society. Amongst all the peoples outside the pale of Jewry, the worship of Satan involved in the worship of false gods was a State institution and was interwoven with all the elements of domestic, social and national life. Man's life, considered in its individual and social, in its domestic and political aspects, was penetrated through and through with the worship of the Evil One. The salvation of mankind demanded that all this should cease. The temples, some of them ancient and venerable, many of them works of great architectural beauty and objects of civic and national pride, were to be abandoned and allowed to fall into ruin. The whole system of established idolatry had to disappear and with it the vast number of endowments, trading concerns, vested interests, and institutions that were linked up with it and which secured to it the allegiance of a whole host of interested persons. With the overthrow of paganism would necessarily go the destruction of a great number of vested interests. The tumult created at Ephesus by the manufacturers of the images of Diana, when their trade was threatened by the success of St. Paul's

[14] *S. Th.* III.   Q. 1, A. 6.

teaching, illustrates this point.[15] The public amusements, the theatre, the army, the literature of the people were saturated with devilry, and all this was to be swept away and supplanted in due course, in all these departments, by the austere Christian spirit—and that, too, not under stress of external force, but by a voluntary renouncement on the part of the heathens themselves !

For it would little avail that the devil should lose his hold on the social framework unless his sway over the hearts and minds of men was overthrown. The devil ruled men by their passions and lusts, which he encouraged them to indulge. He held them captive by the things of sense, by the allurements of the world, by covetousness, by ambition, by revenge and hatred and by the whole array of temporal goods promised on condition of subjection to him.[16] Under the reign of Satan men were hard and unfeeling, without pity or tenderness. The one thing they looked up to was the physical power to dominate, and the one thing they feared was the helplessness of poverty. Their life was divided between pleasure and cruelty. Pride and haughtiness instead of being regarded as defects were cultivated as manly virtues. Weakness was almost synonymous with vice, and all this tended to fashion hearts impervious to the grace of God and to every human feeling.[17] Conversion of heart was for them extremely difficult. What God required on the part of

[15] Acts xix. 23–40.
[16] Cf. Coleridge : *The Public Life of Our Lord*, Part III., par. vi., p. 18.
[17] These statements are weak when compared with the lurid picture of the pagan world that St. Paul, in his Epistles to the Romans, depicts for us. See Rom. i. 28–32.

man as a necessary condition of their friendship with Him was to them abhorrent, for the practice of the Christian virtues of submission, humility and patience would be regarded by them as degrading. They had to learn that what was not degrading for God—since nothing could degrade Him in reality—could not be degrading for them. Turning to God postulated on their part not only a change of heart, but also a change of mentality. Their human values were almost all wrong. In the terse words of St. Ignatius describing the pagan world: " They smite, they slay and they go down to Hell." Now Our Divine Lord took upon Him the task of changing all that. It is easy to understand from what has been said that the task He faced was one of appalling magnitude. It was a task before which any heart but the heart of a God-Man would have quailed. Men were to learn to despise that on which they set the highest value—riches; they were to forego that to which they were bound by a thousand ties rendered strong and tough by centuries of evil conduct—the gratification of their sensual passions— and they were to acquire the knowledge and practice of what was unknown even to the greatest of their philosophers—humility. Poverty, at least of spirit, and detachment were to replace the passionate pursuit of wealth ; mortification, sensual self-indulgence ; submission, haughty insubordination ; and humility, pride. God, Who created us without our will, would not save us without our will. He could pay the ransom for our sins a million times over ; we should still remain slaves of Satan did we not use our free will to turn to God. He might multiply His three years' teaching one hundred times over. He might extend by His miraculous power, over the whole earth, to the ears of all men, the accent of His voice. His doctrine, so high, so holy, so recommendable by its sweet reasonableness, so perfectly satisfying to all the aspirations of human nature, would have fallen on deaf ears. Did He support His teaching by miracles that would eclipse the wonderful ones that adorn the pages of the Gospel, still men would have remained obdurate in their errors. And in fact how very few, if any, did His Miracles gain to His cause during His life ! What little effect the astounding miracles that we daily witness have on ourselves ! Morally speaking, men could not be converted even by a God become Man, were He to confine His action upon them to teaching and the exercise of His infinite power over nature. Almighty God saw all that in His Wisdom and prescience. He saw that men's corruption could be cured only in the fire of suffering. Looking upon suffering with horror and abhorrence—rebelling against it—not being able to understand its place in the economy of THE WORLD—they suffered and blasphemed and lost themselves. They must learn to understand, to esteem and love that which they loathed—they had to learn to suffer and to praise. In the present order of nature suffering is God's instrument to work out the purification of our souls and to destroy the obstacles that oppose themselves to our salvation—the concupiscence of the flesh, the concupiscence of the eyes and the pride of life—attachment to the things of this world—to creatures—to our own ease and pleasure—and finally attachment to ourselves. How could He reconcile man to suffering ? It seemed impossible. His love found a

way. It was by presenting to man a suffering God.
Man was to be weaned from riches and pleasure and
ambition by the example of a God, poor, suffering and
humble. The salvation of man is the explanation of the
life of poverty and suffering elected by Our Lord.

CHAPTER II

THE NATIVITY OF JESUS IN BETHLEHEM

" For a child is born to us and a son is given to us."—Is. ix. 6.

The dominant note of the actions of The Lord Jesus is their thoroughness—the characteristic feature of His human character was its simplicity. He had undertaken the task of rescuing mankind from the abyss into which it had plunged, and He began that task from the very moment of His Conception. From the instant in which the Word was made Flesh, there was not a single moment lost before the attack was opened against the forces that held man in bondage. The task of Jesus was not only to undo the dishonour inflicted by the sin of men on the Majesty of God, by giving to that Divine Majesty the honour due to it from man : it was not only to expiate by His sufferings the criminal indulgence of sin : His task was not confined to meriting for His fellow-men by His life and especially by His death the divine life that had been forfeited by the Fall : Jesus had besides all this to revolutionise the world He had come to save. His work was not merely to rectify the ideas of His countrymen with regard to the nature and character of the Messias, but of all men with regard to human values taken in all their amplitude.

The saving of mankind involved the transforming of mankind. The instrument of this transformation of mankind was nothing else than the human life of the Saviour, with the incidents, the actions, the experiences, the reactions and the sufferings that marked that life. It was on a human nature that the task of changing human nature devolved. " It should needs be, then, that in this human nature, the Christ should undergo the sufferings and accomplish the actions which were to bring a remedy to sin. Now the sin of men consists in nothing else than in a turning from God to yield an attachment to material things which makes them oblivious of spiritual things. The purpose that the Son of God, in assuming the nature of man, had, was to show by His doings and sufferings that men ought to count as nothing temporal woes or temporal blessings lest through an inordinate love of ephemeral realities, they should be indifferent to and detached from spiritual realities." [1]   In these words quoted from St. Thomas it is to be noted how the great theologian stresses the point that the weapon by which the overthrow of Satan was to be effected and man released from his thrall was nothing else but the life experiences ending in death of a human being. As David going forth to fight Goliath disdained the trappings and arms of Saul and was content with a mere sling and a stone, so the Son of God entering into the fight with Satan disdained to arm Himself with aught else but a humanity in all things like the humanity of ordinary men—save sin alone. Jesus Himself in the course of His life frequently stresses this point in that He almost invariably loves to call Himself the Son of Man. He insisted on His sheer humanity. It is that humanity divested of everything except Divine

[1] St. Thomas : *De Rationibus Fidei*, Chap. VII.

Grace and the Hypostatic Union—that humanity naked as it were—that flung itself on the forces of evil which held the world in their grip and that vanquished them. The Sacred Humanity in achieving the revolution of mankind drew upon no meretricious helps. It was not supported either by wealth or station or force or any worldly prestige of any kind. His origin was obscure, His parentage was humble, His nationality despised.[2] It was the human character of Christ by itself alone (belonging, of course, to the Divine Person) that changed the face of the world.

The enemies of Christianity very often blame it for what they call its pomp and display : the charge, however, that is most frequently levelled against the followers of Christ by their adversaries is that they show a preference for the mean, the sordid and the degraded. The unbeliever is wont to decry Christianity as destructive of human dignity owing to its cult of poverty, obscurity and lowliness. The manner in which some pious writers deal with this theme, it is to be confessed, gives some colour to this charge, for they extol all these things as if they were good in themselves. They dwell with eloquence on the poor and humble circumstances of Christ's life and eulogise lowliness of station and wretchedness of circumstances because of Christ's choice of these things. There is in many writers a slightly false emphasis in all this. Poverty and lowliness of station are not good things in themselves ; they are in their own nature indifferent, as are wealth and high station. The poor and lowly are not necessarily, by the fact of being poor and lowly, virtuous : nor are the

2 *S. Th.* III. Q. 35, A. 7 ad 3.

noble born and the wealthy, through the accidental circumstances of their position in life, fatally vicious. It is true that Our Lord dwells on the difficulty of the rich man's entry into the Kingdom of Heaven : but He does not state that the poor man enters therein with promptitude and facility. He states that the way to heaven is strait, narrow and difficult for all, whilst admitting that, owing to men's proneness to pursue the advantages of station or fortune, riches and worldly position do actually prove a greater stumbling block than poverty to the pilgrim in his progress towards heaven. When Our Lord is said to love poverty and all its attendant circumstances one must understand clearly what is meant. This predilection of His must be considered in direct relation to His life's work and only in the light of that relation can it be understood.

God made man to be great. The fact of His foreordaining man to be His own adopted child, sharing the rights and privileges of His only begotten Son, is proof of this. What greatness can be compared with that of being princes in God's Kingdom, " heirs indeed of God, and joint heirs with Christ ? " [3] This is man's high destiny—a truly magnificent one even if it be conditioned. The continuation of the text quoted gives the conditions, and they are full of significance. Yes, we are co-heirs with Christ, " yet so if we suffer with Him, that we may be also glorified with Him ".

Man being called to greatness, it is not wrong for man to thirst after greatness. He errs and defeats his end only when he satisfies that thirst in a mistaken manner. The penalty of his error is severe. His desire

[3] Rom. viii. 17.

is thwarted and instead of becoming great, he suffers deterioration and a shrinkage of personality. This appetite for greatness is more fundamental in man than his appetite for pleasure, notwithstanding all appearances to the contrary. It would seem as if wealth and all the satisfactions that wealth provides were the great and universal lure for mankind. But there is a desire in him more universal still, and more radical. Each man cherishes the secret ambition to be " somebody " and shrinks more from the fate of being " nobody " than he does from hardship, pain and poverty. The saints are no exception. St. Madeleine Sophie Barat, when told contemptuously by her brother that she was of no worth, resolved at least to be " great " in humility. St. Teresa of Lisieux, unable to accomplish the great feats of mortification of the other saints, would be at all costs *great* in love. The Saviour Himself was truè to humanity in this : He would not abide for Himself a greatness that would be purely adventitious and borrowed. He jealously guarded His innate greatness from the least suspicion of its owing aught to the external conditions of life, such as position, riches, powerful connections and the rest.[4] He came to men and for His appeal to them He drew solely on the resources of His Humanity equipped only with what it received from God, and borrowing nothing from the world of men. Jesus was the one man that truly merited the title of

---

[4] Cf. *S. Th.* III. Q. 35, A. 7 ad 2. *Christus florere voluit secundum virtuosam conversationem, non secundum carnis originem. Et ideo in civitate Nazareth educari voluit et nutriri* : which may be translated thus : Christ aimed at distinction through the practice of manly virtue and not through (the merely accidental circumstances of) high birth. Hence He would be brought up and educated at Nazareth.

"The Great." He was conscious of it, and there was no arrogance, only dignity, in this self-consciousness. In the course of His career He confronted the great men of His day, the princes of the people and the political representatives of the Roman power. In all His dealings with them, whilst being flawlessly courteous and deferential, there is a quiet assumption of unquestioned superiority. There is never the slightest indication, when He treats with the powerful and the wealthy, that He felt at any disadvantage because of His poverty, His humble trade or His country origin. He suffered from many things—He never suffered from what in modern jargon is called "the inferiority complex." Wealth, influence, power—all these, He felt, would complicate the appeal of His Humanity. He therefore shrank from all these things, and chose poverty, lowliness and obscurity. *He would influence men solely by what He was, not by what He might have.* Christ's love of poverty was simply the expression of His splendid independence of wealth and its advantages. One of the aspects of His task was to lead men back to the knowledge, the love and the pursuit of that true greatness to which they were called. *He had to teach them that they were great, not by what they had or what they did, but by what they were.*

Man had erred gravely on this question. He conceived his greatness, and consequently the satisfaction of the fundamental aspiration of his being, to be in the extension of his power over as great a number as possible of the created goods of the earth. Man, as was pointed out in the last chapter, hungered after wealth, pleasure and power as being the constituent elements of his greatness. He judged that he would find the happiness for which every rational creature craves in the possession of these things and in the power to enjoy them independently of any higher authority than his own. The pursuit of greatness and happiness along these lines led to the universal disorder and degradation outlined in the previous chapter. This result of man's ordering his individual and political life according to his false views was inevitable. For, as Jesus practised and taught, man's true greatness and his highest liberty consists in his complete independence of what is created and in his utter subjection to the Uncreated. Detachment from creatures and loving submission to God alone give man the greatness and happiness he instinctively aspires to. Sanctity, or greatness of character—for they are actually the same thing—does not consist in anything external nor does it depend on it: it is to be found entirely in the interior. The presence or absence of this world's goods, good or evil fortune, easy circumstances or hardship, health or sickness, protection from or exposure to the unkindness of the elements, or the perverse wills of men, these things in themselves cannot take from or add to us. *What counts is how we bear ourselves in face of them, and to what account we turn them.* " We can all cultivate a divine sweetness even if we live in a hovel. We should prefer not to be there : that is perfectly natural, but as it is impossible to dictate the evolution of the world with a word, and equally impossible to abolish suffering and privation with a wave of the hand, we must face all the circumstances and vicissitudes of life with the strength which God gives us. We must not seek the Good merely in riches and wealth, but in poverty and sickness as well. *The source of Goodness which we so desperately need, lies within ourselves, and it is for us to tap it.*[5] Men before the time of Jesus Christ placed everything in unfettered freedom of action and in the abundance of material goods. This conviction that man's worth, and in consequence the favour of heaven, was indicated by worldly possessions was so deeply rooted that God Himself condescended to regulate His dealings with His Chosen people, to a certain measure, in accordance with this prejudice. God's favour to the Jews was signified to them by temporal prosperity, His displeasure was manifested in defeat and disaster.[6]

Now Jesus, with unerring wisdom and insight, judged that all the things that men shrank from, namely, poverty, pain and powerlessness, though these things did not of themselves generate in men true greatness, yet could be made a powerful means to the achievement of true greatness of soul : He saw, too, that worldly advantages, the things so passionately pursued, proved a serious obstacle to man's true elevation, through his inveterate tendency, due to the loss of equilibrium in his nature, to become, first, attached and then enslaved to the things of this world. The servitude to the material meant the loss of that sovereignty over the world and that independence of all but God that the Almighty destined for man.

This view of things is the key to the teaching of Jesus. It is the burden of all His instructions. It is the

[5] Prohaszka : *Meditations on the Gospel.* p. 122. (Sheed & Ward.)
[6] This error of regarding temporal prosperity as a sign of heaven's favour was curiously revived in the Puritanical, Industrial England of the nineteenth century.

explanantion of His mode of life. Christ, as Man, aimed at leading a life of power, or in modern phraseology, a life of personality. He meant to lead a life of greatness and He meant that the circumstances of His daily life should be a foil to that greatness. He willed that men should acknowledge His life to be such; " which of you shall convince Me of sin " [7], He said to his enemies, and they could not take up His challenge. His life was deliberately arranged to show that human greatness and dignity borrowed nothing from external circumstances, from temporal influence, temporal pomp or temporal goods, but lay entirely in the inner perfection of the soul, in which sense is submitted to reason, and reason to God. Christ showed that greatness was not incompatible with, but could rather be enhanced by poverty, suffering and even ignominy. This lesson, with characteristic zeal, He lost not a moment in conveying to men. To wean them from the things that were turning them aside from their last end, and, as a means to that end, to change their standard of values, He straightway placed Himself in those positions and in that condition which up to that time, even for the people of God, would appear to deprive a man of all greatness, worth and esteem. " In Bethlehem we see true greatness of soul, which opposes itself in its sublime humility to the conceit and pettiness of the worldly spirit. Christ brushes aside all pomp, frippery, tinsel and everything which flatters the senses; and like the clear, icy stream which, issuing from the glacier's foot makes for the rocky valleys, and dives swirling into the depths, He presents humility to the world as sublime

<hr>

[7] St. John viii. 46.

and victorious strength. We must never confound
the unassuming strength of humility with dullness and
indifference. Christ, Who is frequently described in
Scripture as an eagle, is the perfect type of sublime
humility ! " [8] Man judged that his perfection lay in
shaking off every restraint and in emancipating himself
from subjection—even to God. The Word, to correct
this error, " emptied Himself, taking the form of a
servant ".[9] He Who was sovereignly free and independent makes Himself a captive and a bondsman. His
innate greatness of soul, " His virtue and perfection
turned the outward dishonour of His bonds into orna-
ments of glory."

Our Lord might have been brought into the world as
Adam was in the full glory of perfect manhood—He
preferred to be born of woman like every one of Adam's
descendants and to pass through the humiliating stages
of the weakness of conception, babyhood and infancy
before arriving at man's estate. He elected to lie for
nine long months in the imprisonment of Mary's womb.
Scarcely is He incarnate, when He is captive, and this
captivity was in no small way irksome. For ordinary
children it means no suffering, no sense of restraint,
for they do not enjoy the use of reason till long after
their conception. For Jesus it was otherwise. From
the first moment His glorious soul issued from the
creative hands of God, it possessed the full and perfect
and unimpeded use of its faculties. Hence He could
feel to the full the extreme irksomeness of His prison
house. That this was a truly sublime act of condescen-

[8] Note, Prohaszka, *op. cit.*, p. 128.
[9] Phil. ii. 7.

sion to our humanity on the part of the Son of God is evidenced by the fact that the Church extols it in the greatest of her hymns of praise. " *Tu, ad liberandum suscepturus hominem, non horruisti virginis uterum*," thus she addresses the Word of God in the Te Deum.[10] The words of Holy Church are weighted with meaning, and she will not glorify except what, in the eyes of the Holy Spirit Himself, is worthy of glorification. But Our Lord, Who is so thorough in everything He does, would be a man in everything, save alone in that respect which was impossible—namely, sin. Hence He would pass through the touchingly human stages of conception and birth.

The circumstances of that birth, if contemplated, will reveal another striking characteristic of the mode of acting of Our Lord. God has given the elements—all the things of His creation—their natures, properties and their laws; and these things act with absolute necessity, and without any regard for individual men. Accidents happen indifferently to saints and to sinners. An earthquake or a volcanic eruption will ruin the property and destroy the lives of the good as well as the bad. God makes His rain to fall and His sun to shine on the just as on the unjust. The Almighty has given men free will; in that gift is involved the power to misuse the freedom of action it imparts. The perverse use of free will on the part of wicked men will affect their fellows adversely, not only the reckless, but the God-fearing. What is more, men, even with the best will, are dull of perception and prone to make mistakes. Hence

---

[10] Thou, when about to undertake the liberation of mankind, didst not shrink from the Virgin's womb.

it frequently happens that God's rational creatures have to suffer through the well-meaning stupidity of others. It can come to pass that men will suffer greater misfortunes from the mistakes of others than from their malice. Nature punishes error as surely as it punishes sin. Natural laws obey no moral considerations. This is the condition of things in a fallen world. The just man must not, because of it, allow himself to be betrayed into grumbling, detraction, repining, anger or revenge—into anything that will hurt the soul. His consolation in the accidents of life must be that nothing external, however untoward or harsh, can hurt the soul, and therefore rob him of his real and lasting good.

Our Lord has given us the supreme example in this. His life has taught men in striking and forcible fashion that harsh circumstances can cause a man no evil and may be turned into an instrument of real good. Every incident of His life, bitter and repugnant as it was to His sensitive nature, served only to manifest and bring out into higher relief the innate greatness of His character. He accepted everything—but allowed nothing to betray Him into the least imperfection of conduct. By becoming Man He threw Himself into the stream of circumstances and allowed it to work its way with Him. He was treated just the same as any other of His creatures of the same birth and station would be treated both by the forces of nature and the wills of men. He became the prey of the laws of the physical universe of which He Himself was the Author, and of the perverse use of the free will which was His highest gift to His rational creatures. He, as well as we, had to submit to the disorder that followed on sin. The elements were rude

to Him as well as to any other child of Adam.   The
wickedness of man dealt with Him more cruelly—far
more cruelly, in fact, than with the most helpless of
His rational creatures.   He has given a magnificent
example of courage and endurance in submitting to
all these things.   He allowed nothing that happened to
cause His Soul to give back the slightest reflection of
the evil that passed before It and pressed against It.
The surface of that soul never reflected aught but the
unvarying goodness and magnanimity of God.

It was decreed that God the Son should be born in
Bethlehem.   Mary and Joseph lived in Nazareth when
the number of her days was accomplished.   At such
a juncture the journey from Nazareth to Bethlehem
was fraught with hardship.   It was a journey which
neither the unborn babe nor His parents would have
chosen to undertake, especially at such a time, had
choice been left to themselves.   Naturally, He Himself
would have preferred to have been born in His own home
town amid the conveniences, simple as they necessarily
would be, that the circumstances of His family permitted.
Mary must have been very loath, and must have found
it exceedingly painful, to set out in the condition in
which she was—expecting the birth of her Child at
any moment.   What mother would not have been filled
with anxiety and distress at such a juncture?   She felt
it all keenly.   Yet she, already so perfectly attuned in
will to the dispositions of the Child she bore, did not
allow the unpleasant necessity under which she laboured
to diminish her trust in a kind providence or betray her
into grumbling against the tyranny of Cæsar.   Joseph
on his part, was painfully distressed at the toilsome

journey to which he was obliged to expose the unborn
Babe and the Babe's Mother.   But they were all three
the victims of circumstances : they were a poor family,
without any influential persons favou able to them near
the Roman Procurator.   Augustus was all-powerful ;
his edict had gone forth ; it must be obeyed by his
subjects.   Joseph had perforce to go, and it was not
suitable that Mary should be separated from her spouse
at such a time.   She could not but accompany him.
The names had to be recorded by a certain date ; the
Romans brooked no delay ; to resist would involve
them in more hardship ; therefore they had to set out.
And so Our Lord was brought into this world away
from His own home, through the imperious will of one
of His own creatures, and one who was far from being
the best—a very unworthy man indeed, judged by
Christian standards.   What a lesson for us !   But someone may say : " It was Our Lord's own choice, He
could have arranged otherwise if He liked."   Of course
He could : He need not have agreed to save mankind—
and so He would have been spared all this !   It is quite
true.   Neither was He obliged to create the world, nor
the men that inhabit it ; and then He would not have
to redeem them at all.   But because He is good and
wanted others to enjoy the immense happiness He
enjoys Himself, He called creatures into being.   For
His own glory and their own merit He gave them free
will—what if they abuse it ?   It is not His fault, but
theirs.   In the creatures' possession of free will is involved
the power to use it rightly and to use it perversely—to
use it or to abuse it.   And when as a fact they abused
their powers and fell, He could have left them in their

fallen state. If He wished to save them, it was again *His goodness*. And if He chose this particular way of doing it, it was *His wisdom* that was at work. In no other way could it have been done so effectively. But all these things being supposed, *i.e.*, His creating man to share His own happiness, their sin and rejection of their great destiny, their powerlessness to recover it and His desire to come to their aid and save them—all the rest followed as things must follow, given the nature of men and of things. God, foreseeing that men would treat Jesus at His coming as they actually treated Him, did not impose any necessity on them to act as they did.

So Our Lord having, for our sake, chosen to be the child of poor parents of Nazareth, everything else followed as a natural consequence. If Mary were as the rich ones of the earth she could have bribed the scribes to postpone her enrolment; being poor, she was dragged from her home ruthlessly by the Imperial edict. Neither she nor Jesus had any choice in the matter. And when they arrived at Bethlehem it was the same thing. The Bethlehemites were not exceptionally uncharitable; they were probably on the whole much more hospitable than the average citizen of our Catholic cities. But they had an eye to business—they had to live. When an opportunity presented itself of turning an honest penny, why not avail themselves of it ! In the severe competition for shelter that prevailed in Bethlehem at the time it would be very inconvenient to receive a person in Mary's condition. These people were not bad, they were not harsh, they were simply, like ourselves, persons of an ordinary average goodness.

They, like the average human being, were somewhat insensitive to the approach of the supernatural. Did Mary present herself in a Catholic town at the present day, and knock at Catholic doors looking for admittance, in similar circumstances, what reception would she be liable to meet with? She probably would excite some sympathy, but would most likely meet with the same " hospitality."

But it will be urged—it is all God's own fault. Why did He not come in some other way, more worthy of His greatness and His Majesty? Why did He come in such a miserable guise! Or if that was His peculiar fancy, why did He not at least announce His coming? This is the objection of the shallow and the superficial— the objection of him whom St. Paul styles the sensual man. " But the sensual man perceiveth not these things that are of the spirit of God; for it is foolishness to him, and he cannot understand; because it is spiritually examined." [11] These last words of St. Paul contain the key to the mystery. It can be asserted, *a priori*, that the mode in which God presented Himself to men was the mode that was most becoming to God. It is not for men to dictate or to determine for God the ways of His coming. The Creator's way, not the creature's, is bound to be, *a priori*, the wisest, the most fitting and the best, in the circumstances. The divine element in things, not being detected, is not due to God's being disguised but to man's dullness of perception as regards supernatural things. In fact it is as difficult for men to acknowledge the true divinity in power as in weakness. Men deny the divine origin of the miracles that take

[11] 1 Cor. ii. 14.

place before their eyes, and they deify the State or Humanity or Reason. It is not the unusual but the regularly recurrent thing that men are insensible to the neighbourhood of God when He lives and moves amongst them. The divine Church of Christ is like a beacon in the world to-day. Do men, in large numbers, " sense " it as divine ? It is true that it is disguised in human vesture. So it is true that God was thickly disguised when He came on earth, but the disguise did not prevent some intimations of the divine from making their way through—for those who were spiritually in a state of receptivity. If men fail to react appropriately to the approach of God, because of the disguise in which He presents Himself, it is not due to the impenetrability of the disguise but to the impenetrability of their spirits to the divine rays. The fault is not in the disguise but in themselves. They deal humanly with what is divine because they are not sufficiently spiritual, because, as St. Paul puts it, the divine manifestation is not detected as divine unless it is spiritually examined. It is because of men's earthly, unspiritual notions that they look for God's coming amidst the blare of trumpets and in the glare of publicity—as is the way of coming of what they deify. Yet a moment's reflection should make us realise that humility and lowliness are more worthy of God than empty show and feverish bustle. If God were to become man at all, we should expect His coming to be utterly human. It is because men's thoughts are not God's thoughts nor their ways His ways that they expect God to move enveloped in conditions outside the ordinary human measure. They fail to see the obvious truth, namely, that if God were to become man, He would become so in a very thorough fashion, with the thoroughness of God. The thoughtful should expect to find that, if God were to become one of us, no man would be as perfectly and truly human as God made man. *The unspiritual look for God in the strange and the singular : it would be more reasonable to expect to find Him in what is common and universal.* But men make God to their own limited views, according to their own purblind notions, and so to their own great loss. Because of this they miss Him. Hence it is that even if Jesus had given some sign that was of God, or if Mary had proclaimed her great dignity, both the sign and the proclamation would meet with precisely the same obtuseness and incredulity. *Nothing can be so perfect a sign of God made man as perfect humility—* and that sign was before the eyes of the Bethlehemites. But these like the average of mankind were not alive to this truth. They were not attuned to the supernatural. They were all given up to amusement and excitement. The great influx of Jews and Romans, the natural desire to put away the thought of political subjection that the gathering signified, the natural enthusiasm of crowds—all combined to plunge the little city into a whirl of dancing and festivity. It was all very legitimate. It was an extremely natural thing that they should be thus engaged at God's coming, but the unfortunate thing was that this natural activity made them insensible to His approach.

And yet they were not exempt from fault. God blamed them [12] and they suffered a great loss through their

[12] It is difficult to read the words in St. Luke's gospel, viz., " She . . . laid Him in a manger *because* there was no room for them in the inn," without detecting in them a note of implied and sorrowful reproach.

spiritual obtuseness. Strange as it may appear, He expects and demands that men should be sensitive to Him even under the thick disguise of His lowliness and humility. If He was turned from those doors that night, it was not His fault : the fault lay on the side of the inhospitable householders. It was a moral one. They did not lack keenness of vision, but they were wanting in purity of soul. God's coming into men's lives is ever a supernatural event, and it is not detected by the eyes of the body, but by those of the soul. Given up to an exterior life, abandoned to immortification—knowing nothing but what the senses revealed—the Bethlehemites observed nothing but a poor carpenter and his poor wife, nothing betokening the divine or the heavenly. God offered many of them that night the glorious privilege of sheltering under their roof the Queen of Heaven, and of having their home the theatre of the birth of the son of God. For want of an interior life, for want of supernatural instincts, they lost that chance, which was never again to be offered to them.[13] But we must not be hard on them. Day by day, and many times a day, we are doing the same thing. Inasmuch as we are not leading a supernatural and interior life, it must needs be so. God presents Himself to us in a thousand ways—in good

[13] Of course this does not imply that it was demanded of the Bethlehemites that they should recognise Mary explicitly as the Mother of God, and her child as God Himself. For this there would be needed a special revelation as afterwards in the case of St. Peter at Cesarea Philippi. What is meant is that here God was truly present and men were expected to react appropriately, that is, in a spiritual, not in a merely natural (or sensual, according to St. Paul's use of the term) way to that presence. To God's advent into their lives, whatever be the mode of that advent, men are required to react obediently, reverently, submissively, charitably, humbly—as the occasion demands.

inspirations—in calls to a life less natural and more heroic—in temptations that are meant to purify and not to be a cause of sin, in interior pains, in family afflictions, in difficulties in our work, in misunderstandings with others, in sickness, in discomforts and pains of every kind, and above all in the ever-recurring calls of duty and obedience—*and as regularly we fail to find God in these things*. Nothing but their external physical aspect strikes us. The reason is the same in our case as in that of the inhabitants of Bethlehem. Our dullness of spiritual perception is due to want of recollection, absence of mortification, and a life, in great part, exteriorised. Without an interior life, it is impossible to discern God in the highways and byways of this life.[14] If our prayer were what it should be, that is, a familiar and intimate converse with God, we should know His ways, recognise Him when He presents Himself, and never miss our chances of taking Him into our souls. God is continually inviting people to enter into the intimate relations of close friendship with Him. If such relations do not exist, it means simply that the door has been shut in His Face and His pleading rejected as was His unvoiced pleading in the bosom of Mary on that inhospitable night at Bethlehem. If Jesus is not to be found within human hearts, it means that He has been shut out.

The conduct and bearing of Mary and Joseph in their fruitless quest give us a great lesson as to how we

---

[14] Cf. the following passage from Bishop Prohaszka's *Meditations on the Gospel*. " Our Lady was not admitted into the Inn, because Bethlehem was full—full of foreigners and visitors, full of gossip and clamour. There was no room for her. Our hearts, too, can be like Bethlehem, with no room in them for God. They make place for everything, but God."

should bear ourselves in the disappointments of life and under the rebuffs of fortune. If we analyse our thoughts with regard to these events we shall find that we have been accustomed to look upon the whole scene, and in fact all the scenes of Our Lord's life, as a carefully arranged stage-play. Joseph was to go from door to door, and each householder was to refuse, but all was to happen in accordance with a previous understanding. We should be careful in studying Our Lord's life to dismiss this thought from our minds. *It is true that all was foreseen—but it is equally true to say that nothing was pre-arranged in the stage sense. All things fell out just as freely and naturally as if God foresaw nothing.* Joseph's asking was not make-believe. *It was earnest and sincere.* Each rebuff cut him to the heart. Yet his manner does not change—his pain and disappointment have no power to ruffle the tranquillity of his great holiness. Anxious as he was to secure a shelter for Mary, his request never degenerated into an unmanly importunity. He asks with humility but not with subservience, and accepts his refusal with dignity and without recrimination. For, in the successive disappointments, he sees God's Will and he instantly conforms himself to it, knowing it to be best. So should we make our petitions, too, our demands for this or that—ready to accept, *with perfect resignation*, whatever God should decide. If we do not get what we desire, we should thank God that we have failed to obtain what might have proved hurtful to us. And even our best interests will always be found to have been served by this conformity to God's will. As in the present case, the cave of Bethlehem that God's Providence provided for the shelter of the Holy Family was after all the most suitable place to be the scene of God's birth, although we should never have thought it so before the event. On reflection, and contemplating the nativity in the full light of our knowledge of what the Son of Mary is—" Who," as St. Paul says, " was predestinated the Son of God in power according to the spirit of sanctification " [15]—we can see how incongruous would any other place have been, how perfectly congruous the cave itself was for the birth of Jesus. He Who was the Immense should not be confined within the narrow walls of a town, and He Who was *infinitely rich* would be demeaned by dependence on any of the creature comforts of earth. There is only one joy to be looked for on earth, only one thing that attracts Him, one thing that calls forth His complacency : it is the souls and hearts of the holy and the pure. Even in the cave He found that comfort and that joy in Mary and Joseph. For the rest, the poverty, the silence, the abandonment were what perfectly became Him as God made man.

Having searched the town in vain, Joseph tried to find a shelter in the public caravansary that is to be found in every oriental town of any size. It is usually in the form of an open gallery, roofed over and enclosing an open court. The floor is slightly raised and strewn with straw ; it is meant to provide a shelter for those wayfarers who are too poor to secure more suitable accommodation for the night. This is " The Inn " spoken of in the Gospel. It is quite characteristic of Joseph that he tried to secure a corner of this shelter of the poor for Mary and himself. *They were not ashamed*

[15] Rom. i. 4.

to consort with the humblest and to partake of their lot.
But even this miserable protection against the winter's
night was denied them. It was thronged when they
arrived—the floor of the gallery, closed on the exterior
and open on the side of the court, was entirely covered
with the mats on which those who had arrived already
were to repose for the night. The court itself was filled
with the beasts of burden. Doubtless several of the
kindlier disposed—for the poor are as a rule charitable—
would have freely vacated their places out of respect
for Joseph and sympathy for Mary. *As they were not
in Bethlehem for amusement or pleasure their hearts would
not be so hard, nor their perceptions so blunt as those of
the householders.* Joseph, who would not put anyone
to inconvenience for himself, gratefully declined these
offers, and directed his steps into the country to see if
he could fare any better.

One cannot help feeling glad that there was no room
in this crowded inn. There is something repugnant in
the idea of Our Lord's birth taking place amidst such
thronging and confusion, noise and bustle. The
character of God, and therefore of the God made man,
is tranquillity. He cannot abide feverish agitation,
disorder and the glare of publicity.

There were no unkindly thoughts either in Joseph's
mind or that of his spouse as they left the inhospitable
town behind them and wandered homeless towards the
hills in the neighbourhood. Their attitude was one of
absolute submission to the providence of God. They
had done their best to find a roof, they had insisted as
much as was becoming without being importunate,
and if they had been refused it was because God had

so permitted. They wasted neither words nor thoughts on the blindness, inhospitality or avarice of the Bethlehemites. They probably did not question their actions at all, and if in any way their thoughts returned upon what had taken place, they probably found excuses for the townspeople. But most likely they looked upon the whole thing as being the natural consequence of their condition in life, their poverty and their belated arrival. Regarding it as such, they bowed their heads in submission to Divine Providence, and placed their trust in God. Their trust was not misplaced—God Who takes care of the little birds directed their steps towards a natural grotto of which there were several in the chalk hills in the neighbourhood, and which were used as a shelter for cattle. It was to one of these bleak, windswept caverns that the Holy Family found its way—in the darkness. For a great part of the night had already been consumed in their unavailing search. Joseph did what little he could to introduce some degree of comfort into the cave—and there, at midnight, *in the silence, obscurity, abandonment and cold, but in perfect calm and quiet,* God came forth into the world. Certainly, never was child of Adam born in direr circumstances. Mary and Joseph must have been smitten to the heart at the plight in which the Son of God, the Lord of Heaven, found Himself, and at the chilling welcome that was extended to Him by the world which He had come to restore to happiness. They did what they could to compensate Him for this coldness, by the warmth of their affection, and it was not without success. It is true that the exposed cavern was cold ; chilling draughts were wafted into it from the star-lit night outside.

The swaddling bands in which Mary wrapped the Infant afforded but an imperfect shelter against the chilliness of the icy draughts. There is no doubt but that the straw was rough and coarse in spite of all Mary's efforts to make of it a clean and smooth bed for the tender Infant limbs. The manger, to be sure, was a sorry cradle for a King, and that the august King of heaven and earth. Doubtless, it was all very comfortless, but that is only one aspect of the birth of Jesus in the stable. It was not all wretchedness and misery. In this life of the Man-God lowliness and greatness, obscurity and splendour, weakness and power ever go hand in hand, and it is the splendour and power and greatness that dominate. They are but enhanced by the dark shadows of poverty, isolation and suffering. The shadows of the life of Jesus but serve to throw the splendours into stronger relief. The stable was a wretched abode, but in it was a sanctuary as worthy of God as it is possible for a created thing to be worthy of Him. That sanctuary was Mary's soul. In it the Child God could nestle to His heart's content and find delight. He is God and for Him, therefore, spiritual realities are more real than material realities. In His eyes the splendours of His Mother's soul transformed the cavern into an abode of palatial splendour and beauty. The mother love of Mary wrapped the soul and heart of Jesus in a mantle of warmth that was grateful in the extreme. God had never before experienced the like from a human person. Mary lavishes tenderness mingled with adoration on the Child. She ministers to Him the warmth, the light, the comfort, denied by the cavern. Joseph's affection and adoration were a pale but still a true reflex of the

love and worship of Mary. It is not easy to satisfy
God. The saints, even great ones, find Him exacting
in His requirements. Yet here God was satisfied. He
could ask no more from these two than they had given.
For they had given without niggardliness. They had
given all that their hearts and souls were capable of.
The hostelry in which the new-born God found shelter
was not, after all, such a mean one. It was the greatest
and the most beautiful that our earth has seen or ever
will see. It was not all lowliness and sordidness that
surrounded the nativity of the Saviour. Man could not
take from Him His greatness, nor could the humble
circumstances to which their blindness condemned Him
obscure it. He was great, in spite of all that man could
say or do or judge and His greatness burst in splendour
through the lowly conditions of the Nativity. Trumpets
proclaim the birth of princes. Never did earth re-echo
to strains comparable to those that announced the birth
of the Great Prince of Heaven, Mary's Son. Never
was such a radiance diffused through the palaces of
kings as flooded the wide spaces in the centre of which
was found the manger. Men may not, but God always
does recognise true greatness, and He sets His seal
upon it. Of Jesus of Bethlehem, as of Jesus of Nazareth,
it can be said : " For Him, hath God, the Father,
sealed." [16]

The cave of Bethlehem is an exact presentation of the
paradox of Christianity. It is austere and forbidding.
Even in the daylight and under the bright sun the cavern
would look miserable and uninviting. In the darkness
it was positively repellent. The glimmer shed by

[16] St. John vi. 27.

Joseph's lantern was not strong enough to shed a cheerful light; it served but to reveal and to bring out into relief every harsh and rude feature. The sides dripped with moisture and showed bare and jagged. Through openings in them, here and there, the wind moaned dismally. The strong draughts increased the natural chilliness of the place. The floor was uneven and covered with straw that had been trampled to filth by the animals. What was in the rude manger, though clean, was coarse and prickly; it scarcely tempered the hardness of the few planks for the Infant limbs. The dripping of the water and the sounds of the animals as they stirred in their rest, falling on the ear, intensified the general feeling of comfortlessness. And all these things, the cold, the darkness, the roughness of the straw, the unpleasant odour, concentrated their arrows of suffering on the tender Body of the Baby that had just been born in this inhospitable place. Sensitive in the extreme, the Child-God quivered with pain, and broke into infant wails. He willed to be as an ordinary child. *He was not yet at the age when, as our Model, He would control His feelings and support His sufferings without flinching.* And all who wished to be with Jesus—to come close to Him—were drawn into these miserable surroundings, first Mary and Joseph and then the shepherds. They all had, in order to get near Him, to suffer the same cold, the same misery, the same abandonment—to share in everything which provided a marked contrast to the scenes that were taking place in the village above. From it floated down the pleasant sounds of revelry and feasting. Every house was brilliantly illuminated and the lights shone on faces that were bright with laughter and excitement. The rooms glittered with vessels in which were set out delicate things to eat and drink. The cheerful music set the young people dancing, whilst the old exchanged confidences with their friends who had come from a distance. An agreeable warmth pervaded every house. Each one vied with the other in the effort to gratify every sense and to dispel in a whirlwind of gaiety and pleasure the tedium of life. How they would have shuddered at the dreariness and discomforts of the cavern in the chalk cliff ! The cave and the city ! What a remarkable contrast ! In the city seems to be all the "*joie de vivre*"; on the hillside nothing but misery and discomfort. Yet which of the two groups of personages enjoyed the greater happiness ? Need we ask ? The revellers find dissipation but not happiness, and in the very act of enjoyment are filled with a sense of dissatisfaction.

Who is there who has not experienced the hollowness and emptiness of even the most intoxicating joys of earth ? How many repeat after Solomon, after having gratified every sense, " Vanity of Vanities and all is vanity," save to serve God and Him alone.[17]   On the other hand, what intense happiness is to be found at the side of the manger ! The very absence of everything calculated to please the senses leaves the soul free to enjoy itself more largely. In Bethlehem little concession is made to the body, " for it is the setting for the soul ". It is not of that which benefits the body, but of that which benefits the soul that all men stand in need. This is the lesson preached eloquently by the silent

[17] *Imitation*, Bk. I, Chap. I, 3.

Babe. The two who were there understood the lesson well, above all did His Mother. She bent over the manger, and as she enveloped the Child, her Child and her God, in her arms, torrents of happiness surged through her heart. The glow within her radiated from her eyes and her face shone with a light which bathed the Infant and in which His glance found a resting place. The hours sped for her. Utterly absorbed, she loved and adored Jesus with a vehemence which neither the Cherubim nor Seraphim could match. Her love was an adoration and her adoration was a mother's love. She was rapt in a tumult of emotions which were a commingling of homage, praise, love, tenderness, joy and exultation. Her gladness would have ravished her soul from her body were she not so spiritually strong. Joseph's pain and anxiety disappeared in a torrent of joy that overflowed his calm and deep soul as he knelt in worship before his foster Child and his God. The shepherds, too, far removed as they were from the holiness of Mary and Joseph, entered into a happiness, one moment of which infinitely outweighed in satisfaction years of such pleasure as their more favoured brethren (as the world would think) tasted in the city above. And yet all these were in contact with these physical discomforts from which Jesus was in the same instant suffering so bitterly. Were they insensible to those things to which He was so keenly alive? In a sense they were, for all these material things seemed to have turned their cruel points on the Infant Saviour, whilst from Him was diffused a joy and happiness which flooded the souls of His worshippers with delight. He seems to have taken all the sting out of poverty and pain, by suffering them Himself. His faithful disciples—real Christians—often feel nothing of them owing to the intense happiness they derive from their union with Jesus. The pleasures of this intimacy render them almost insensible, certainly indifferent, to pain. This is the secret of the saints' contentment in the midst of trials and persecutions. This is the secret of the strength of the martyrs in the midst of their intolerable torments.

To us, too, it may be given to feel, in a little measure, something of all this. But if we are to share the experience of Mary, Joseph, the Shepherds, and the Kings, we must learn to rise superior to our sensuality, and to scorn a life of self-indulgence. The cave is not tender to the body: it is rude to the sensibility: it is hostile to the love of ease and comfort. It seems hard and repugnant to deprive ourselves of the warmth and light of life, of everything that seems to make life enjoyable— ease and comfort, leisure, society—in a word, all things that worldly people esteem, and that are comprehended under the heading of riches, pleasure and power. The Christian life on the other hand has a cold and harsh and forbidding appearance. Yet, if we once deliberately make our choice, we shall find that all this austerity is in the exterior and that the whole-hearted practice of Christianity and the full acceptance of its conditions give a happiness and contentment that fill the soul. Was there ever a man who had completely surrendered his will to the will of God who could not confess that he was supremely happy? Was there ever a worldling who could say with truth that the pleasures of sense ever left him otherwise than with a dissatisfied craving which

they were unable to satisfy? It is only those *that lead
an interior life* that ever in this world taste real happiness.
Out of one hour of their life they get more value than
do superficial Christians out of years. *They really
live*—the men given to exterior things merely *exist.*
It is a source of sadness and surprise for interior souls
that of the vast number that are called to follow Christ,
so few enter into His Society. They pity them for
what they miss—when they do not boldly and resolutely
turn their backs upon the lighted city and cast their
choice for the dark cave. The friends of Jesus realise
that conventional Christians, if they would but resolutely
brave the rudeness of the stable, cast themselves on
their knees beside the rough manger and, fixing their
gaze on the face of the Child, allow themselves to be
wrapped up in the sense of His presence and wholeheartedly accept His values, would taste a happiness
that could not be destroyed or even assailed by the
worst miseries of human life ; for in that contemplation
they would learn—taught by the eloquent silence of
the Infant Jesus—that all that this earth can give is
nothing and that the life of God, or the life with God, is
everything.

CHAPTER III

THE COMING OF THE WISE MEN

*" We have seen his star in the East, and are come to adore Him.
. . . Opening their treasures they offered Him gifts ; Gold, frankincense and myrrh."*—ST. MATT. ii. 2–11.

ST. PAUL tells us " that all scripture, inspired of God,
is profitable to teach, to reprove, to correct, to instruct
in justice ; that the man of God may be perfect, furnished
to every good work ". [1] Every individual soul is created
to acquire, by the aid of God's grace, interior justice,
and through it, intimate knowledge of and union with
God. All dealings that the Lord has with the soul have
a purpose, no other than this. He is not uninterested
in our temporal plans, objects and cares, but their value
in His eyes is entirely judged by their aptitude to further
the main purpose of our life on earth—growth in holiness. If He sends us worldly success and prosperity,
it is not because He has a desire to see us play a brilliant
and agreeable *rôle* in the theatre of life, but that He sees
in our character or temperament something which
demands these advantages in order that the service of
our Creator may come easier to us. This is true, of
course, only where temporal blessings are willed by God
for us, and not where they are the fruit of human endeavour put forth, and human talent exercised, without

[1] 2 Tim. iii. 16–17.

any desire to have the one or the other or both regulated by God's views in view of our spiritual welfare.   God weaned the Hebrews from sin and drew them to Himself by temporal favours—so much so, that these temporal favours were for this people the sign of their conduct being agreeable in His eyes.   In our own times we see many favours of a temporal nature, as health of body, successful issue of undertakings and a certain measure of worldly goods granted by the Lord, according to the prayers of the faithful.   Lourdes is the perpetual theatre of these temporal favours.   But compared with the few who are gratified in this manner, how great is the multitude of those who are treated otherwise and left in their mental distress or their bodily ailments ! Yet the same divinely benevolent purpose directs the granting or the refusal of the prayers that ascend to God's throne through the intermediary of His Saints.   When the Father in Heaven visits His children with sorrow and failure, it is not for any satisfaction that He finds in their sufferings—which on the contrary excite His compassion—but for the purpose of breaking down the obstacles that separate their souls from Him ; the removal of these obstacles He sees to be morally impossible in any other manner.   This, of course, is true only of those trials which are disposed for us by divine providence and which enter into God's plan in our regard.   We have no such guarantee with regard to those we bring on us by our own wilfulness.   The history of the Jewish race is a sad instance of the fate that befalls groups or individuals that involve themselves in disaster through their own perversity.   There is great spiritual advantage attached to the sufferings endured in submission to God's will : these advantages are not attached to the sorrows that are experienced through opposition to His will.[2] St. Peter writes to the early Christians : " For this is thankworthy; if for conscience towards God, a man endure sorrows, suffering wrongfully. For what glory is it, if committing sin and being buffeted for it, you endure ? But if doing well you suffer patiently, this is thankworthy before God." [3]

God will always give to His children the grace to turn to spiritual advantage either adversity or prosperity. The adversity itself or the prosperity may not be ordained for us by His will. Many of the sufferings that men have to bear in life are certainly due to activities that are not and would not be willed by Almighty God. He cannot will the wrongdoing which is the cause of suffering : He merely permits it. It is relatively easy for good souls to submit to what He positively ordains. Much greater difficulty is experienced in accepting bravely and patiently and without sinful anger, bitterness and revolt, what He merely permits. Pious persons gladly submit themselves to God : they often have a great reluctance to submit to God's representatives enjoining something which is not manifestly and may not be at all in the designs of God in their regard.

---

[2] Of course there is no grace or benediction attached to the sufferings brought on us by our own wilfulness. The sufferings that the bad thief brought on himself by his crimes earned for him no blessing or healing of soul. On the other hand, God is always able to draw good out of evil, and if we humbly accept the pains and sorrows that come on us through our own blindness or perversity, He can turn them into instruments of sanctification for our souls. He can make even our sins, if we accept their aftermath of suffering in a spirit of expiation and compunction, serve to procure our spiritual good—as happened in the case of the good thief. Cf. *S. Th.* I.   Q. 22, A. 2, c. and ad 4.

[3] 1 St. Peter ii. 19–20.

Theoretically they accept St. Paul's statement that, " to them that love God, all things work together to good ".[4] But when put to the test they fail in faith and consequently in submission because they do not discern that God is able to procure good for them through the evil that comes by the mistakes, self-will or perversity of others, of which they may be the victims. It is not easy to detect the intimations that God gives to us through the happenings of life. Our feelings and passions and emotions prevent us from grasping clearly the instructions that Our Father in Heaven wishes to convey to us through our life's experiences. But things come to us more distinctly, and the lessons of existence lose their obscurity for us, if we exercise ourselves to see in what is narrated in Scripture a dramatic and vivid presentation of what each, in his own individual capacity, in some measure, goes through, in his spiritual pilgrimage. The Holy Spirit addresses each one of us through the medium of the inspired writings. In all that He has dictated to the authors of Scripture we can be sure that God intends a certain teaching to be conveyed to our souls. The events set forth in the Old Testament and in the New are not narrated for the purpose of imparting to us merely historic or scientific information. The purpose of the narration is wholly spiritual—to " instruct us in justice ".

The lessons taught by Scripture are not exclusively of a universal or general import. Not only are groups and nations instructed by them in the ways of God ; the individual soul, too, can, if it meditates with faith and humility on the word of God, discover in that Word

[4] Rom. viii. 28.

a well-defined picture of what the soul meets with in the vicissitudes of the interior life and can be instructed by that picture as to the manner in which it is to act if it is to make all its experiences contribute to its growth in union with God. But it is not always easy to find in a particular incident a " sacramental," as it were, presentation of an individual spiritual experience. In some cases the application presents considerable difficulty, as for instance, in the story of the Magi, found in the Gospel of St. Matthew. It is easy enough to grasp its significance, when regarded in its universal aspect, especially when taken in conjunction with the prophecies that heralded a Messias, royal and glorious. Everybody knows that the call of the Magi typifies the vocation of the Gentiles to the Church of God. But to penetrate more deeply into this mystery and to read therein an experience common to a multitude of souls demands a deeper understanding of God's way of manifesting Himself to His creatures, and a keener discernment of His actions in human souls.

God is never idle, and His great work is not creation, but re-creation. Jesus said, " My Father worketh until now ; and I work." [5] Jesus implies that for God there is, in a sense, no sabbath. There was a sabbath as far as regarded the work of creation : there is no sabbath for the activities involved in the re-creation. The divine energy of these activities is employed on all rational creatures, but it does not effect them merely externally nor yet in a general way. God's work is interior, and is directed to the soul with a view to re-creating it to His own Image. Each individual claims the attention

[5] St. John v. 17.

of God, and that Divine attention is given to that creature as totally and as unreservedly as if it were the only one on the earth's surface. Waves of thought, of feeling, of vague desires, of indefinable dissatisfactions, rise incessantly in the soul from its depths. We assign them to some immediate, obvious, secondary cause and we fail to trace these spiritual phenomena to their rightful source, namely, the action of Almighty God. If we were mortified, detached and recollected, we should be quick to seize God's action in the moods we experience in our moments of quiet thought and reflection. But the tragedy of our lives is that we so frequently fail to seize God in action. It is not that we wilfully and deliberately choose not to see Him. It is quite the contrary. We are all eagerness to gaze upon His countenance, and to see Him at work in the universe outside and within ourselves. But He does not show Himself distinctly. He and His action are hidden and so escape us. God is a Hidden God, and must be so for us. He manifests Himself obscurely. God does not hide Himself from us purposely or to make approach to Him more difficult. He desires revelation of Himself to us, and approach to Him on our part. God in His approach to us but tempers His brilliancy to accommodate it to our weak and diseased spiritual vision. He, as it were, takes care not to hurt our soul's sight. But He aims at revelation through the dimmed radiance. The Incarnation, which is the utmost concealment of the Godhead that there is, or that can be—except that of the Eucharist alone—is the greatest revelation of God.

That we are dull of perception is certainly not due to the mode in which God reveals Himself, but must be

traceable to our own fault. It is the poor quality of our
faith that is responsible for this dullness. We do not
take God on His own conditions. We are always given
to imposing ours on Him. We have a tendency to
decide for ourselves what shall be the sensible exterior
vesture of God's message. We clothe that message
with a garment woven of our own ideas and imaginings,
and we reject the material selected by God Himself for
His revelation. God takes certain created forms to
manifest Himself to us, namely, words and actions.
We do not accept them. We have an inveterate tendency
to substitute for them our own forms—the creation of
our petty, narrow, earthly conceptions of the divinity.
Perversely " we look for a God that will conform to
our formulæ ". We strive to compress Him and to
contract Him to these moulds of our thought, and when
He fails to fit we are prone to judge that here in this
case God is not. We seek Him, then, in the conditions
created by ourselves, and of course fail to find Him.
We do not seek Him in the conditions determined by
Him, and so He passes by, without our recognising
Him. His mind and ours do not agree, and this is the
reason of all the misunderstandings with God from
which we suffer in the course of life. His ways are not
our ways, nor our thoughts His. What happened to
the Jews is happening to countless souls daily. The
Jews knew where the Messias should be born. They
were able, without hesitation and without doubt, to
inform strangers and pagans of the place of His birth.
" There came wise men from the East to Jerusalem,
saying, Where is he that is born King of the Jews ?
And they said, In Bethlehem of Juda. For so it is

written by the prophet : And thou Bethlehem, the land
of Juda, are not the least among the princes of Juda :
for out of thee shall come forth the captain that shall
rule my people Israel." [6] The priests and the scribes
answered correctly, but all the evidence goes to show
that they did not themselves discover the Messias,
whose whereabouts they disclosed to the Magi. The
pagans and strangers had vision where the people of
God were blind. It was because the latter had created,
out of imaginations heated by racial prejudice and
national pride, the glorious pageantry in which the
promised Redeemer was to make His dazzling advent.
They had arranged the circumstances of His appearance,
and when He did not come in the form their imagination
had woven for Him they gazed on His face, unseeing.
Not so the Wise Men. They took God on His own
terms. He chose a certain mode for His manifestation,
and they acknowledged Him as God in the lowliness of
the guise in which He appeared. *They looked on a
Babe and they saw God.* Their faith was superb.

Faith according to St. Paul is " argumentum non
apparentium ",[7] which may be translated the clear
showing forth, for the person having faith and because
of it, of the unseen. It is a power of keenest vision in
the soul by which it penetrates through the veil of
created circumstance, and discovers the God that was
enveloped in obscurity. It is a supernatural faculty of
discerning the divine through, and in, the human. It
is a sensitiveness of an intellectual kind to the presence
of God in things and in conditions, which show them-

[6] St. Matt. ii. 1–6.
[7] Heb. xi. 1.

selves to the unspiritual as purely human. The faith here spoken of is what Cardinal Newman will describe " as a *practical perception* of the unseen world ".[8] It is a strong participation in the piercing intuition of God Himself. It is a divine gift of insight. It was given to St. Peter in a remarkable manner on the occasion when, seeing with bodily vision what the other apostles saw, he, nevertheless, discerned what no bodily sense or reason revealed. He, unbaffled by his natural vision of eye and intelligence, saw God in the Man by Whom he was questioned. " Blessed art thou, Simon Bar-Jonah, because flesh and blood hath not revealed it to thee, but My Father, Who is in heaven." [9]

If we wish to see God day by day our faith must be of a better quality than we ordinarily give proof of. Our constant prayer should be for an increase of Faith, echoing the words of the Apostles, who said to the Lord : " Increase our Faith." [10] To see God we must believe in God *Incarnate*. " He that seeth Me," He said, " seeth the Father also." [11] To believe in God Incarnate is not merely to believe that under the human vesture is the Godhead, but to believe *as strongly that this human vesture, in all its particulars, belongs to and is the apt clothing of the divine*. It is to believe that if God the Son is to be discovered on earth by men, He is to be found clothed in all the elements of this Humanity and in all its circumstances, and in all its conditions. It is to believe not only that God became Incarnate, but to believe also that God literally reveals Himself to us

---

[8] *Parochial Sermons*, III., 79.   (Italics mine.)
[9] St. Matt. xvi. 17.
[10] St. Luke xvii. 5.
[11] St. John xiv. 9.

in the thoughts, judgments, doings and endurings of the
Sacred Humanity. It is to believe that the life of Jesus
amongst men is the divine way of living on earth and
that that divine way of living on earth is a perfect earthly
reflection of the divine way of living in the centre of
the Blessed Trinity. " Philip," said Jesus to his
apostle when eager to discover and gaze upon God the
Father, " he that seeth Me, seeth the Father also." [12]
To believe in God Incarnate is not merely to accept the
Divinity of Jesus Christ ; it is to accept His Humanity
also ; it is not merely to believe in His Godhead, but to
believe in His Manhood, too. It is to believe not only
that He is divine in the way God is divine, but to believe,
as firmly, that He is human in the way men should be
human. We falter more easily in this latter aspect of
belief than in the former. For to accept Him as human
is not merely to accept Him as man—that He had a body
and soul like ours—but it is to accept and to subscribe
to all His views on life on earth and his whole theory of
human values. It is not only to believe in the reality
of God's human life, it is to hold firmly that the human
life of God is the only true human life or perhaps,
better, the only life that is truly human : it is to be
convinced, in consequence, that every life of man that
deviates from its standards and principles is a false
human life, and false to proper human standards in the
exact measure of that deviation. To grasp firmly and
to hold unhesitatingly to this truth does not come
easily to us. We admire Our Lord, we think Him
magnificent in the circumstances, but we are tempted to
look upon His attitude towards things in general as

[12] St. John xiv. 9.

somewhat exaggerated, and unnecessary and, of course, unsuited to the conditions in which our human life is cast. To accept Him totally and not partially (the Jews accepted Him in His miracles; they rejected Him in His powerlessness) demands a reversal of many of our standards of evaluation, the shedding of a lot of our prejudices, and the taking of extraordinary risks, involving, it may be, the loss of all that nature clings to. We are faint-hearted before this absolute renouncement, and our faint-heartedness effects in us a kind of spiritual obtuseness. And yet this absolute renouncement of our habitually earthly standards of life, and the complete acceptance of those of Jesus, is the price we have to pay for our Epiphany, which means " Manifestation ". If a man sets himself to accept and live the Gospel in its totality, he will not fail to see God, daily, and many times a day, as the saints did, in the form of created persons, incidents or things.

That the three wise men were able to discern in the form of a helpless babe, lying in an earthly Mother's frail arms, under a miserable roof, the King of Kings, the great Redeemer of the human race that had been spoken of in prophecy for centuries before, was a truly marvellous thing. It is a proof that they must have been men of very pure lives and to a large extent immune from the corruption of the world in which they lived. Gifted with great science, as their name implies, they must have had clear and docile and simple minds, minds eager to acquire the truth and ready to submit to it, no matter how much it might conflict with the traditions and prejudices of their race. They loved truth, and their studies were pursued to discover what was true and not what they would like to be true and what would fit in with their preconceived or inherited opinions. Their scientific investigations were, therefore, pure and disinterested. This gave them a deep insight into the reality of things and the power to discern the emptiness, hollowness and superficiality of the life that surrounded them—its false values, its idle pursuits and its love of the superficial and the unreal. Pure hearts, strong and docile intelligences and aloofness from unreality, these were the characteristics of the three wise men. This effected in them a great detachment from the comfort, the riches and the luxury that surrounded their high station. They were ready to submit to the Reality in whatever guise this should present itself, and were too free from passion, prejudice, from self-love and self-seeking in all its forms, to seek to impose on It the forms of their own mind.

Their docility of mind and their purity of heart made them receptive of God's graces. Knowledge of the ancient prophecies had spread from Palestine over the eastern world which had been brought into relation with it through political and commercial channels. The Scripture tells us that the prophet Daniel while in captivity in Babylon was made head of all the magi and wise men of the kingdom.[13] From him the Jewish expectation of the Messias was known to the learned. Hence we can understand how all men of thoughtful and meditative lives were expecting a Redeemer, who should restore what the heathen imagination called the " Golden Age ". The Magi, too, like the others, were

[13] Daniel i. 20; ii. 48; v. 11.

anxiously scanning the signs of the times to read therein some indication of the coming of the "long expected of the Nations". But purer of heart than the generality, and with souls more sympathetic to spiritual aspirations, they looked to the promised Saviour, not merely for the cessation of temporal evils but also, and perhaps more so, for the reformation of religion and morals. At the time that these Sages of the east were pursuing their deep studies into the nature of things, the whole civilised world was agitated with vague expectations of something great and decisive in the destinies of the world, about to take place. When, therefore, in their nightly watchings a new heavenly body, of remarkable and unwonted radiance, came into their ken, they were prepared to recognise in this brilliant luminary the star of the ancient prophecies. Moved by an interior grace, they regarded this celestial apparition as the portent heralding the arrival of the Saviour of the World. At the same moment God touched their souls with a secret inspiration which moved them to leave their homes and to follow the guidance of this star to the land of Palestine, where the Redeemer was to make his appearance. This they knew by the ancient prophecies. From the terms which they used on their arrival in the holy city—" Where is He that is born King of the Jews? For we have seen His star in the East and are come to adore Him "—it is evident that their response to the touch of grace was prompt and unhesitating, and that they set out on their quest without any delay.

And yet, can anything be more strange in itself? Their undertaking would seem to the worldly-wise most foolhardy. Why should they leave their magnificent homes and the ease of a cultured and studious life, to go to pay their respects to One whom they knew not ? The journey was long and would entail hardship. Even if they were drawn by the hope of acquiring some higher religious knowledge, some deeper certitude about the World beyond the world of sense, some more sublime truths, had they not already acquired a pure religion and profound wisdom by their prolonged studies and their ascetic lives ? It is most likely that to these wise men were not wanting prudent friends who strove to dissuade them from setting out, pointing out the magnitude of the sacrifice they were making and the very problematic return that was to be theirs for what they were giving up. Why should they exchange what was certain for what was doubtful ? They knew the blessings they enjoyed, they had no surety with regard to those that were promised. Why renounce home and wealth and royalty, with the reverence and affection of those dependent on them, in order to pay homage to a King, Whose powers and prerogatives were set forth in the prophecies in enigmatic and perplexing terms ? But the deep faith, the sincerity and the simplicity of the Magi triumphed over all these too reasonable objections. The folly of their faith silenced the difficulties presented by human reasoning, and they set out, laden with rich gifts, to present themselves to the new-born King.

The whole story is romantic in the extreme. The wonderful faith of these men passes all belief. The splendour of their coming, their rich presents, their kingly service to the Babe of Bethlehem, seem somewhat out of keeping with the austere and rather severe outlines of the rest of the Gospel story. Their appearance in the pages of St. Matthew is like a sudden burst of glorious sunshine, breaking in a flood of glory, through a sky wrapped in a mantle of sombre grey. There is a picturesqueness, a quaintness and unexpectedness about the incident of the Eastern Kings that is in striking contrast with the severity, the simplicity, the " ordinariness " that, if we set the miracles apart, characterises the rest of the Gospel story. The entry of this Eastern cavalcade into the picture is like something that the Divine Child used His Divine Powers to bring about in order to charm and delight the imagination of the children of earth. In fact, there is something eminently childlike in the prompt unquestioning faith of the Magi, in their ready acceptance of a wonderful heavenly portent as the normal indication and accompaniment of the .great happening they were called to witness. As they hastened on their way, they must have been filled with high expectancy ; their imaginations must have formed glowing pictures of the wonders that awaited them at the term of their journey : an event heralded in such a striking manner, by a heavenly body of unparalleled brilliancy, must surely be attended by circumstances of magnificence such as the world had never yet seen. An adventure which began with such radiant promise would surely end in a still more brilliant realisation. As, with the star flooding with light their path at every step, they drew near to Jerusalem, their souls must have been raised to the highest degree of bright expectancy. To find the people of the Holy City utterly ignorant of the great event which had drawn them from the remote East must have been a rude shock

and must have had a chilling effect on the warmth of
their imaginations. It did not, however, cause their
faith to waver. As soon as they had learned from the
accredited custodians of the ancient prophecies that
Bethlehem was the birthplace of Him whom they sought,
they set out immediately for the City of David, and
were sustained and encouraged by the presence and the
light of the heavenly guide that directed the course of
their journey. " And the star went before them, until
it came and stood over where the child was ; and seeing
the star they rejoiced with exceeding great joy. And
entering into the house they found the child with Mary
his Mother." [14]

Their long quest had come to an end. Were they
disappointed with the unexpected manner of its termina-
tion ? As they saw the humble roof under which the
Child was, and as they perceived the lowly simple
condition of His parents, were they taken aback ? Had
they any misgivings ? Were they harassed by any
doubts ? Did they entertain any regret for having
embarked on this enterprise against the counsels of
human prudence ? Was it merely a poverty-stricken
helpless infant, who attracted no attention, and was
surrounded by no pomp of circumstance, that they
had come so far to see and to worship ? Were they
expected to discern in this humble babe an object of
their kingly homage ? It was the supreme test to which
they were put, and their magnificent faith triumphed
over all appearances. Their hearts responded loyally
to the touch of grace, for they were unprejudiced and
ready to concede to God whatever form He should

[14] St. Matt. ii. 9, 11.

choose for His manifestation. They did not presume to quarrel with God's choice. The star was the outward sign by which they recognised the Ruler of the Universe and the King of men in Mary's child. All their views were rectified and they understood in a flash that the sovereignty to be exercised by this child was to be mainly spiritual, not material—a sovereignty to be won not by the forces of the flesh but by the forces of the spirit.

It came home to them that it was a great, universal, spiritual religion and not a vast, crushing, material empire that was to be established on the earth; and they realised that this was the interpretation to be applied to all the ancient prophecies concerning the Messias, and therefore, " falling down, they adored Him, and, opening their treasures, they offered him gifts, gold, frankincense and myrrh ".[15] It was at the prompting of a divinely given instinct and under the influence of a divine illumination that they made for their offerings this selection from amongst their treasures. There is a deep symbolism in the gifts. By them was manifested in a most expressive manner their grasp of the nature of the Kingship to be established by Christ and of the economy of that salvation for which the world was sighing. The gold typifies understanding or, better, wisdom. These learned men, wise hitherto with the wisdom of worldly science, were now instructed in the wisdom of God which is always foolishness to men.[16] Being enlightened interiorly, it was given them to enter into the views of God with regard to the reconstruction

[15] St. Matt. ii. 11.
[16] Cf. 1 Cor. xii. 7–16.

of the world. The frankincense, which in its odoriferous fumes aptly expresses the exhalation of prayer rising from the human soul, was an appropriate offering to One in whom they recognised their Sovereign Lord. The wise men worshipped and expressed their total dependence on this apparently helpless infant held in its Mother's arms. The myrrh, because of its bitterness, is the symbol of mortification. Because of its preservative qualities it signifies the salutary effects exercised by suffering in combating the corruption left in nature by original sin. The myrrh suggests the suffering life and the painful death that awaited the great King to whom they offered their homage. It shadowed forth the saving effects of that passion and death. Moreover, it symbolised the *rôle* that suffering was to play in transforming the King's followers to the likeness of their Head. The offering of myrrh was a gesture on the part of the wise men expressing their understanding, and their acceptance, of the cross as the means of bringing about the salvation of mankind.

Rarely has there been faith like to that of these three Eastern potentates ; rarely has faith been so severely tested and so magnificently triumphant. It would be difficult to find faith in the Gospel like to theirs. By their faith they left their homes, by their faith they followed the star, by their faith they consulted the heads of the Jewish religion, and by their faith they recognised in the Babe of Bethlehem the Desired of the Nations, the Saviour of the World.[17] In accepting this child, enveloped in obscurity, poverty and suffering from His birth, as their King and their Lord, they

[17] Cf. Hebrews xi.

accepted His standards of value, His concept of life, and His principles of action. Some thirty years later the Jews failed to discern the promised Messias, even when confronted by the testimony of the holiness of His life, the wisdom of His teaching and the power of His miracles. What a contrast their incredulity, in face of such evidence, presents to the faith of the kings who discern their King and their Lord under the form of a tiny babe, born in a stable and swathed in swaddling bands ! The conduct of these oriental kings teaches us a deep lesson. God manifested Himself to them in a manner for which all their previous life, their tastes, the customs of their country must have left them utterly unprepared. With their oriental views they looked for an Epiphany of grandeur, and they were confronted with one of abject poverty. And yet they did not fail to recognise the Divine, nor were they baffled by the unexpected disguise, by His humility of circumstance, nor by the defiance of all earthly prejudices and standards of valuation. Their purity of heart, their sincerity of mind, their love of truth and reality (no matter how much truth might conflict with their own views and feelings) and finally their great humility were what made them receptive of the gift of the wonderful faith given them by God.

There are daily Epiphanies in our lives. The grace of God is ever pointing out to us where the Child is. And we look at the outward circumstances, the mean disguises, the, to us, unworthy surroundings ; we decide that God cannot be *there* where the star stands, and so we pass on and miss the Manifestation. God is always wrapped in the same garments in which He was enveloped at His coming into the world and in His passage through it.   To us He always presents Himself in what thwarts the concupiscences of the flesh, in what contradicts our self-will, in what wounds our self-love, in a word, in pains, and trials, and disappointments, in sorrow, in opposition, and in failure. He expects us, as He expected the kings, to recognise Him under these habiliments.   Every cross in our life is, as it were, a reliquary .containing God.   If we embrace it with faith it will open and reveal His Presence to us.   When too much influenced, too much governed, too much determined by human external appearances, we decide that surely God could not and would not take such a form for His Manifestation, we fail in faith, we have not the docility and the simplicity of the Magi. It is for God, not for us, to determine the mode in which He offers Himself to each human soul for worship and for fealty—worship as to its God, fealty as to its King. Jesus comes to us in everything that tends to mortify our self-love and our pride, in everything that tends to break down the obstacles that prevent the development of our interior life, our growth in the vision and in the love of God.   He manifests Himself to the religious in the uncongenial task, the irritating opposition, and in the uncouth companion—in all the multiple disabilities, annoyances, and inconveniences arising for us from the failure or imperfection of creatures.   But at every conjuncture God wishes us to discover Himself, however disconcerting be the guise in which He comes.   It is not easy—it requires a strong faith to see Him in the long, dull sequence of squalid, obscure and pointless miseries that *condition* our daily lot.   In the dullness and weakness of our faith, we pause disconcerted before the humble appearance ; we decide that God is not there and pass on our way. We are always looking for Him elsewhere, in different circumstances, in other surroundings and in more gracious conditions. When men, moved by grace, turn from the ordinary routine life and resolve to give themselves wholly to God, they are prone to judge that all difficulties are overcome after the initial act of surrender to the Will of God and renouncement of creatures has been made. They think that henceforth life will be a smooth, tranquil development of the life of grace in their souls. And they expect God so to arrange life that no harsh and distracting conditions will intervene to complicate and disturb the soul's quiet converse with Himself. The incident of the Magi teaches that hardship, anxiety, pain and harsh circumstance must always prepare the way for the discovery of the child in its Mother's arms. We do not find the herald of God or God Himself in easy circumstances. The Child of Mary, many years later, warned His hearers of this, saying : " But what went you out to see ? a man clothed in soft garments ? Behold they that are clothed in soft garments are in the houses of kings." [18]

[18] St. Matt. xi. 8.

CHAPTER IV

THE MOTHER OF JESUS IN THE TEMPLE

" And thy own Soul a sword shall pierce."—St. Luke ii. 35.

THE first days of our Blessed Saviour on earth must have been ones of ecstatic joy for Mary. During those forty days of seclusion which the law imposed on her she tasted to its fullest measure the happiness of motherhood. She had given birth to a Son, and the Babe she held in her arms was none other than her God and her Creator, whilst He was at the same time flesh of her flesh, and there ran in His veins her own most pure blood. Exempt from all the pain and weakness which is the lot of all other mothers since the sin of Eve, she was, from the very first moment, able to lavish on Jesus all the care and attention that His helplessness— the helplessness of the Omnipotent—needed. Every service that His Infant state demanded of her was given with wondrous promptitude and solicitude. To feel God powerless in one's arms and to be able to minister to His wants would be, in itself, sufficient to bewilder any soul less strong and less simple than Mary's. She did not pass her time in motionless adoration. *Her maternal attentions to the needs of her Child were her worship. She never for an instant lost sight of the Babe in her adoration of her God, nor did her deep realisation of the Godhead cause her to forget for a moment the necessities of the Child.* The physical tie which bound her to Jesus, the natural maternal instincts which such a tie created, would make it impossible to lose sight of the fact that the Being that nestled in her arms and looked to her for help, protection and sustenance was her Child. The absolute independence of the God did not dim her perception and full realisation of the complete dependence of the Babe. But this profound sense of the reality of the Infancy of Jesus did not cloud her vision of the power and the glory and the divinity that lay hidden under the frail, fleshly envelope. Her mother's love became mingled and identified with the creature's most perfect love of its Creator. She had not two loves of Jesus in her heart, the love of a mother for her child and the love of a creature for its God. The latter simply passed into the former, undergoing, in the passage, a marked transformation. In the Mother's love for her Child the creature's love of the Creator was touched with a marvellous devotedness, tenderness and reverent familiarity. How grateful she must have been for the law which bade her, though it did not bind her, to wrap herself up in that deep retirement, where she could, without interruption, allow herself to be penetrated through and through with the joy that inundated her soul.

Mary's uninterrupted bliss did not last for long. As is usual in the case of all God's spiritual consolations, her joy was a prelude to a trial which was to plunge her into the deepest grief. The Levitical Law ordained that every mother that had borne a male child should, after forty days of seclusion, redeem her right to take part once more in the service of religion by the offering of sacrifice. The women of Israel were considered to have contracted a legal stain in childbirth, and for this reason were obliged to offer a young pigeon or a dove as a sin offering. By this sacrifice was taken away their legal disability and after the offering of it they were free once more to attend the ceremonies of the divine worship. The sacrifice of atonement was followed by one of worship and thanksgiving. A young lamb, or in the case of the poor, still another dove or pigeon, was offered in holocaust to the Supreme Being. It was a solemn protestation by which the young mother acknowledged God as the Source and Author of her own life, and that other fresh young life that God had made her instrumental in bringing forth. These sacrifices made, the law furthermore enjoined that the child, if it were the first-born, should be consecrated to God. Originally, amongst the theocratic people, the first-born male child was, in virtue of this primogeniture, destined to exercise the sacerdotal functions on behalf of his family. He was consecrated to God from his birth. The establishment of a definite sacerdotal caste by the setting apart of the tribe of Levi for the service of the tabernacle took away the *raison d'être* of this custom. But still, God, to mark His absolute rights over His people and to engrave deeply on their memories their deliverance from the bondage of Egypt, when all the first-born of men and animals were, on their account, afflicted with death, claimed the eldest male child of each family as His own. That the child might be in a position to be brought back to the bosom of his family there was demanded from the parents a ransom of five shekels. The coming of Jesus signified the passing of the priesthood of Aaron. In the presentation [1] of the Son of Mary there returned the primitive signification of the offering. In what a perfect sense was He, the eldest born of Mary, consecrated to God and the divine service ! How absolutely did He belong to God ! How perfectly was He priest on behalf of His family—which was the whole human race !

Mary had not contracted any stain in bringing forth her Child. The Body of Jesus had been formed outside all the ordinary laws of conception, and in a miraculous manner, by the Holy Ghost. Although really and truly His Mother, she preserved her virginity unimpaired. She was a virgin before, during and after the delivery of Our Lord. She did not, therefore, come under the prescriptions of the Law ; yet it never occurred to her to demand exemption from its application in her regard, on the grounds of the privilege that had been bestowed on her by God.

She had conceived solely by the operation of the Holy Ghost, and so preserved the fairness of virginity whilst acquiring the glory of motherhood. Yet, so far was she from wishing to proclaim aloud her great and incomparable dignity, that she chose rather to hide it from the eyes of men by humbly submitting to the law that weighed upon the daughters of Israel. In all the scenes of the sacred infancy transmitted to us by the skilful and artistic pen of St. Luke it is instructive to note the close association between the Mother and

---

[1] Fillion notes that the Greek word used by St. Luke and translated by the English term " present " has a religious meaning. It responds to a Hebrew word which was used to designate the offering of sacrifices with blood-shedding and those without blood-shedding. It literally means—to bring near to the altar. *Vie de N. S. J. C.*, Vol. I., Chap. III.

the Child. The same characteristic is to be observed in the narrative of St. Matthew. Of the Magi, he says, that "entering the house, they found the child with Mary His Mother ".[2] Now the grouping of these two thus constantly, as if they formed a certain unity, is not unintentional. Neither is it due to the physical state of dependence in which the infant actually was with regard to her who had given Him birth. It is literally true that He needed the help of her sustaining arms to be presented to the gaze of His worshippers. But this natural necessity is not the reason for the insistence of the inspired writers in grouping together the mother and the child in all these incidents, when the infant is the centre of admiration, praise and worship. The close association of the two, so strongly stressed, points to a certain inseparability between them in the function which was to be the life-work of the Child. The two were to be as one in realising the purpose of the existence in the flesh of the Son of the Most High. This being so, it is eminently fitting that this intimate outward association should be a visible sign of inward unity of sentiments, tastes and aspirations. The external closeness marks the inner oneness. It is remarkable how naturally, from the moment of the Incarnation, the interior dispositions of Mary harmonise with those of her divine Child. Instinctively His ways become hers. The dispositions of the Mother easily mingle with and melt into those of the Child. What His tastes would inspire in the way of action becomes her choice. Her ways perfectly reflect His. She instinctively enters into His predilections. Jesus in a spirit of humility and

[2] St. Matt. ii. 11.

in obedience to the law, from which He was exempt, willed that for Him should be paid the ransom that was customary in the case of every first-born male child in Israel. In a similar spirit of humility and obedience Mary submitted herself to the rule of purification which she had no obligation to undergo. She practises the same self-effacement and observes the same silence as her Child. The words said about Jesus and the actions done concerning Him do not betray her into opening her lips and proclaiming aloud to all the wonders of which she holds the secret. She veils herself in modesty and retirement; she says nothing; she allows the incidents to speak for themselves; she watches and adores the action of Divine Providence in regard to her Child, and is content to store up all these things in her mind, in order to meditate on them at her leisure and to probe ever more deeply into the unfathomable mystery contained in every incident of the human-divine life that is gradually manifesting itself before the eyes of men. So now, too, after the forty days of her seeming purification were accomplished she preserves a complete silence on all that has taken place within her, leaving the revelation of it to the moment determined by God's Providence. Angels, Elizabeth, Shepherds, Kings, Simeon and Anna, all in their turn speak and proclaim aloud the glories of her Divine Son, Whose splendour is reflected on her who gave Him birth; *she* is silent and buries herself in profound meditation on all she sees and hears.

Her virginity was very dear to her. So dear was it that she was ready to forego the wonderful privilege of the Divine Maternity rather than surrender it, and yet

she is content to have it known only to God and herself,
and to pass before men as one who had foregone that
virginity for the bonds of marriage and the dignity
of motherhood. She maintains the same silence and
reserve when she stands before the Jewish priest and
allows him to make the legal sin offering on her behalf,
although she is absolutely sinless and exempt from
all that concupiscence which is the fruit and the punish-
ment of sin. Only God Himself saw the depths of
humility in her soul; only the Child she held in her
arms could sound the deep abasement involved in the
humble acceptance of the conditions of existence that
enveloped her as a daughter of a sinful race, even though
she herself was sinless.

Who of those that saw her passing that day up the
steps of the temple, mounting from the Court of the
Women to the entrance into the Court of Israel, could
suspect that this modest, unassuming, poorly clad, if
dignified, Jewish mother was in anything distinguished
from those others who on that same occasion were,
with her, pressing towards the gate of Nicanor to
fulfil the same legal obligation as she. Nothing in her
revealed to the careless glance that the humble and
unassuming Nazarene, bringing the offering of the two
poor turtle doves, was in very truth at that moment
the Queen of them all, the Queen of the whole universe,
the Sovereign of the invisible world of spirits, the
Mother of the great God, Who was Ruler and Judge
of all in Heaven and on earth and under the earth.
That quiet exterior, from which there radiated an
indefinable grace and dignity, revealed nothing of all
this. And it is ever so. Nearly all that is great and

noble, elevated and divine in the world of souls, is as a rule destined to escape the notice and observation of men. It is only the eye of faith, purified by prayer and close union with God, that can pierce the disguise and perceive the divine realities that lie concealed in what seem to be the ordinary things of this world. It is only the practised eye of the saint, trained to observe objects in the immaterial atmosphere of the super-natural world—so disturbing for the ordinary vision of the ordinary unsanctified human being—that can discern Jesus Christ in the poor, in the outcast and in the abandoned ; it is only he that is accustomed to close and constant communing with God that can see the action of God's Providence in the vicissitudes of human life, and that can read the wonderful realities of God's grace that are contained in the very least symbols and rites of our holy religion. St. Teresa could say with truth that she felt she could gladly die on behalf, not of the faith, but of the very least rubric prescribed in the ceremonies in which that faith expresses its worship.

What a wonderful contrast Mary, in her reserve, presents to our way of acting ! It requires constant effort on our part to keep in check our desire to make parade of every gift or talent that is ours by nature or by grace. Even really spiritual persons are not exempt from some anxiety lest their qualities should remain in obscurity. They fear that they themselves may not be able to turn their qualities to account unless they are credited by men with the possession of these qualities. Mary's example should save us from this foolish and idle fear. If we seek but one thing only, namely, to abide in union with God and seek only His esteem and regard, we can be certain that God will on His side make such use of us and our talents as is most conducive to His glory. We must, like Mary, wait for God's manifestation, and in the meantime carefully guard from the eyes of those around us those gifts, whatever they be, with which we may have been favoured by God.

There is a tradition that there was a remarkable resemblance in feature between Mary and Jesus. However this may be, we can be certain, from the testimony of the Gospels, delivered to us in many a suggestive trait, that there was a wonderful likeness between them in lineaments of soul. Jesus had shown His predilection for poverty by His choice of the place and circumstances of His birth. Mary, who had brought Him to birth in her mind, before bringing Him into the world, was quick to learn, and prompt to put in practice, the lesson conveyed by this choice. Poverty and lowliness are a hard election, a harder election than suffering, because they entail greater disabilities in the eyes of our fellow-men, even in the eyes of the good and high-minded amongst them. Poverty, no matter how one may wish to ignore the fact, does carry a stigma with it, and a certain shame. It should not be so. It is unnatural that it should. But the fact remains. The great bitterness of Poverty lies in this, that it carries with it a certain powerlessness, helplessness and dependence on others. Patronage and not esteem is the lot of the poor. And human nature shrinks from the one as much as it hungers for the other. Poverty takes from man many of the possibilities of achievement—as achievement is understood by mankind. To noble natures it is easy to give and it is distressing to have to receive. The poor have little means of giving, few opportunities of bestowing help or conferring favours. Under the disabilities that attend the absence of this world's goods it is difficult to preserve one's dignity. It is much easier to be dignified in suffering than in poverty. It was these very disabilities that weigh so heavily on the poor that determined the choice of Jesus and, as a consequence, that of Mary. We are not surprised to find her coming to the temple bearing in her hand two doves—the offering of the poor. It is significant that St. Luke is not content with remarking that she offered the usual sacrifice, but that he takes care to note that her offering was that of the very poor. We see, of course, at a distance that poverty did not detract from but rather enhanced the nobility of Jesus and of Mary. But at the time and in the judgment of those around them was it the same? Is it not our own instinct—the instinct, that is, of nature, though not of grace—to be condescending towards the poor and to treat with them as if, in truth, the absence of worldly means did lower a man's dignity and worth? Is it not the instinct of the man who is well-to-do, even though he be fairly religious minded, to regard his less fortunate fellow-man as one who is not quite his equal as far as human values go? It takes all the force of the example of our Heavenly Mother to rectify in us this false view, this false attitude towards life. But with that example before him, who does not feel stirred to love and esteem not only detachment of spirit, but real and actual want, should God send it? The Christian, having before his eyes the vision of God Incarnate and of the creature nearest to Him on earth evincing such a predilection for what St. Francis poetically terms his " Lady Poverty," has no excuse if he continues to give his esteem to wealth as such and to repute the poor, because of their poverty, as of less worth than himself. It is the characteristic of all great souls to rise superior to this ignoble prejudice.

True holiness consists in the sympathetic entering into the views and feelings of Our Blessed Lord. How different Jesus would have been for us had He chosen to come in the guise of wealth rather than in that of poverty ! For the vast majority of mankind condemned to a life of lowliness and want, He would have been a God removed from them, not an Emmanuel, a God dwelling with them, and sharing their life and their hard lot. But to the poor, all come with ease and without constraint—rich and poor alike. The poor are eminently accessible, whereas wealth, owing to the inequalities it generates, invariably erects a barrier, even when the rich are not very worldly or overweening. Poverty, it is true, has its rewards. To be sure, it makes us powerless, but in Christ's Kingdom power is made perfect in infirmity. St. Paul could say : " I will glory in nothing but in my infirmities." [3]

When Jesus, in the hands of the priest, had renewed interiorly the unreserved offering of Himself to God in sacrifice that He had already made at His entrance into the world and when Mary had, in lowliness, obedience and humility, conformed herself to the requirements of the law, the whole Mystery of the Presentation was not consummated. Before Mary left the temple she

[3] 2 Cor. xii. 5.

was to be called on to make a sacrifice that was to cost her more than did the renouncement, in the estimation of men, of the real dignity and the true wealth that was hers, in virtue of her high prerogatives. In the holocaust of the second dove she gladly prostrated her whole being before God, and offered herself unreservedly to the purposes of the Divine Will. God took her instantly at her word. *The unalloyed joys of her Motherhood were of short duration.* As she was making her way forth she found herself confronted by an old man of holy and venerable appearance. With a confidence and reverent assurance which she could not resist he took the child from her arms. Gazing on the infant face, and his whole countenance illumined by prophetic fire, gladness and enthusiasm, he cried aloud: " Now Thou dost dismiss Thy servant, O Lord, according to Thy word, in peace. Because my eyes have seen Thy salvation, which Thou hast prepared before the face of all peoples : a light to the revelation of the Gentiles, and the glory of Thy people Israel." [4] Whilst Mary was contemplating the wondrous vision that was opened up to her mental gaze by this glorious prophecy, the eyes of Simeon were turned from the face of the Child and fell on the Mother. It is hard for us to know how far Mary's vision had, up to this moment, pierced the veil of futurity and seen what lay before her Divine Son. She had read and pondered on the oracles of the prophets relating to the Messias. Many of them spoke of glory, but several also set forth details of suffering and ignominy. God did not reveal all to her from the beginning ; she dimly surmised what was to be. She had too much spiritual

[4] St. Luke ii. 29–32.

understanding to be carried away, as her countrymen were, by the predictions concerning the Messias, which seemed to promise a career of earthly triumph and glory. The visions of the prophets that unfolded scenes of bitter suffering and final rejection were for her the ones that more literally than the others set forth the earthly destiny of her child. She had forebodings of what was to come. It is to be remembered that Mary's great dignity did not freeze or etherealise in her the natural instincts of a mother's heart. Hence it was that she would strive to drive her heavy forebodings into the background of her consciousness. Her maternal love would wrestle with her fears and seek to conquer them. She would be moved by her love for her child to believe against her own spiritual convictions. It is a different thing to labour under the foreboding of an impending woe and to be brought face to face with the bitter reality. Whoever has seen on a human countenance the impression of anguish which suffuses it as dire previsions of some great sorrow harden into certainty can realise what Mary underwent as the concluding words of Simeon's prophecy smote her ears. He said : " Behold this Child is set for the fall, and for the resurrection of many in Israel, and for a sign which shall be contradicted. And thy own soul a sword shall pierce, that out of many hearts thoughts may be revealed." [5] As Simeon's words penetrated to her consciousness, her soul was flooded with light and the shadows that had hitherto clothed the harsh reality disappeared. She at last grasped in all their significance those texts which set forth the history of a Messias destined for pain and

[5] St. Luke ii. 34-35.

death. The Messias is now her Son, and she realises
that her own Child is to undergo, at the hands of His
Own people, contradiction and trial and a rejection
culminating in a cruel death. For some only, not for
all, was her Son to prove a Saviour : for many, through
their own fault, He was to be an occasion of utter and
irreparable spiritual disaster. "And Simeon said to
Mary, His Mother ; Behold this Child is set for the fall,
and for the resurrection of many in Israel, and for a
sign which shall be contradicted." [6] Her mother's heart
was wrung with anguish as the sword of this bitter
prophecy was plunged into it and as it turned in the deep
wound it made. It was the first of those Seven Sorrows
by which her soul was crucified with a crucifixion that
resembled that of her Son. She shuddered when she
saw what she should be called on to bear. She knew
that it was demanded of her that she should acquiesce
in the awful dispensation of Providence that was presented to her in vision. She realised that it would be
asked of her not merely to allow the Divine Will to
pursue its course or merely submit to that Will in its
dealings with Jesus, but also, over and above all that,
to identify her will with that Will of God, and to make
the voluntary sacrifice of the gift that had been placed
in her arms. She was asked to will the sacrifice of Jesus.
It was an incredibly hard thing to ask of a mother.
It was much to ask her to accept—but to will it ! that
was something which would be demanded only of a
sanctity like Mary's. And her sanctity did not flinch
before God's demand. And when her will surrendered,
a depth of calm and peace possessed her soul, that

* St. Luke ii. 34.

wonderful peace and calm which always follows on a sacrifice generously made for God. Her heroic act had instant compensation. She was rewarded by a closer degree of union with Jesus, which carried her sanctity to still greater heights. In spite of its pain, her soul was plunged in joy—the joy of possessing Jesus more closely. Her having Him did not exempt her from pain, but it excluded all sadness. God deals with us as He did with Mary; every fresh and great gift He bestows on us is but a prelude to a more pressing call on our spirit of sacrifice. He gives to us in order to prepare us to give to Him more largely.

This Mystery of the Presentation, although of such tragic intensity, is not without some light that relieves the gloom. As was said, not one of the mothers who mounted the temple steps by Mary's side realised that she was walking beside one who carried God in her arms. Not one of them saw the greatness that was veiled in that modest exterior. Yet Jesus did not pass by entirely unnoticed. In the joy that irradiated the souls of the prophet Simeon and the prophetess Anna, Mary had a glimpse of the glory and the gladness that, to men of good will, would be brought by the coming of her Son. In them she saw all those for whom He would not be a sign to be contradicted but a sign to be followed with loyalty and enthusiasm. In these two holy souls Mary saw verified the conditions which prepare the way for the discovery of God on earth. Anna, after the few years of her happy married life had sped by, gave herself up to the conquest of her flesh by a career of sustained mortification. By obliging her imagination and her thoughts to dwell day by day

on God and the things of God, she had obtained a great
mastery over her inner faculties. In this her soul had
gained an immense freedom to devote itself to spiritual
things, the animal instincts were subdued, and self-love
was starved. Sternness to the flesh and resistance to
the unreasonable demands of the sense life impart a
great freedom of spirit and clarity of inner vision.
The reward of mortification is an acuity of spiritual
sight. With the subjugation of bodily passions and
desires goes an intensification of the spirit of faith.
Those who deny themselves valiantly see clearly in
the things of God. So it proved with the prophetess
Anna. She had spent long years in mortification of the
flesh and in prayer. The result was that her soul
responded instinctively to the presence of God. She
recognised who the child was and its mother and she
spoke of Him " to all that looked for the redemption of
Israel ".[7] Simeon, like Anna, had passed his life in
self-denial and in the study of divine things. His self-
denial took the form of detachment from and aloofness
with regard to merely earthly interests. Earth had lost
its grip on him. He swung free from its attractions.
Valuing nothing but God, death had no terrors for him :
because for him it would not mean a sundering or a
snapping of ties. He wanted only one thing on earth
and that was to behold with his eyes the promised
redeemer. Completely detached from, and therefore
soaring above earthly things, his eyes were able to
discern clearly the vision he longed for when at last it
presented itself to him. To the perfectly detached there
is given an unblurred and undimmed vision of spiritual

[7] St. Luke ii. 38.

realities. Our vision is faulty because we wish to fix, with our regard, other things along with God. Simeon was heard beyond his desires. It was given him on earth not only to see Jesus; he was allowed to hold Jesus in his arms. At the contact his soul overflowed with peace and happiness and earth and all it contained lost all significance in his eyes, and he could say : " Now Thou dost dismiss Thy servant, O Lord, according to Thy word in peace."

We, too, may look for the great grace that was granted Simeon. He has shown us how to prepare for and merit it. The desire of our hearts should be to see Jesus. There is only one path that will lead us to the vision. It is the way of detachment and of prayer. Prayer, according to the great St. Teresa, means a constant, loving and familiar intercourse with God. This adapts the soul for seeing Him when He shows Himself to it. The vision may be deferred for a long time for us— Simeon had to wait until age had come upon him— but if we persevere the Lord will come to us, too, some day. His Mother will place Him in our arms, and a great sigh of peace and happiness and supreme contentment will be breathed forth from our soul. At that instant, earth with all its joys, its trials and its sorrows will fade away before our eyes. The world will no longer hold any attraction for us; all its ties will be snapped. Our life may not be at an end, but our life's desire will have been satisfied. We may be asked still to linger on the earth, but we shall move there as if not belonging to it, and at each moment we shall be able to repeat in our hearts those words of Simeon so filled with contentment. " Now Thou dost dismiss Thy servant, O Lord, according to Thy word *in peace*, because my eyes have seen Thy salvation, which Thou hast prepared before the face of all peoples : a light to the revelation of the Gentiles and the glory of Thy people Israel." [8]

[8] St. Luke ii. 29–32.

CHAPTER V

THE EXILE OF JESUS IN EGYPT

" Out of Egypt have I called my Son."—St. Matt. ii. 15 ;
Osee xi. 1.

When God, in view of fulfilling His loving designs
of mercy with regard to men, determined that the time
had come for making His appearance amongst them,
He condescended to beg a shelter from them. Through
Mary, His mother, and St. Joseph, His foster-father,
He requested the protection of a roof-tree beneath which
to be born. His request was denied. He had given all
to men and the little He asked for was churlishly refused.
He did more than give them all. When men had squandered their spiritual substance and wasted their divine
heritage, He came, at incalculable cost to Himself, to
give them back what they had wickedly squandered.
His surpassing generosity was met by surpassing
ingratitude. God, as a rule, is little welcome amongst
His creatures. There was worse to follow. The initial
churlishness and ingratitude rapidly hardened, first, into
an uneasy resentment at His presence, and then into a
positive hostility to His life. Jesus was not, for long,
allowed to remain undisturbed in such a shelter as His
parents had succeeded in securing for Him after His
first chilling reception upon the earth. The powers of
this world were in instant clamour at His neighbour-

hood. Their jealous fears could not brook the presence
of One whom they felt, in a vague way, to be their
enemy. It is strange that an infant so winsome, so
appealing, so full of tender love towards the creatures
whose companion He had made Himself, should be
regarded as a dangerous foe. Yet, so it was. Herod
resolved on the death of the Child and planned a crime
of appalling proportions and inhuman cruelty to secure
that he would not be baulked of his prey. To compass
his ends he did not hesitate at a massacre of all the male
children of Bethlehem and the neighbourhood who
might have attained the age of the new-born king of the
Jews. Obscure, hidden, unassertive, unpretentious as
that king was, He could not but be involved in the
general slaughter. Neither his blamelessness nor his
refraining from urging his royal claims would save him.
It will be said that this cruelty and hostility aimed at the
infant Christ were individual to Herod himself. Jesus
became a prey to them owing to the purely accidental
circumstance of His being born in the dominions of this
violent, suspicious and heartless monarch. Why should
the blame of this attitude towards Jesus, peculiar to
Herod, be placed upon the world? Such reasonings
proceed from a very superficial interpretation of the life
history of Jesus Christ. One will fail entirely to understand either that history or the whole sequence of events
that have issued from it in the course of time if what
befell the Son of God on earth be regarded merely as
the outcome of an accidental conjuncture of circumstances, of persons, of place and of time. It is only in a
limited and restricted sense true that what happened to
Him was the outcome of the particular combination of

events in which historically He actually found Himself
placed. From the Fall, has the world ever treated its
God otherwise than in a manner which is an exact
counterpart of the way He is treated in this mystery of
the Flight into Egypt? Is not God always in some
measure an outlaw in His own world? What befell
Him was not due to something transient and ephemeral
but to a spirit that transcends all passing conditions of
time, place and individuals. Of course, to express
itself and to enter into action, the spirit must clothe
itself with concrete and accidental circumstances. These
vary with the ages, but the spirit itself ever remains the
same and unchanged, as a substance under the perpetual
changing of the accidents. Herod was but the spearhead
of this spirit driving against the incarnate God, not
because of the human in Him but of the something
other than human behind the flesh which by a kind of
blind instinct it sensed as being present there. This
evil spirit could not analyse what it sensed, but it could
hate it. God is never safe with His rational creatures
until these creatures begin to bear some supernatural
resemblance to Him. Men are never easy in His vicinity
as long as they are acutely conscious of His utter unlikeness to them in standards of values and in appreciations
of the relative worth of things. And they envelop in
their dislike Him and all who are close to and bear a
likeness to Him. Mary and Joseph were caught in the
storm that stirred against the divine child.

The wise men had taken their departure, prudently
not taking the route that would lead them back to Herod.
Hardly had the sounds of the bustle of their departure
died away in the distance when the sleep of Joseph

suffered a rude disturbance. An angel came to Him in the dead of night and sharply and peremptorily aroused him from his slumbers, saying: " Arise and take the child and His mother and fly into Egypt . . . for it will come to pass that Herod will seek the child to destroy Him." [1] Joseph, with a start, awoke to a world in which customary and agelong values were completely reversed. What could possibly be the meaning of the panic fear that the words of the heavenly messenger seemed to imply ? Was not the child whose safety was menaced that one with regard to whom it had been said to him : Joseph, son of David, fear not to take unto thee Mary thy wife, *for that which is conceived in her, is of the Holy Ghost* and she shall bring forth a Son : and thou shalt call his name Jesus. *For He shall save His people from their sins.*[2] ? It is to be remembered that the spouse of Mary had grown to man's estate under the Old Testament. As was the case with every holy Israelite, his mind was steeped in the sacred books of the race. The glowing imagery of the inspired writings coloured his imagination and his thoughts. The God whom he had learned to worship was the Mighty One at Whose coming the enemies of His Name were scattered as chaff by the whirlwind. He was the God Whose outstretched right hand had wrought wonders of all kinds in the interests of His chosen people. Jehovah was He before Whom " the Gentiles are as a drop of a bucket, and are counted as the smallest grain of a balance . . . the islands are as a little dust ".[3] The outstanding attribute

---

[1] St. Matt. ii. 13.
[2] St. Matt. i. 20, 21.
[3] Is. xl. 15.

of the God Whom he revered was one of overwhelming
and irresistible power. Joseph was aware that the child
who was entrusted to his care was of heavenly origin
and was not conceived of earthly seed. He knew that
to that child had reference all those grandiose titles
with which he was acquainted from the prophecies of
Isaias : " For a child is born to us, and a son is given
to us, and *the government is upon His shoulder :* and
His name shall be called, *Wonderful, Counsellor, God
the Mighty,* the *Father of the world to come,* the *Prince
of Peace* " [4] Apart from certain distressing happenings
that had occurred owing to the incapacity of the ordinary
public to recognise Him Who was in their midst, the
events that took place since he took Mary for his wife
confirmed the judgment he would have formed of the
greatness of the Son of Mary. The shepherds had
related to him their experiences on the night of the
Nativity, when they saw the heavens flooded with light
and heard the exultant strains of the heavenly choirs.
He himself had just seen the first signs of the homage
that mankind was to pay to the new-born Prince of Peace.
The adoration and the gifts of the kings were the pledge
of greater things still to come. It was true that the
prophecy of Simeon hinted at dark and painful issues :
yet these events, in spite of the dark shadows that
attended them, were certainly to be on a scale of heroic
grandeur. The child was to be the centre of mighty
happenings and had a *rôle* of great power to fulfil. And
now there breaks in on these reflections what looked
like an affrighted messenger from heaven, with words
that plainly spoke of a danger that was imminent. " It

[4] Is. viii. 6.

would look as if alarm had spread through all heaven before it communicated itself to earth." [5] The expression used by the angel speaks of urgency. His warning is not merely to withdraw into Egypt but to " fly " there. There is evidently no time to be lost. It is as if this child of heaven needed to save Himself and could with difficulty succeed in doing so. His departure was to be in haste and under cover of darkness. Could anything be more upsetting to ordinary calculations and so bewildering in its implications? There was in this something to test the strongest faith. A parallel may be drawn between the situation that confronted Joseph at this juncture and that in which Mary found herself at the moment of the Incarnation. It was a test of faith of unimaginable difficulty for the young Jewish maiden to believe that she was chosen to be and could become Mother to the everlasting and eternal Son of God. Mary underwent this test triumphantly. Well might Elizabeth exclaim in admiration of her : " Blessed are thou that hast believed, because these things shall be accomplished that were spoken to thee by the Lord." [6] It was now the turn of Joseph to be tried, and tried severely. If this child was what he purported to be, why should he have to use darkness and haste to escape from the clutches of a mere creature like Herod ? Being what He was according to the angel's previous announcement, why could He not wrap Himself in obscurity if He disdained to make use of power and in this way evade His enemy ? Why should He, the Son of the

---

[5] St. Petr. Chrysolog. Sermon 151 as quoted by Bossuet in his panegyric on St. Joseph.
[6] St. Luke i. 4.

Most High, have recourse to the precaution of weakness ? Did all the power lie with the tyrant, and was the child of heavenly origin all powerless ? If so, how could this be reconciled with the magnificent titles given Him by Isaias ? How could the great God be placed in the ignominious position of fleeing before the face of His creature ? Was He as helpless as those divinities that the psalmist spoke of with such fine scorn and biting irony ; " they have mouths and speak not : they have eyes and see not : they have ears and hear not . . . they have hands and feel not, they have feet and walk not : neither shall they cry out through their throat." [7] If the son of Mary were as dependent on human hands for his security as were the idols of the Gentiles, could He be true God, and the Son of Jehovah ? Such would be the reflections of merely human reasoning, which constantly shows itself as incapable of understanding the humanness of the Son of God as of apprehending the divinity of the Son of Man. There is no indication of any such reasonings having traversed the mind of Joseph. As in the case of Mary, his faith emerged triumphant from the rude trial to which it was subjected. It is true that there was demanded of him an adjustment of mind to meet a situation in which the manifestations of the God of his fathers were evidently to be of a character far different from what they had been during the history of his people from the time of the Exodus out of Egypt. It is wonderful how rapidly not only the mind of Mary but that of Joseph was initiated into this new world with its strange and paradoxical, if coherent and consistent scheme of values—a world in which what was weakness with men

[7] Ps. cxiii. 5, 7.

becomes strength, what was helplessness becomes power, and what was folly, wisdom. For in the world as being reconstituted by Jesus " the foolishness of God is wiser than men : And the weakness of God is stronger than men ".[8]

Mary and Joseph are admirable in their interior realisation of the " humanness " of Jesus, whilst to their faith His divinity was not for a single moment obscured. Joseph rose from his sleep in haste, and giving immediate heed to the warning of the angel, he took the child and the mother and made a hurried departure in the favouring darkness. The route which, according to tradition, he took was that which would lead him in the shortest possible time out of the dominions of Herod. He does not rely on prodigies or any super-natural intervention to secure the safety of himself and those in his keeping. Reliance on divine providence and ordinary foresight, calculation and prudence were the things in which he placed confidence. It never occurred to him that he could call on resources that were in their nature divine. The means he looked to in order to effect his purpose were such as any of those parents in Bethlehem whose children's lives were menaced by Herod would have to employ. To the poor, the obscure and the defenceless in face of the hostility of the great ones of the earth there is no resource except in hiddenness and flight. Hence it was that Joseph made his way rapidly southwards and plunged into the desert of Pharan. A toilsome and hazardous journey of many days lay between the holy family and safety. The hurried departure left Joseph little opportu-

[8] 1 Cor. i. 25

nity to make adequate provision for the hardships that awaited him. The Son of God whom he protected would be helpless and powerless in his arms. He would make no move of any kind either to provide what was necessary for the journey or to alleviate its hardships. Jesus brings not only uneasiness to His enemies but also trouble to His friends. If close contact with Him means joy, there also comes with it sharp pain. The anxiety of Joseph during that long flight of six hundred miles on foot across, for a great part, arid and trackless wastes must have been extreme. Many a time it was not possible to find shelter for the night, and the way-farers had to protect themselves as best they could with the poor wrappings they had with them against the chilliness of the night. Frequently, too, the food would fail and the heart of the holy patriarch would be wrung with anguish as he contemplated the silent suffering of his spouse and heard the pitiful wailings of the infant. The way he trod was marked profusely with memorials of the extraordinary interventions of God in favour of His people on their way out of the bondage of Egypt. No miraculous event signalised God's flight when He was driven from the land of promise and forced to seek shelter in that very country from which He had in the old days rescued His people. No savoury manna dropped now from the heavens or cool refreshing water gushed from the rocks. Jesus, even when the time came to manifest Himself to the world, never used His miraculous power for the satis-faction of His own personal needs. He fed the multitude in the desert and the narrative implies that He did not Himself partake of what His goodness prepared for the

others. When after His long fast in preparation for
His Mission He felt the pangs of hunger He repelled
the suggestion of Satan that He should cause the stones
to be made bread, preferring to trust Himself to divine
providence.[9] There was all the greater reason now that
there should be no outward sensible sign of the divine
power that was concealed under the infant form.   Apart
from the consideration that the Saviour would not
exercise the omnipotence that was at His command,
to evade the ordinary disabilities of a human life such
as He had chosen, it was in the designs of God that for
thirty years the Son of Mary should not present, except
to the eyes of faith, anything that would indicate the
presence of the more than human in Him.   St. Thomas
writes : " It is by faith and humility that men derive
from Christ the benefits that He procures them.   To
favour this, Christ did not begin His teaching in boyhood
or adolescence but in the ripe age of manhood.   This
aided faith, because the growth in bodily stature and
powers from year to year manifested the reality of His
humanity.   Lest this development might be regarded
only as apparent, not real, Christ *willed not to manifest
His wisdom and His power, until He had attained the
perfection of manhood according to age.*" [10]   To meet the
ordinary vicissitudes of a humble existence, He brought
but the ordinary resources of humble circumstances.
And this law ruled not only for Himself but for those
who were in closest spiritual contact with Him.   It is
true that the Lord does occasionally intervene in a
miraculous manner to help His saints, but this interven-

⁹ St. Luke iv. 2–4.   St. Matt. iv. 1.
¹⁰ *S. Th.* III., Q. 39, A. 3 ad 2.

tion is exceptional. Ordinarily they are left to battle with life's circumstances as best they may. As a rule things are not made easier for them than for others, but more difficult. It was the practical experience of this that drew from the great St. Teresa the remark, half-loving, half-petulant, that this being the case, it is not to be wondered at that the Lord has so few friends. Joseph and Mary were now being practically instructed in this law of things. Rapidly they learned the lesson. They would have wondered more at a manifestation of something that would be a departure from the ordinary and common than they would at the ordinary and common itself.[11] The head of the holy family knew well that the safety of his charge depended on his foresight, energy and resolution. He knew that he would have to exercise all his intelligence to evade the dangers that beset them. There was no fatalistic waiting on divine providence on his part, no inactive and sluggish leaving it to God. Decision, promptitude, prudence and determination stamp his actions. There was no weak repining at the hard lot that was his. It was abundantly clear to him that, though the providence of God watches over all, men must use their natural forces and capacities to surmount the difficulties with which they are faced. Joseph, versed in the science of life, recognised that struggle and endeavour have their place in God's plan as an aid to progress and development and that it is through trials manfully borne that man's soul grows in force and virtue.[12] The true Christian

---

[11] Cf. their astonishment at the incident in the temple when Jesus was twelve years old : " And seeing Him, they wondered."—St. Luke ii. 48.
[12] Cf. Prohaszka : *Meditations on the Gospels*, p. 210.

is one who endeavours to escape not the trials of the
world but the contagion of the world. Jesus Himself,
on the eve of His death, voiced this guiding principle
when He prayed to His Father for His disciples, saying :
" I pray not that Thou shouldst take them out of the
world, but that Thou shouldst keep them from evil." [13]
But though Joseph was not spared any of the hardships
that such a flight as this into Egypt would present, he
enjoyed one great consolation through it all.   He
carried Jesus with him. The Saviour does not mitigate
but He compensates for the sufferings which His friends
are called on to endure on His behalf. To have Jesus
with one in the struggles of life is the solution of life's
problems. If a man has to meet them alone, he is overcome by them : if he faces them in company with Jesus,
he is formed, purified and perfected by them. Trials
yield him virtue in this life and glory in the next. All
this Joseph learned in his secret communings with the
divine infant in the depths of his soul. Hence he faced
manfully the painful situation thrust on him by circumstances and looked for no exemption from the trials
with which it was attended. Hence it was that it was
only at the expense of much fatigue, constant anxiety,
frequent alarms and painful effort that he succeeded in
bringing his charges to safety in one of the cities of
Egypt : this city, according to tradition, was Heliopolis.

Painful and difficult as was the flight, its successful
issue did not bring the sufferings of the Holy Family
to an end. Their arrival in Egypt was but the beginning
of the sharpest and most bitter suffering of all endured
in this incident. For many long months they had to

[13] St. John xvii. 15.

experience the anguish and the distress of exile. They
had to live away from their own home and their own
kinsfolk and spend their days amongst a people alien
to them in race, in manners and in religion. They had
nothing or next to nothing in common with the men
amongst whom they dwelt. Even those who have
voluntarily renounced their home to seek a fortune in
distant lands find themselves a prey to longings for
return to the place of their birth, when the novelty of
the strange land and of the mode of life of its people
has worn away and the fever of gain has passed. How
much more poignant are the regrets for the homeland
on the part of those who have been forced by tyranny
and much against their will to leave it behind. The
hearts of Jesus and Mary and Joseph were not insensible
to any legitimate human feeling or emotion, and it
cost them much, in consequence, to exchange their home
in Palestine for the land of Egypt. In their case, as
being Jews, the natural love of country would be
deepened and intensified by the religious and historical
associations connected with almost every rood of the
land of promise. It was in all its length and breadth a
holy land. The aroma of the divine presence clung to
every corner of it. The land had been selected by God
for His people and had been given them by Him when
the appointed time had come. Almost every place-
name recalled some kindness on the part of God to
them or was hallowed by some past manifestation of
divine power, beneficent or avenging. If with these
historical associations account be taken of the stout
wall of separation that the theocratic laws and ordinances
reared between the Jew and the stranger, one can form

some idea of the strong spell which his native land exercised over the imagination of the Israelite and the strong hold it had on his affections. Jesus, Himself, as is clear from many a trait in the Gospel, experienced this attraction strongly as He grew to man's estate. Mary and Joseph must have, day by day, felt in their hearts all the yearning so touchingly expressed by the sacred writer in the Book of Psalms : " By the rivers of Babylon, there we sat and wept ; when we remembered Sion. On the willows in the midst thereof we hung up our instruments. For there they that led us into captivity required of us the words of songs. How shall we sing the song of the Lord in a strange land ? If I forget thee, O Jerusalem, let my right hand be forgotten." [14] The bitterness of exile does not diminish with the passage of time ; it tends rather to become more acute, especially in the case of sensitive and loving hearts. When the sting of poverty is added to the pain of separation, the feeling of loneliness and isolation that sweeps over the exile is apt to be overpowering. Even in sympathetic surroundings poverty is hard to bear : it becomes still more difficult when it has to be borne in the midst of strangers to whom one is not bound by any ties of kinship or neighbourliness. The charity that is readily extended to the hapless ones of one's own race is but grudgingly given to the alien. The latter is made to feel painfully that he has no rights where he has come to dwell—scarcely the right to sympathy. It is true that there is a likelihood that Mary and Joseph found some of their own race in the Egyptian city where they took up their abode. But it is also most likely that

[14] Ps. cxxxvi. 1–5.

the Holy Family shrank with characteristic delicacy from intruding their wants and their miseries on those for whom life may have been as hard a struggle as it was for themselves. Joseph would strive to eke out an existence by the exercise of his profession, and that would mean that the most of his dealings and his daily intercourse would be with the idolatrous Egyptians. Their rude ways, their false culture and their unspiritual philosophy of life would jar continually on the spiritually refined soul of the holy Israelite. There was no inconvenience of residence in a foreign land and amongst an alien people that the members of the Holy Family did not experience to the full. Christians, whom fate may oblige to endure the pangs of separation from home and country, will find consolation in the thought that Jesus Himself and those most dear to Him deigned to drink to the dregs the cup of sorrow, which they find so bitter to taste.

One of the heaviest trials that the head of a family is called upon to endure is that of uncertainty for the future of himself and those committed to his care by divine providence. On Joseph the task devolved of finding, day by day, sustenance for Mary and her child. The first weeks in Egypt, presenting, as they must have done, great difficulties in supplying the immediate wants of the Holy Family, must have been especially trying. In his effort to set himself up in a strange land and to secure a market for his labour, the spouse of Mary must have met with many a check and many a disappointment: he must have experienced moments of bitter uncertainty in which the future must have appeared black indeed. His little household was not fed by the

ravens. It depended on human efforts, human resources;
on human industry and human energy. Many a dawn
must have come for Joseph, in which the day held out
anything but bright prospects for himself and his charges.
Many an evening must have found him wearied out with
fruitless endeavours and unrequited efforts. It is
exceedingly bitter for a man, who is willing to provide
for those dependent on him by the labour of his hands,
to be unable to find work for his hands to do. Inaction
and the sight of the suffering of those dear ones, for
whom that inaction spells want, distress and hunger,
is a bitter experience for the honest and upright working
man. Unemployment is more crushing to his soul than
the very hardest toil. How many, in our days, find this
grim spectre attend their daily, despairing trudgings to
and fro—exactly like a dark shadow! Joseph, almost
certainly, must have borne this sorrow during the days
of exile in Egypt. It must have frequently smote him
to the heart to see his two charges look to him for what,
with all his good will, he was unable to give. Though
providence, as the event proved, never failed them, the
existence of these three must have been, at the best,
precarious. There must have been days, and even whole
periods, when absolute want stared them in the face.
It is most likely that God allowed Joseph and Jesus and
Mary to suffer all the trials that, in the ages to come,
were to fall to the lot of the poor—of people of their
own condition in life. Unemployment for the earnest
worker is a far greater hardship than sickness or disable-
ment. Those who experience it, and their numbers are
great, need the example of the Holy Family to bear
up with fortitude under this great trial. The heads of

families who have to face the harassing problems of finding the means to educate and provide for their children will find in Joseph a sympathetic advocate and helper—for he, in his own lifetime, had to face the solution of this same difficult and sometimes agonising problem.

The Catholic who, by circumstances, is obliged to quit his own land, finds one great comfort in the isolation he suffers when living amongst those who differ from him in language and mentality. In the familiar rites and practices of his religion he establishes contact with those around him and annihilates the distance that separates him from what had been the ordinary setting of his existence. In the presence of the Blessed Sacrament he establishes contact with home and kindred. There the feeling of loneliness and isolation is much mitigated if not quite dispelled. But for Mary and Joseph, banishment from Palestine meant the deprivation of all the essential practices of their religion. There was for them no participation in the divine worship which was carried out in the temple of Jerusalem : it was only in spirit that they could be present at the regular sacrifices of the law and at the great religious festivals of the Jewish cycle. They felt this loss keenly. Father Faber remarks with great penetration that the greater became the sanctity of Mary, the more she clung to the religious rites and practices of the law, even to the most unimportant of them. The same is true, in due proportion, of St. Joseph. This is the ordinary characteristic of eminent holiness. To the piercing gaze of deep faith there are laid bare the realities of the supernatural world, with the importance that belongs to and the spiritual advantages which are attached to the slightest observances instituted by Almighty God. " The saints in their sublimities are for ever returning to the wise littleness and childlike commonplaces of their first beginnings. It was, therefore, a keen suffering to Mary to be deprived of the outward ordinances of her religion. Her spirit pined for the courts of the Temple, with its crowd of worshippers, for the old feasts as they came around, for the stirring and soothing show of the ceremonial of the law, and for the sound of the old Hebrew Scriptures from the reader's desk within the Synagogue." [15] Mary's soul literally hungered for the practices of the true religion. The regrets of Mary and Joseph for the rites of the law were rendered all the more poignant because of the daily contrast between these rites and the sights and sounds of a debased and debasing worship which constantly assailed their senses and froze their souls with horror. It is impossible for us to conceive the spiritual nausea that these holy souls, who had the true God in their charge, felt in presence of the false worship of the Egyptians. They must have experienced a profound sense of relief when the time of their exile drew to a close and they were free to return once more to their native land. Their souls echoed the words of the psalmist : " our soul hath been delivered as a sparrow out of the snare of the fowlers. The snare is broken and we are delivered." [16]

After the lapse of a period which is variously estimated, some making it consist of two, others of four, and others still, of seven years, an angel again appeared

---

[15] Faber : *The Foot of the Cross*, Chap. III.
[16] Ps. cxxiii. 7.

to St. Joseph in sleep, saying: "Arise and take the child and his mother, and go into the land of Israel. For they are dead that sought the life of the child."[17] The foster-father of Jesus directed his steps towards the hills of Judæa. But the rule of Archelaus made Judæa an insecure abode for the divine child, and Joseph, being warned by another message from heaven, directed his steps towards Nazareth. Thereafter, except for one brief instant of light, as when a solitary lightning flash cleaves open a sky of darkness, a pall of obscurity descends on the career of the Son of God on earth. The patriarch Joseph disappears in the depths of that obscurity, after he had played his part as chief actor in this incident of the flight into Egypt. It is interesting to note how easily, simply and readily he assumed the leading *rôle* when it was a case of protecting the life of his charges. Without a deprecatory gesture he plays the part of a man. The very simplicity of his character made it easy for him to assume without awkwardness the *rôle* of leader in a group which comprised two persons of such transcendent dignity as Jesus and Mary. His very humility made it easy for him to issue commands to these exalted personages. And his humility suffered no wrong but rather acquired increase in playing this high *rôle* which was thrust on him by circumstances. Mary, on her side, in spite of her own great dignity and personal wisdom, deferred in all things to the decisions of her spouse. The successful evading of Herod, the surmounting of the difficulties of the flight, the securing of the necessaries of life in Egypt, and the bringing back of his charges unharmed to Nazareth—all this manifests the wisdom

---

[17] St. Matt. ii. 20.

of God in selecting Joseph to be the spouse of Mary and the protector of Jesus. He was not only a just man : he was, as well, an able man. The whole of this episode shows that he was quick in decision, energetic in action and resourceful in the solution of difficulties.

CHAPTER VI

THE LIFE OF JESUS AT NAZARETH

" For neither did His brethren believe in Him."—St. John vii. 5.

It is quite true to say that it is by the cross and passion of Jesus that we are redeemed. The faith teaches that it is by the death of the Saviour on the cross that to men has been restored the dignity of the divine adoption and that from Satan has been wrested his usurped princedom of the world.[1] But it would be a mistake to consider the passion in isolation from the rest of the life of Christ and out of all relation to it. It would give us a false view of that life were we to regard the passion as alone entering into the Divine economy of redemption and as having nothing but an accidental connection with the thirty years that preceded the public life of the Saviour. That Divine Life constituted a totality and an indivisible unity, each part of which has a vital and intimate union with every other part. It is through, and by means of, and in virtue of that life taken as a whole that our salvation has been achieved, and each several mystery of Our Lord's life had its part to play in the work of the redemption.[2] Each had its redemptive

---

[1] St. John xii. 31 : " Now shall the prince of this world be cast out."

[2] Cf. "It was the plan of God . . . that the whole life of Christ and the violent death which crowned it, should be, in an indivisible manner the ransom and the salvation of the world." Terrien, S. J. : *La Mère des hommes,* Part I, p. 175.

effect on humanity, though all were meant to lead up to, to prepare, and to converge on the great tragedy of Good Friday. Every path in Our Lord's life led towards the hill of Calvary; Calvary, in turn, projected its shadow over every mystery and *simply set forth in letters of vivid flame and blood what each expressed in more sober terms.* In other words, Jesus was redeeming us when He laboriously planed wood in St. Joseph's workshop as well as when He faced the awful ordeal of the passion. The Hidden Life played its part in the salvation of mankind no less than the public life with its *dénouement* on Calvary. Without the passion the Hidden Life would not have been accepted by God—in accordance with His eternal Decree that by the death alone of His Son should men be redeemed; but without the Hidden Life redeemed mankind would not have been taught how to exercise in the ordinary circumstances of average life the virtues displayed in such an eminent degree in the passion. Men had not only to be restored to life, they had to be taught to live.

By the death of Christ we were restored to that supernatural condition which we had forfeited by Adam's sin, but it is through the *example of and by virtue of the life of Christ that we are enabled to walk worthy of our Divine vocation.* It would have been useless for us to have had salvation won for us were we incapable of profiting by that salvation. Were we to dwell under the impression that access to God would be for us only through the accomplishment of works on a heroic scale, the endurance of sufferings that would bear some resemblance to those of the passion, the courage of almost all would fail. But heaven is not thrown open

exclusively to men of heroic calibre. Jesus, in His
goodness, has traced for us a human existence which
is easy for all to imitate and at the same time one which
is eminently pleasing to God. It must needs be a
manner of existence pleasing to God, seeing that God
made man chose it for Himself, and in all things, as He
tells us, He fulfilled His Heavenly Father's pleasure.
" For I do always the things that please Him." [3]

Our Lord had a threefold purpose to fulfil when He
came on earth. He had to restore to men, by meriting
it, the grace that had been lost to them by Adam's sin.
He was to complete and perfect Divine revelation,
making known to mankind all that it was destined to
know concerning God, God's inner life, and His relations
with the world He had created ; and finally, He had to
set before men an example of the human life they should
lead if they were to please God and arrive at their final
supernatural end. To the latter object He consecrated
thirty years of His life—whilst to the task of vindicating
His Divine mission and instructing men in the Divine
secrets He devoted but three.

How utterly different are the proportions of Jesus'
earthly career from what we should have expected.
There was a stupendous work to be accomplished—
namely, to undo the effects of some thousands of years'
estrangement from God and to revolutionise completely
the individual life and the social life of the whole world—
and there was such a short time to do it ! Yet of Jesus'
short span of time on earth only one-eleventh apparently
was given to the accomplishment of this great undertaking, whilst by far the greater part of it was frittered

[3] St. John viii. 29.

away, as man would judge, in what seemed to be doing nothing. But such was the choice of a mind flooded with Divine light, and it must be therefore one of profound wisdom. Those thirty years at Nazareth, far from having no bearing on the salvation of mankind, must on the contrary have been most effective in the accomplishment of the task Jesus set Himself to do. Of course, they will always remain for us full of mystery; but though we cannot penetrate fully into the secrets of their mysterious efficacy in the regeneration of the world, still a study of them under the illumination of faith will cast some light on the wonderful ways of God to man.

Our Lord could not have chosen a more obscure place in Palestine in which to pass His life. Nazareth was one of the most insignificant villages in a land itself insignificant and, at that time, playing no important part in the world's affairs. The little town lies midway between the Mediterranean and the Sea of Tiberias, about sixty miles north of Jerusalem. It is surrounded on all sides by hills, and in this way is cut off from easy communication with the rest of the country. Evidently owing to this its people were rude and rustic; they enjoyed but a very poor reputation for culture, refinement and enlightenment amongst their own countrymen. The outspoken Nathaniel asked contemptuously: " Can anything of good come out from Nazareth ? " [4] And yet it was amidst this uncultured, uneducated and boorish people, and in this backward little town, lying outside the broad highways of social communication, that Jesus elected to spend the greater part of His life.

4 St. John i. 46.

The village itself was obscure, the life which the Saviour of men led there was still more obscure.

Nothing in Our Lord's life is so extraordinary as its simplicity. That God should live a human life on earth, and live it in such a way as not to manifest anything that would differentiate Him from the ordinary run of men is the most striking proof of the thoroughness with which God became man. And it was not as if He were hidden from the eyes of His fellow-men, and led a life of the utmost seclusion as John the Baptist did, before the day of his manifestation to Israel. Jesus lived in a small town almost completely screened off from the outer world. In communities of such a kind, whose interests are narrow and whose horizons are limited, there is no secrecy possible. Everybody knows all that concerns his neighbour and the affairs of one family are a subject of interest and discussion for all. The life of each individual is passed in the light of the day and under the gaze of his fellow-townsmen. When we speak of a man residing in a remote country village far from the main highways of social and commercial intercourse as leading an "obscure" or "hidden" life, careful attention must be given to the meaning of the word obscure or hidden. Jesus led a hidden life in the sense that He played no part whatsoever in public or national events. His life was not obscure in the sense that nobody knew how He spent His days. Everybody in that little village community knew how He passed His time and had Him under constant observation. What is more, the occupation of Jesus brought Him into daily contact with His neighbours. He was a workman, rendering public service to all, and the workshop, in

which He passed the greater part of His day, admitted
clients at all hours. In those circumstances the Son of
God lived and worked, spoke and conversed with men,
shared the vicissitudes of village life, and took an active
part in the affairs of the synagogue, around which that
life gravitated ; He did this during the period of His
boyhood, youth and manhood, and yet He appears in
the eyes of others nothing more than an ordinary man,
somewhat quiet and dignified perhaps, with a certain
reserve that combined firmness with an open candour
and sincerity ; men saw that He was a careful worker,
a devoted son, and of a blameless life—and that was all.

So completely free from singularity was His existence
in Nazareth, so utterly simple was the conduct of Jesus,
so uneventful and devoid of remarkable incident were
His days, that the Nazarenes were filled with astonishment
when the news of the stir He was creating after the
baptism in the Jordan began to filter through various
channels to the secluded hamlet. They could with
difficulty connect these wonderful sayings and doings
with the young carpenter that had lived so long in their
midst : " Is not this," they said, " the son of Mary,
the brother of James, and Joseph and Jude and Simon ?
Are not also His sisters here with us ? " [5] These cousins
of His were people of the most ordinary type, nephews
and nieces of His Mother ; He Himself had shared their
family life, and was in no way distinguished above them.
It is impossible, they judged, that there could be anything above the ordinary in the young man about whom
there was so much talk. Had He not grown up under
their eyes during the greater part of thirty years and

[5] St. Mark vi. 3.

during all that time had they seen in Him anything whatsoever to distinguish Him above His fellows? Not only were they surprised; they were positively incredulous; and Jesus faithfully interpreted the incredulity of their thoughts when He said to them: " Doubtless you will say to Me—as great things as we have heard done in Capharnaum, do also here in thy own country." [6]

Not only His neighbours but even His own cousins, who had lived in intimate contact with Him, failed to penetrate the disguise of His Humanity; so perfectly human was He that they could see nothing in Him but the man. "If," they said, "Thou do these things, manifest thyself to the world." [7] This *if* with which they preface their solicitations to Him, to seek distinction in Judæa, shows conclusively that they could not bring themselves to credit Him with any exceptional or miraculous power. And St. John makes the somewhat sad comment: " For neither did His brethren believe in Him." [8] So blind were they to the superhuman in the personality of Jesus that when the crowds began to follow Him, attracted by the grace and persuasiveness of His word, they concluded with the habitual stolid dullness and incomprehensiveness of men in the presence of the supernatural that He had taken leave of His senses; and they judged that the attraction He exercised was nothing else than the idle curiosity and interest excited by the strange doings and sayings of a person beside himself. " And when His friends had heard of it (namely,

[6] St. Luke iv. 23.
[7] St. John vii. 4.
[8] St. John vii. 5.

of His being so pursued by the crowd that He was not left time even to take food) they went out to lay hold on Him. For they said, ' He is become mad '." [9]

Such was the judgment on Jesus of those who were most intimate with Him ! The world is always true to itself, and it is ever blind where God is concerned. It looks for Him in signs and wonders and He presents Himself as one of themselves—and they fail to recognise Him. Since everything in creation down to the most insignificant thing is an object of industrious attention on the part of God and is of importance in His eyes inasmuch as it has engaged His omnipotence, it is consonant with reason that God should be more at home in the ordinary and everyday things than in those that are exceptional and that mark a departure from the habitual course of the universe of things He has created. We speak of God being present in the humble and the ordinary. The terms are to be found fault with. Everything is wonderful that God has made and nothing is really ordinary in the sense in which we use the term. A flower or a tiny insect is a marvel. The Bethlehemites of old turned God from their doors, ignorant that it was to their God they were refusing shelter ; the inhabitants of Nazareth shut their hearts and minds to Him, failing to see that it was to God Himself that their town had extended its hospitality for thirty years. It seemed incredible—but the testimony of the Gospel is there, explicit. *Certainly God has achieved nothing more wonderful than this, that He should live a life so perfectly simple and natural and human that men should never detect in it, during thirty years, anything divine.* Its very

[9] St. Mark iii. 21.

simplicity proved a stumbling block for His countrymen as the ignominy of His Passion proved a scandal for the Gentiles.

And yet this life in which the Galileans saw nothing wonderful was one of absolute perfection. Men judge as great only those things which are stamped with external show and splendour. God has a different standard of evaluation. Each act of Jesus was an object of infinite complacency for Him—on account of the great charity in which it had its origin. Though all interior, the life of Jesus was one of wondrous force and power, and each year of His hidden life played as great a part in the redemption of mankind as any of the last three up to and exclusive of the Passion.[10] His human greatness as ours consists in the depth of union of the soul with God, and is proportioned to the measure in which God's life is participated in by the soul. Greatness does not consist in the amount of external achievement. Works of great magnitude, if they are not based on and founded in charity, have no value of a supernatural kind in the eyes of God. Not only have they no value in His estimation, they have little worth, even in themselves. Proceeding from a purely human source, they partake of the transient nature of their origin. Such works, no matter how apparently brilliant and successful they may appear for a time, have within them the seeds of decay. They cannot last. *Only that can endure which has the principle of Divine life in it— only that is truly great which has its origin in a soul filled with the grace of God.* And even the most trivial act

---

[10] The Passion is excluded because of the Divine decree that mankind was to be actually redeemed by the Passion and Death.

that proceeds from such a soul shares the greatness of its origin. Hence it is that Our Lord's life, which was apparently so meaningless, was one of great force and power. It was all interior, springing from the fountainhead of Grace and therefore all divine. *Every pulsation of that life was a mingling of a divine and imperishable leaven with the mass of human destinies.* It was eminently a divine life, as divine in the least of its details during the period of seclusion as in the accomplishment of the great miracles that distinguished its latter days.

Furthermore, though Jesus might have at any moment of His life left His home and undertaken the task which was to issue in His own death but in the life of mankind, still since He wished to be in all things like us, He underwent the preparation that human ways and conditions demand of us for the accomplishment of any great work in God's service. No one, however great or gifted, no matter how well endowed by nature or by grace, can carry through successfully any great work of God, unless a long and careful discipline is first submitted to. It is by union with God in prayer that there is derived light to see the course of action to adopt and it is through the reception of God into the soul that there is acquired the divine strength to carry it through. These thirty years of silence were the natural preparation for the three of activity ; in the career of the servants of God it is from the hours of silence and communing with God that is derived the efficiency that marks the hours of active service.

The lesson to be drawn from all this is important. *It is not what we do that matters in God's eyes so much as how we do it ; it is not what we effect that He regards, but what we are.* An action of the most trivial kind, as far as human estimation goes, may be wonderfully pleasing in God's eyes, if it proceeds from a soul in which charity is great, and grace abundant. A series of such acts extending over years, and all of them utterly devoid of external importance, but done in a spirit of love for and devotedness to God, imparts to the soul that power which enables it to face the most arduous labours in God's service and to undergo great sufferings in His cause. *To accomplish great things, we must be great.* And all greatness in the supernatural order consists, for us, in the development of sanctifying grace in our souls. No outstanding achievements are necessary for this ; the most humble tasks if done with obedience and through charity contribute effectively to that growth. Hence it is that the Evangelist takes care to remind us that " Jesus advanced in wisdom, and age, and grace with God and men ".[11] This was His preparation for the great mission.

Only once during the thirty years was the veil of obscurity that enveloped them lifted, and that was for a moment to show Jesus in the Temple listening to the doctors of the law and asking them questions. On this occasion Jesus was about His Father's business.[12] Can we not conclude, then, that the subject, which occupied His mind and about which He interrogated the Masters of Israel, was the great work which the Father had given Him to do ; is it not safe to conjecture that He conversed with the doctors concerning the Messias, the Saviour of Mankind and concerning the

[11] St. Luke ii. 52.
[12] St. Luke ii. 49.

mode of His redeeming mission ? This mysterious incident in the Temple gives us an insight into the preoccupations of the mind of Jesus. He said later on, in an enigmatic sentence : " Wheresoever the body shall be, thither will the eagles be gathered together." [13] The thoughts of Jesus are as eagles. Men, whose inner life is all given up to some object which is of supreme interest to them, betray, at times and inadvertently by a word which escapes them, their interior preoccupation. The thoughts of Jesus were constantly occupied with God, God's Glory, God's plan of redemption and God's desires in regard to Himself. In the Temple it is as if He were betrayed for a moment into revealing what was constantly uppermost in His mind. Meditation on God, His ways and His designs, was the great occupation of Jesus during the thirty years. So it must be with us. If we are to profit by a life of retirement and obscurity—of quiet and external inaction —and make it serve as a preparation for one of later achievement, we must make it one of intense interior activity. That activity must be a constant and loving interchange of thought with the God-Man accompanied by a desire to penetrate ever further by the light of faith into the knowledge of the Divinity, as revealed in His sacred Humanity.

The eighteen years that followed the brief revelation in the Temple are briefly summarised by St. Luke in the words—" And He went down with them, and came to Nazareth and was subject to them." [14] These long years of obedience and subjection were a set-off to the rebellion and self-assertiveness of the first man.

[13] St. Luke xvii. 37.   [14] St. Luke ii. 51.

There is something extremely touching in the contemplation of this subjection of the Lord of all to two of His own creatures. What a condemnation it is of our unwillingness to submit our actions and our judgments to the control of others! Jesus was obedient not only in some respects; from the moment that He left the Temple at the age of twelve until He left His home at the age of thirty there was not a single deliberate action of His which was not done at the bidding or in accordance with the desires either of St. Joseph or of the Blessed Virgin Mary. He never did the least thing of His own will and through the exercise of an independent judgment. All was done under subjection to authority and in the exercise of the virtue of obedience. And in spite of the perfection of those two, under whose care He lived, their commands cannot always have been perfectly consonant with His views; for their wisdom was infinitely removed from His. It is true that when they directed Him as their child, they worshipped and looked to Him as their God, and hence in all things they sought to issue their orders in conformity with the Divine Will. But the mind of the creature can never view things precisely as God views them; and in Jesus dwelt the fullness of the Godhead substantially. The views and judgments of the parents of Jesus, perfect though these persons were, could not possibly be always in complete accord with those of Him Who was Son of God as well as Son of Man. That this is no mere supposition is proved by the words of the Gospel saying—" *And they understood not the word, that He spoke unto them.*" [15] That their lives,

---

[15] St. Luke ii. 50.

and especially the life of Mary, were spent in a constant
effort to approximate ever nearer to His point of view
is evidenced by the statement twice repeated, " And
His Mother kept all these things pondering them in
her heart." [16]   But in the meantime, in the absence of a
perfect understanding of her child, Mary was obliged
to issue orders and He elected to obey.

How easy, after this example, we should find it to
carry out instructions given us by those set in authority
over us even when these instructions do not coincide
with our views and judgments !   *Jesus knew that He
was doing what was highest in not choosing to do what
was best : He knew that it was more pleasing to His
Heavenly Father that He should adapt Himself to the
limited vision of His creatures than that He should follow
the dictates of the highest wisdom.*   And in truth those
years of silence and self-repression, though seemingly
so wasteful and unfruitful, continue to exercise a saving
and sanctifying virtue down the ages and will do so
until the end of time.   Our own activities should follow
the same principle.   There are generous souls, who,
feeling themselves possessed of great supernatural
lights and endowed with qualities that would enable
them to exercise power and influence over others,
are all impatient to put their talents at the service of
God, and chafe at what they deem idleness and inaction.
They err in this.   The good we effect is not done at
the time that we are in activity, nor is it in virtue of
that activity ; it depends wholly on the degree of union
with God which prepares and accompanies it.   A slight
act of self-repression, of blind submission, of sacrifice

[16] St. Luke ii. 19 and 51.

of the light of our judgment to the darkness of faith, being wholly steeped in the supernatural, is far more efficacious in the deifying of the world than any amount of feverish activity; *it is a divine element contributed to the reality of this world;* as such it is permanent and will continue exercising its saving influence long after the author of that act has passed to his rest. Jesus might not have returned to Nazareth after the three days' loss; He might have continued the instruction begun in Jerusalem and laboured for twenty-one years instead of three; but would He have achieved more? He certainly would not. For we know that the economy of His earthly career was that which was most apt to secure the purpose aimed at by His mission, namely, the redemption and sanctification of humanity. The vast majority of men are destined to pass their days in humble obscurity; a life of brilliancy could not be an example for them. Whereas on the other hand those years of simple, ordinary, unpretentious life at Nazareth, which, while being distinguished in nothing exteriorly from that of the humblest of village artisans, was still one of Divine perfection, is for all who are not called to external distinction a wonderful consolation, strength, light and encouragement.

It was a life of prompt obedience. Our Lord seems to have a special predilection for prompt, ready and unquestioning docility. Faith is always shown in the Gospels as exercising an extraordinary attraction on the Heart of Jesus. Now prompt and unqualified obedience cannot exist unless Faith is strong and deep. Jesus loves a Faith that is strong, deep, vivid and penetrating; for without such a faith He cannot be appreciated rightly and loved with ardour. Transformation into Him demands a faith of this kind. For our power to penetrate into the mysteries of the life of Jesus and reproduce those mysteries in our own life is fundamentally conditioned by our belief in Him as true God and true man with a whole-hearted acceptance of His views and a strong loving trust that He can conform us to Himself.

Not even after St. Joseph's death did the existence of Our Lord undergo much change, unless that it became more laborious. For the support of the family and its care of the poor devolved, then, entirely on His shoulders. He had to work hard in order to keep Himself and His Mother and to have something to give to others less favoured still by fortune than themselves. Unremitting toil became His lot, and the soft hands of the boy became roughened and hardened with the constant pressure of the tools of His trade. Work could not have been plentiful in the confines of that narrow village and it is likely that He had, often, to go abroad to look for employment. He had to face rebuffs from those who needed not His services, and discourtesy and rudeness from those who employed Him. The Nazarenes were not a polite people. As He handed over to His grumbling clients the accomplished tasks, He had to hold forth His hand to receive His wages, the meed of service rendered. There is something inexpressibly touching in this picture of God receiving from His creatures the wages He earned in their employment ! And so passed the time until the day came when He was to leave His home and begin that struggle with Satan which was to end in the overthrow of the

Archfiend's Empire, in the redemption of mankind from slavery, and in the death of the Redeemer.

A monotonous life, one would say, but this would be a very superficial judgment; monotony consists in the dull repetition of acts, uninteresting, devoid of significance and all stamped with the character of sameness. But there is no monotony in the soul's relations with God. Each act in which it expresses its love for its Creator is fresh with the freshness of novelty; each communication of the love of the Creator to the creature comes with all the charm of a new revelation. Each step forward in the knowledge of God makes it seem to us as if we had never known Him before. And the external material acts which proceed from the soul enjoying this intimacy with the Lord partake of this quality of freshness and novelty. Although to the senses each little task of the day resembles in all respects that of the day before, yet, in reality, these tasks that recur are not the same. Acts springing from and animated by charity vary with the variations of charity. The newness and freshness given by a greater love in the doing far surpasses the newness given by a material change in the occupation. The love of God is never stationary. It grows with each act done in the fullness of the actual charity possessed by the soul. Hence for the saint the task of to-day, which materially resembles the task of yesterday, is clothed with all the charm of novelty, for it is transmuted and transfigured by a greater love. All men naturally desire to be great. To achieve greatness it is not necessary to seek it afar or to ascend into the heights in its pursuit. It lies at our door and is within the reach of all. It is found by bringing a great love of God to bear on the doing of the most ordinary of life's tasks. Our Lord in His hidden life has shown how we may attain to greatness and perfection in the accomplishment of the humblest of life's duties.

CHAPTER VII

THE FOSTER-FATHER OF JESUS

" Joseph, Son of David, fear not to take unto thee Mary, thy wife."—St. Matt. i. 20.

THAT Joseph was a man of holiness we know from the Scriptures : of the nature and characteristics of that holiness we have little direct testimony. The Evangelist, St. Matthew, says of him, that he was a *just* man,[1] assigning to him a quality, which in the language of Scripture, always implies the possession, in a harmonious balance, of the moral and Theological Virtues. The term is applied to others—as for instance, to Zachary and Elizabeth,[2] and it is therefore no indication of there being anything in the quality of Joseph's holiness which would distinguish it from, and exalt it above, that of the other virtuous persons mentioned in Scripture. In the absence, therefore, of all direct evidence, it is from an enquiry into the providential part Joseph was called on to play, in the economy of the Redemption, that we are to derive our knowledge of the greatness and of the characteristics of the sanctity that distinguished the head of the Holy Family.

When God directly assigns a definite mission to a creature, especially a mission having a close and intimate

---

[1] St. Matt. i. 19.
[2] Cf. Gen. vi. 9 ; St. Luke ii. 25 ; Acts i. 23.

relation with the Incarnation, He owes it to Himself to impart to that creature a measure of grace proportioned to the importance of the *rôle* to be fulfilled. It would be thought that, starting from this easily accepted principle, Sacred writers would, from the beginning, have formed a lofty conception of the measure of Divine Grace meted out to one who was privileged to be the Spouse of the Mother of God, and to exercise all the rights and functions of parental authority with regard to God's Son. Yet, strangely enough, this is not so. Joseph, called by God to cast the veil of obscurity over the mystery of the birth and the early years of Jesus Christ, has had his own greatness enveloped in the shadow, which it was his function to project on the persons committed to his care by Almighty God. The very nature of his mission is the very cause of the hiddenness of his sanctity. The constant care of the Church to put clearly in evidence the miraculous virgin birth of the Saviour, during the first centuries of the Church's history, caused the figure of Joseph to remain in the background in the writings of the early Fathers. But when, in the course of time, after the successive heresies, attacking now the divinity, at another time the humanity of the Saviour, had been overthrown, the Theology of the Incarnation had been fully developed and the virginity of Mary clearly established, the Spirit of God inspired saints and spiritual writers to turn to a study of the mission and of the sanctity of the third member of the Holy Family. Devotion to him then rapidly developed, and the investigations of the theologians revealed the solid foundation on which it is based.

St. Thomas [3] lays it down as an indubitable principle
that when God in a special manner elects a creature
for some special function, having a relation to the scheme
of Redemption, He endows the object of His choice
with dispositions by which it is equipped to fulfil
worthily the ministry to which it is called. The grace
accorded is in proportion to the dignity of the office
to which the creature is called, and this grace is sanctifying (gratum faciens) where personal holiness is
required for the due acquittal of the obligations attached
to the office. (When God's election is absolute, not
conditional, it infallibly attains its purpose.) St. Joseph
was predestined absolutely by Almighty God to be
the protector of Mary's virginity and to watch over
the early years of the Incarnate God. The duties which
fell to his lot in consequence of his vocation brought
him into and necessitated the closest and most intimate
relations with the Source of all Sanctity—Our Lord and
Saviour Jesus Christ. Eminent sanctity and sanctity
of a singular kind was demanded for the due discharge of
the office committed to St. Joseph by divine providence.

Joseph has been called the foster-father of Our Divine
Lord—but he was bound to Him by a tie far stronger
than is implied by this term. The Scripture, when
the context requires mention of the two holy spouses
together, refers to them as *the parents of Jesus*.[4] After
the prophecy of Simeon, St. Luke records that *His
Father and Mother* were wondering at those things
which were spoken concerning Him.[5] As the true

---

[3] *S. Th.* III. Q. 27, A. 4.
[4] St. Luke ii. 43.
[5] St. Luke ii. 33.

and lawful spouse of Mary, St. Joseph was meant by God to have the privilege of exercising, as his right, in virtue of his virginal marriage, the parental office in regard to Mary's Child. The union of these two, Mary and Joseph, was ordained in the designs of God for the education of Jesus. Joseph was necessary to this work of supreme dignity and importance. The Son of God, in becoming Man, deigned to assume all the conditions of the nature He assumed—including the helplessness and dependence that characterise its early years. The Child needed the strong care and watchfulness of a father to be preserved from the dangers that threatened His existence whilst still in His infancy. Mary could not of herself, owing to the conditions with which custom and convention invested the lives of women in the East, provide the protection and furnish the means of safety that the situation demanded. Neither could she supply, of herself, all the conditions that were needed for the due upbringing of her Son during the years of His boyhood and His adolescence. A large share of this work naturally devolved on the Father by whom the young Nazarene was to be formed to the duties and tasks of a man's life and initiated into the social and religious obligations which were incumbent on a Son of Israel. As God had planned the salvation of mankind, the function of Joseph was one not of mere convenience but of necessity in the working out of that plan.

Joseph was chosen by God the Father to take His own place, in regard to His Divine Son, during the early years of that Son's sojourn on earth—" qui et vir justus est datus, ut unigenitum tuum, Sancti Spiritus

obumbratione conceptum paterna vice custodiret " [6]
—as we read in the Preface assigned to the Mass in
honour of St. Joseph. Having, therefore, to exercise
the function of father with regard to Jesus he was
endowed by God, with Whom all things are real,
with all a father's tenderness and love for Him Who
was confided to him as his Child. St. Chrysostom
says that there was given to Joseph by the Lord all
that can belong to a father without prejudice to virginity.
He experienced with regard to the Son of Mary all
the strong, quiet, deep, tender emotion that stirs a
father's heart towards his own child. What, by nature,
Joseph was not, with regard to Jesus, he became by
affection. Jesus revered and obeyed him, and since
everything in the family at Nazareth must have been
perfect—destined as it was to be a perfect exemplar of
family life for all time—the direction of Joseph must
have been such as merited the reverence and esteem
of even Jesus.

The good towards which marriage is directed, in
the plan of God, is not merely the generation, but
more especially, the proper upbringing and education
of children. For this reason the union between Joseph
and Mary can be said to be the most perfect of conjugal
unions—for it was formed (and was demanded) for
the training and upbringing of the Divine Child in
the way ordained by Providence. Without it Jesus
could not have been reared in the manner that was
postulated by the plan that had been formed for redeeming mankind. This marriage, therefore, secured what,

[6] Who, adorned with justice, was deputed to guard, in the place of the
Heavenly Father, Thy Only-begotten Son, conceived by the operation of
the Holy Ghost.

according to the Christian view, is the chief and good of marriage, namely, the suitable training and education of the Child.[7]

The nature, then, of Joseph's mission demanded of itself that he should be supernaturally united with the Source of all Grace, the God Incarnate—by a union which in its force, intensity and intimacy, is surpassed only by that through which Mary is bound to the fruit of her womb. It is this which brings us to a realisation of the sanctity of Joseph.

We can form a conception of his holiness by analysing the notion of sanctity itself and by instituting a comparison between the holiness of Jesus and that of the two beings who, on earth, were most closely united to Him. The holiness of a soul is in direct proportion to the grace inherent in it. And holiness is nothing else than union with God—the closer the union the greater the holiness. It is the function of Grace, precisely, to effect this union between the soul and God. It is the action of the faculties, transformed and elevated by grace, that perfects this union and unites the soul more completely to God. The more perfectly our two faculties of will and intellect are subjected to and informed by the activity of Grace, the more closely they bind us, by their action, to God. Charity, that is the supernatural love of God (not merely natural love nor mere philanthropy), is that which excites, intensifies and sustains this activity.[8] Love urges us to cleave

---

[7] *S. Th.* IV. Sent. Dist. 30. Q. 2, A. 2 and 4.

[8] Gratia conjungit nos Deo per modum assimilationis, sed requiritur ut uniamur ei per operationes intellectus et voluntatis. Q. un. A. 2. Ad. 7.— Grace unites us to God by assimilating us to Him ; but it is imperative that we be united to Him by the operation of will and intellect.

to the object of our love in thought and affection. It
is because God, as He is in Himself, is, when loved,
the term or object of these operations of will and intellect
—because He, as it were, is held and possessed in His
own substantial Being by them, that He is said to dwell
in the souls of the just. And St. Thomas says, " Grace
is produced in man by the presence of the Divinity,
as light is produced in the air by the presence of the
sun." And just as the nearer an object is to the sun,
the more fully does it receive its light and heat, so
likewise, the more closely the soul is brought to the
Principle and Source of Grace, the more powerfully
does it participate in the virtue of that principle. There
is effected in the soul by this approach—this drawing
nearer to God—wrought by charity, a resemblance
to the Divine Being in perfection and in operation.
The soul becomes more and more like to God in form
and feature, so to speak, the more closely it is attracted
to Him by charity.

No union to the Divinity can be conceived closer
than was that enjoyed by the Sacred Humanity of
Jesus—united Hypostatically as it was to the Second
Person of the Blessed Trinity. Hence, His Soul was
a perfect mirror reflecting in its human acts the Divine
Perfections and the Divine Operations. Christ had
the plenitude of sanctifying Grace : this grace in its
quasi infinitude flowed from the union with the Divinity,
as light from the sun.

The grace of the Divine Maternity in Mary created
in her an intimacy with God that comes next in perfection to the intimacy effected by the Hypostatic Union.
Her grace is, to the Divine Maternity, proportionately

as is the grace of Jesus to the Hypostatic Union. Christ is the Principle of Grace in a twofold sense: He is the Principal Cause of it as God, the Instrumental Cause of it as Man. By her Motherhood, Mary is brought into the most intimate relations with Jesus that is possible for a mere creature. No union can be closer than that of Mother and Child. And as we have said, the nearer one is to the principle of a thing in any order, the more perfectly does one participate in the effects of that principle. Since Christ is the Instrumental Principle of grace as Man, and Mary is so intimately united to the Sacred Humanity (since she furnished It with the material elements of Its Being), it follows that she receives in the most perfect manner the grace that comes to us through that Sacred Humanity.

After Mary, no human being was brought into closer or more intimate relations with the Incarnate Word, the Source of all Grace, than Joseph. It follows as a consequence of the axiom already enunciated (that the nearer one is to the principle of a thing in any order of effectivity, the more fully does one receive the effects of that principle), that the grace of Joseph must come next in greatness to that of Mary. Joseph was not merely the guardian of Jesus, not merely His foster-father; *he was as the lawful spouse of Mary, the legal Father of Christ*. God *would not* place him in such a position without giving him the dispositions that would enable him to fill it *in all* perfection, and realise in himself the conditions of it according to the measure of reality that was possible. He had, therefore, for Jesus, all the love and tenderness that a father has for his own child. This love was not merely natural affection. It was supernatural charity infused into his soul, enabling him to shadow forth on earth with regard to the Incarnate God the relation that exists in Heaven between God the Father and His eternally begotten Son. Such an earthly shadow of the Procession of the Word must have been productive of a great depth of grace in the soul of Joseph—a grace which gives him a special likeness to the Eternal Father.

Other saints have enjoyed in vision, in a transient, occasional and passing way, commerce with Our Divine Lord. Joseph, in virtue of his office, enjoyed this privilege not in a passing way but in a continuous and habitual manner for many years of his life on earth. And to this intimacy and intercourse he brought, constantly and unvaryingly, the most perfect disposi-tions, the most profound faith and the warmest charity. He brought to it the love of a father and the insight of a soul so divinely illuminated, that not for a single instant was there dimmed for him the radiance of the Divinity, that was veiled by the humble exterior of Mary's Child, Who deigned to address him by the name of Father. Though Jesus learned from Joseph, as a disciple learns from a master, never for one instant, in spite of this bewildering eclipse, this unimaginable reversal of rôles, was the Divinity in Him obscured for the Spouse of Mary. As has been said, whilst it is by grace that we are made like to God, there is required, for the perfection of this resemblance, that we actively unite ourselves to Him by the exercise of the faculties of will and intellect, operating through the infused virtues of Faith, Hope and Charity. Wonderful must have been the resemblance to the Divinity wrought in the soul of Joseph, through the constant, sustained exercise of his profound faith and his deep, strong charity, in respect of Our Divine Lord—especially when it is remembered that the exercise of these theological Virtues extended over many years and did not admit of a moment's intermission.

Perfection in the spiritual life follows the progressive purification of the infused virtue of Faith. Although vision of God, in the proper sense of the term, is reserved for the hereafter, there can be, even on earth, a growing realisation of the presence of the Divinity in the soul. It is not sight—but an obscure knowledge of God, which comes with an ever clearer understanding of what He is not. The intellectual operation by which the created spirit seizes the Godhead is progressively freed from the influence of the natural forms which the intellect must use to grasp Divine things.[9] It is in the growing realisation of the utter insufficiency of these created elements to express what God is—in the growing realisation that He transcends all created perfections even when carried to the utmost limits conceivable —that there is given this dim and obscure knowledge of God, which though obscure, surpasses in clarity the deepest theological knowledge that human genius at its highest can acquire. Joseph's faith was submitted to a purification like to which that of any other saint was not, nor could have been subjected. When Peter, by a grace from on high, was inspired to see the Christ the Son of God, in the Person of Jesus of Nazareth, he was felicitated by Our Divine Lord Himself on the

---

[9] Cf. Saint John of the Cross.   Dark Night Bk. II. c. 9. and Garrigou-Lagrange, O.P.   L'Amour de Dieu et La Croix de Jésus, vol. II. p. 590.

grandeur of this Divine illumination and on the great
prerogative that it was to win for him. " Blessed art
thou, Simon Bar-Jonah, because flesh and blood hath
not revealed it to thee, but My Father Who is in
Heaven." [10] Simon's penetration of the mystery of
Jesus was an intuition of faith—his recognition of the
Christ as being the Son of God was the result of an
extraordinary exercise of this infused virtue in his soul
—so strong, so powerful, so penetrating, that in virtue
of it he was instantly proclaimed to be the very foundation on which the stability of the faith in Christ's Church
was to repose. Yet, Peter's faith was not so meritorious
nor could it have been as perfect as that of Joseph.
Though not based on, it was conditioned by elements,
which were wholly lacking on the part of the Protector
of the Divine Child. Peter had passed many months
at the school of Jesus. He had daily been witness to
the perfection of the Master's life and had for a long
time been subjected to the dominating influence of a
Personality that stood apart from and above the ordinary.
Miracles had multiplied in the Lord's passage, and wisdom
flowed from His lips with an effortlessness that of itself
bespoke a knowledge and a power of mind that was
superhuman. Peter had seen the works of Jesus, had
listened to His teaching and had been in daily contact
with a perfection of life, which imposed itself on mind
and on senses ; hence, his soul was thoroughly prepared
beforehand and made receptive for the illumination of
Faith.[11]

But things were far otherwise for Joseph, and that

[10] St. Matt. xvi. 17.
[11] Cf. Grandmaison : *Jesus Christ*, Vol. II, p. 30.

by reason of the mission that he was called by Providence to accomplish. It was necessary in order that no untimely obstacles should prove an impediment to the working out of God's plan for the redemption of mankind, that an impenetrable veil should be cast over the circumstances of the birth and early years of Jesus. The revelation of the reality of His divine nature should only be gradual and progressive ; men's minds and hearts were to be prepared for the reception of the salvation that He was to bring, and that was so utterly different from that to which they had looked forward, aspired after and hoped for. If He had been revealed to them as Divine in the beginning, the Jews would have doubted of the reality of His human nature, and would have been stirred into a ferment of excitement, in which the expectancy of seeing their national aspirations at last realised might have caused scenes of tumult and revolt. There would not have been time for the difficult and therefore prolonged effort to work that transformation of mind and heart, which was necessary in order that men might be rendered apt to receive the Kingdom of God, such as it was according to the teaching of Jesus. Joseph's marriage with Mary was necessary to hide from profane eyes the mystery of the virgin birth, to save Mary from the tongue of calumny and to provide a protector for the Mother and Child during the years of helplessness of the Latter. Jesus' mission, since it consisted to such a large extent in moulding the minds and wills of men into a new form, could not be begun conveniently by Him until He had reached man's estate. The revelation of what He was could begin only then. His Divinity was to be wrapped in impenetrable darkness during all the years of His infancy and of His private life. It was, therefore, in the Divine plan, that never during the thirty years should the Incarnate God give any exterior manifestation of the Godhead that dwelt in Him in its plenitude. He grew, as St. Luke says, in the normal way, as other children, in wisdom and age and grace before God and men.[12] It was Joseph's very mission to co-operate in securing this hiddenness. And so Our Lord, in His Divine Nature, had to be as hidden for Joseph, as far as exterior signs went, as for any others. The Divine Child never taught him, never revealed to him, by word of mouth, the inner mysteries of His Being. Joseph had to walk by the light of faith alone. So perfect and sustained was the restraint of Our Lord, that on the one occasion when He just slightly drew the veil aside both Joseph and Mary were filled with astonishment.[13] This shows that they had before their eyes and expected to see before their eyes nothing but the apparently human and ordinary. Joseph never saw a miracle, never heard a word of teaching or of power from the Child of his holy spouse. During those years that dragged themselves out slowly for the expectation of Israel he saw nothing that hinted, even remotely, at the realisation of Israel's dreams, or the fulfilment of the prophecies that he knew so well concerning the Messias. These prophecies foretold practically nothing of the hidden life. There was no indication whatsoever from any quarter as to its meaning, its significance, its purpose. Day followed day, and each brought the

---

[12] St. Luke ii. 52.
[13] See St. Luke ii. 48.

same unchanging round of, and alternation of work and prayer. The only change was that Jesus became stronger, more vigorous, more adept in the use of the tools that belonged to His father's trade. He bent Himself with as much assiduity to the acquisition of skill in His craft as if the sole object of His life was to be able to provide support for His Mother when Joseph should be taken from them both. There was no evident connection between this worker's life and the grandiose rôle in the world's history which the Jews of that day attributed to the coming Messias, a rôle based on a mistaken interpretation of the glowing and magnificent imagery of the Sacred Books. We cannot imagine of course that St. Joseph was deceived by such dreams of Israel's earthly glory, for his supernaturally enlightened soul divined something of the nature of the work before the Saviour. Yet even to him there must have seemed little apparent proportion between the work with which Jesus was busying Himself and the task to be accomplished by the Redeemer. Year followed year, and each bore witness to the same apparent inactivity, the same apparent shelving of the great work waiting to be done, the same apparent frittering away of valuable time.

It was necessary that the depository of the secret in which was enveloped the mystery of the Incarnation should disappear from the scene of this world before the voice from Heaven revealed to the son of Zachary in the desert the presence of the Messias promised and announced. So in the obscurity which had surrounded his whole life, Joseph, continuing to the end his sublime mission, rendered his soul to God before Jesus announced Himself to men as the Man-God. He had to close his eyes in death without seeing the manifestation of the desired of Israel. Nothing as far as human reason could see had been attempted, nothing done, unless that this Child who had been entrusted to his keeping had learned perfectly the carpenter's trade and was now capable of providing, unaided, for His Mother's support.

This was a baffling mystery, a mystery sufficient to stagger reason, to make it falter and doubt. Yet during all those years of mysterious silence not only was there no doubt in Joseph's soul but his faith burned ever brighter, purer, more free from admixture of the elements of nature. He was all the time in close contact with the Divinity that was in Jesus, and had of it a perception that never for a moment suffered eclipse. And yet, this dim, obscure vision that his soul had of the Godhead in Our Lord differed only in degree and vividness, from that enjoyed by the saints, in their union with God through faith. But in none of them was this faith subjected to anything like the purification that it underwent in Joseph's case [14]; in none of them was the contact with God so continual and so sustained. Consequently, in none of them did the realisation of what God is—the realisation that comes by the perfecting of faith—attain to the proportions that it reached in the soul of him who took the place of the Eternal Father, in the care of the Son of God on earth. In no saint, excepting Mary, was faith so tried and so perfected as it was in Joseph; in none of them, in consequence, did the vision of God, that is given to men here below, attain to such clearness, force and intimacy.

[14] Cf. Bossuet. Panegyric on St. Joseph. *Sermons*, Lebarq, Vol. III, pp. 652–654.

The development of the Theological Virtues of Hope and Charity goes hand in hand with the development of Faith. It is the strength and vitality of these virtues that determine the grade of sanctity in each saint. From what has preceded, it is evident that they attained in Joseph a measure unequalled in any other : and it is clear, therefore, that his sanctity surpassed that of all others if we except Jesus and Mary.

His close relation with the august Virgin was another source of great graces for him. His marriage with her was a virginal one : in it there was a mutual donation of virginity. Mary committed hers to Joseph as a treasure for him to guard, to protect and reverence. There was a reciprocal surrender on Joseph's part. These two holy spouses were bound together by a deep and pure and chaste conjugal affection, which sprang from the love each bore to the other's purity. To this marriage Mary brought a dowry composed not of the riches of this world, but of the treasures of grace. From the moment of the Incarnation Mary entered into her office of dispensatrix of Divine Grace. To whom ought she to impart in greater abundance these treasures, of which she had the keeping, than to him to whom she stood in such a close and intimate relation and to whom she was so much indebted ? What saint can claim to have had Mary in his debt ? Yet this claim can be vindicated with justice by St. Joseph. Mary owed much to him for the care, the providence and the affection with which he enveloped her and the Child she brought him. To be chosen to play the part of spouse of Mary, the Virgin of Virgins, and the Mother of God, there was already needed an extraordinary purity and sanctity :

to sustain worthily and unfalteringly that lofty *rôle*, there was needed a continuous stream of exceptional graces. Since Mary had the privilege of dispensing all those graces, she must have given them with the utmost generosity to her holy spouse. Everything in this marriage was spiritual and perfect—and since in perfect marriage there is a complete reciprocal donation of goods between spouse and spouse, there must have been given to Joseph in the way of graces all that was in Mary's power to obtain for any creature.

The difficulties which have been brought forward against this pre-eminence of St. Joseph's sanctity can all be explained away easily. The chief one is drawn from the words of Our Lord about St. John the Baptist, when He said that there was not born of woman a greater than John.[15] This would seem to indicate that in Our Lord's unerring estimation St. John stands supreme amongst the saints after Mary. An examination of the context, however, shows that no such conclusion can be drawn from it. Our Lord is not thinking of the personal holiness of St. John, still less is he deliberately setting it over against that of others. He is but contrasting the condition in which John was born with the condition of the prophets who preceded him and with that which is the happy privilege of those born in the New Law. The Lord says that John, as compared with all the prophets of the Old Law, is a greater prophet than any of them, but that, in spite of this exalted position, he is not so privileged as the child who is destined to be incorporated with the Incarnate God, in the waters of Baptism in the new dispensation.

[15] St. Matt. xi. 2.

Another objection is drawn from St. Thomas's commentary on a verse of the Epistle to the Romans : " We ourselves also, who have the first-fruits of the Spirit." [16] Referring this verse to the Apostles, the Angelic Doctor says that they were elected to the highest of human dignities since they were destined to receive immediately from Our Lord the first-fruits of the Spirit, which they were to transmit to others in view of their salvation. Their position as foundations of the Church of Christ—the sole means of sanctification of men, confers, he says, on them, the primacy in the order of grace. From this it would seem to follow that the Apostles were higher in grace than St. Joseph. In reply to this it may be said that St. Thomas was comparing the Apostles with all the saints who were to come after them in the course of ages, as can be gathered from the words which he uses in the context : " Tempore prius et ceteris abundantius." He had not St. Joseph in mind when instituting his comparison, because he was thinking only of the times subsequent to the Apostles, and, besides, in his day, according to the designs of Providence, the prerogatives of St. Joseph were still wrapped in obscurity.

Leo XIII. in his Encyclical on St. Joseph, " Quamquam pluries ", confirms this view.   " It is true," he says, " that the dignity of Mother of God is so elevated that nothing greater can be created. Nevertheless, since St. Joseph had been united to the Blessed *Virgin* Mary in the bonds of marriage, it cannot be doubted, that he has been closer than any other to this supereminent dignity by which the Mother of God surpasses

[16] Rom. vi. 23.

so much all created natures." This view of the pre-eminence of St. Joseph is now the general opinion of the Church, so much so that in 1847, at a time of great trial, Pope Pius IX. extended to the whole world the already existing feast of the Patronage of St. Joseph, to be celebrated on Wednesday of the second week after the octave of Easter. In 1870 the same Pontiff proclaimed this holy Patriarch Protector of the Universal Church. Finally Benedict XV. had composed and prescribed for common use the new Preface of St. Joseph which salutes the saint as " a faithful and prudent servant ", set over God's household.

The universal patronage of St. Joseph is the direct consequence of the mission confided to him on earth. As the spouse of Mary and the guardian of Jesus, during that period of the Saviour's life on earth when He needed care and protection, it is fitting that the care of the Mystical Body of the same Jesus should be entrusted to him, while it, too, is accomplishing its earthly pilgrimage. Because the Word of God on earth was submissive to Joseph and rendered to him all the duties that children render to their parents, there devolved on the earthly shadow of the Eternal Father all the duties that nature imposes on the heads of families—i.e., to be the guardian, the administrator and the legitimate defender of the home of which he is the head. St. Joseph exercised these functions during his mortal life. He applied himself to protect with supreme love and tend with hourly solicitude his spouse and the Divine Child. He saved the Child from death when menaced by the jealousy of Herod, and with commendable prudence and promptitude snatched the

Treasure confided to him away to a place of safety. In the hardships of the journey and the sorrows of exile he was the companion, the comfort and the support of the Mother and the Infant. By his work he earned what was necessary for their support and provided for all their material wants. The holy house which Joseph governed with the authority of a father was, as it were, the Church of God in its infancy. Mary is the Mother of Christ and, by way of consequence, of all Christians, to whom she, as it were, gave birth on Mount Calvary in the midst of the final agony of the Redemption. Jesus is the First-born of many brethren—that is, of Christians who become of His family by that adoption, that was merited for them in the Redemption. This is the reason why all Christians are confided in a particular way to the protection of Joseph. Again the Church continues and perpetuates in a mystical way the life of Christ : it is therefore admirably fitting that the great saint should continue to exercise the function of guardian and protector of Jesus, perpetuating His sojourn on earth in this mystic manner. This patronage of St. Joseph is not without appositeness : across the ages the Church in its trials, its works, its sufferings, portrays to the eyes of faith the very vicissitudes of the mortal life of Jesus. It is fitting that just as of old the spouse of Mary attended to all the wants of the Child at Nazareth and enveloped Him and His Mother with the mantle of his protection, so he should now extend his heavenly protection to the Church and be constituted its accredited defender. In the biblical Joseph we recognise his prototype.[17] As the first brought success and prosperity

17 Gen. xli.

to the domestic interests of his Master and rendered marvellous services to His Kingdom, so the second, destined to be the guardian of the Christian religion, must be considered as the protector and defender of the Church, which is truly the house of the Lord and the Kingdom of God on earth. This protection of Joseph is universal, extending itself not only to spiritual, but to temporal needs as well. St. Teresa says that to the other saints is accorded the grace to succour us in particular necessities, but to St. Joseph, to come to our assistance in all. Therefore in all necessities, both spiritual and temporal, recourse is to be had to Joseph.

PART II

THE VICTORY OF THE VANQUISHED

" Set for the fall and for the resurrection of many in Israel."—
St. Luke ii. 34.

CHAPTER I

THE MOTHER OF JESUS

" The Mother of Jesus saith to Him ' They have no wine.' "—
ST. JOHN ii. 3.

ST. JOHN is the only one of the Evangelists who
transmits to us the story of the incidents that marked
the marriage feast at Cana of Galilee. He narrates the
event in great detail. He notes apparently trivial circumstances, as, for instance, the procedure of the waiters,
the number of the water-pots, their capacity and finally
the remarks made on the quality of the wine by the
master of the feast. To St. John, writing in his old age
and looking back over the long series of years that
had passed, and analysing the gradual development of
the Church, the happenings at this marriage, an ordinary
event in the social life of the Jews, had a significance
that escaped the minds of the other inspired historians
of the life of the Saviour. For them probably the
miracle at the marriage was but one miracle among
many others, less striking than most, perhaps, and
certainly not containing any elements that would
invest it with a special importance. This is not surpris-
ing. Those who live close to historical events cannot
see them in their true perspective nor can they mark
their bearing on other happenings which with them
constitute an important cycle in the history of mankind.

St. John was much better circumstanced than the others, to see the great importance that this miracle of the changing of the water into wine had as revealing and stressing a factor of the highest significance in the economy of the redemption of mankind. The chosen disciple had lived for many years after the crucifixion with Mary, the Mother of Jesus : he had seen the influence she exercised on the growth of the Church and in the distribution of graces that contributed to that growth. In the light of this experience he saw and understood the meaning of the combination of circumstances that attended the miracle at Cana. He saw why it was not wrought by Jesus through a sentiment of pity for a suffering revealed to Him by the sufferers themselves, as in all other cases. Of all the miracles in the Gospel this is the only one in which Mary intervenes. St. John grasped the full import of this intervention. He saw why it was pre-ordained that this intervention should take place. It shed light for him on the whole economy of the Redemption. In that light stood revealed to his spiritual vision the place of Mary in that scheme of divine mercy. The mode of the miracle manifested clearly to him the active part that falls to the lot of " The Woman " in the working out of the salvation of mankind. In the fact that Mary had with Jesus her definite part to play in the accomplishment of the marvellous change of water into wine, St. John traced the working out of the primeval prophecy which linked for ever and inseparably " The Woman " with her seed in the work of the restoration of mankind. " And the Lord God said to the serpent : I will place enmities between thee and the Woman, and thy seed

and her seed : she shall crush thy head, and thou shalt
lie in wait for her heel." [1] It was at Mary's word—
the word of "The Woman"—that was, for the first time,
unloosed the divine power of which Satan was presently
to feel the effects and the manifestations of which
would be the first indication to him of the approaching
collapse of his empire.   Understanding clearly in the
light of subsequent events and in virtue of his prophetic
insight, that the peculiar significance of the miracle at
Cana lay in its being not only a showing forth of the
divine power of Jesus, but also in its revelation of the
rôle of Mary as co-operating in the work of her son,
St. John dwells on it in a very expressive manner.   Having
completed his narrative of the events that transpired
at the feast, he underlines the fact that no miracle had,
in the life of the Saviour, preceded this one of the
changing of water into wine.   "This *beginning of
miracles* did Jesus in Cana of Galilee and manifested
His glory." [2]   Having occasion somewhat later on in
his narrative to make mention of Cana, his mind again
reverts to the miracle that took place at the marriage
feast.   "*He came again therefore into Cana of Galilee,
where he made the water wine.*" [3]

   In itself, as a work of power, this miracle at Cana is
not to be compared with other wonders related by the
fourth Evangelist, as for instance, the raising of Lazarus
from the tomb ; yet it is clear that it was for St. John
one marked with characteristics that singled it out and
gave it a place apart from all the others.   In the light
of ancient prophecy and in the experience of the actual

[1] Gen. iii. 15.
[2] St. John ii. 11.
[3] St. John iv. 46.

fulfilment of these prophecies in the gradual evolution of the Church, St. John understood that the wonder wrought at Cana was invested with a special supernatural significance belonging to none of the other miracles. These were done to prove the divinity of Jesus or to show that the seal of the divine approval was set on His teaching : the incident at Cana over and above this purpose had that of revealing the essential part that Mary, the Mother of Jesus, plays in the economy of the Redemption, and the providential place that she occupies in the life of the Church.

It is remarkable that whilst, on the whole, the life and actions of Mary are left in profound obscurity by the sacred writers, this obscurity is not unbroken by flashes of light. She is, at times, given prominence by the Evangelists and invariably at what may be called the pivotal moments in the life of the Saviour. What is more, when she does appear, it is always with full light thrown on her, the other actors in these scenes (except, of course, her Divine Child) standing in comparative shadow. On each occasion she is the central figure. The attention of the reader is necessarily fixed on her. She dominates the situation. Even in the presence of the great Archangel Gabriel, during the whole of that momentous dialogue on which turned the destinies of mankind, the eyes, as it were, are fixed and the attention of all ages focussed on the face of the Virgin. It is clearly understood that it is her word that will determine the *dénouement* of this most dramatic situation in the history of mankind since the Fall. The brilliant archangel, as a dignified but yet obsequious messenger, moves on the outward rim of that strong

circle of light in which is thrown into powerful relief
the figure of the maiden of Nazareth.[4] When the hour
of the Nativity comes, it is Mary, who, unaided by any
human helpers, gives the Saviour to mankind and who
on mankind's behalf offers the immediate ministrations
that the helpless infant needs. St. Joseph is there : he
is the master of the household, but still he remains in
the dim and shadowy background. " And it came to
pass when they were there, her days were accomplished
that she should be delivered. And she brought forth
her first-born Son, and wrapped him up in swaddling
clothes and laid Him in a manger." [5] When the shepherds came in haste to see " Christ the Lord " [6] whose
birth had been announced to them, it is not stated
simply that they found the child, but that " they found
Mary and Joseph and the Infant lying in the manger ".[7]
And lest this might be thought to be a characteristic
of St. Luke and due to the special devotedness to the
Virgin, which tradition attributes to him, there is the
same note in the narrative of St. Matthew. Narrating
the arrival of the three kings, he says : " And entering
the house, they *found the Child with Mary His Mother.*
And falling down they adored Him." [8] It is as if the
Evangelists were inspired to represent the Virgin in
the attitude of holding forth and presenting the Saviour
to the whole Gentile world, present in the person of

---

[4] One has but to contrast this scene with all others in Scripture in which
angels appear to men.   The difference is striking and obvious.   No matter
how great and holy be the human being who is favoured with the presence
of the heavenly visitant, it is the person of God's messenger that dominates
the situation.

[5] St. Luke ii. 6–7.

[6] St. Luke v. 2.

[7] St. Luke v. 16.

[8] St. Matt. ii. 11.

these three wise men. There is no mention of the
foster-father of Jesus in the scene. And yet immediately
afterwards when there is question of protecting the life
of the Child and saving Him from a pressing danger,
it is St. Joseph to whom the angel appears, and it is
St. Joseph who is the chief actor in the tragic flight into
Egypt. " And after they were departed, behold an angel
of the Lord appeared in sleep to Joseph saying : Arise
and take the Child and His mother and fly into Egypt :
and be there until I shall tell thee ; he arose and took
the Child and His mother by night and retired into
Egypt." . . . " But when Herod was dead, behold an
angel of the Lord appeared in *sleep to Joseph* in Egypt
saying : Arise, and take the Child and His mother and
go into the land of Israel . . . *who* arose and took
the Child and His mother and came into the land of
Israel. But hearing that Archelaus reigned in Judea
. . . *he* was afraid to go thither ; and being warned in
sleep retired into the quarters of Galilee. And coming
he dwelt in a city called Nazareth." [9] It is interesting to
observe how naturally the person of the foster-father of
Jesus assumes, in vigorous and decisive actions, the
chief *rôle* throughout the whole of this episode. When
it is a question of preserving Jesus for His life-work
it is Joseph who holds the principal place, but when it is
a question of that life-work itself, then it is that Mary
steps into prominence. That she is necessarily involved
in, and has a definite part to fulfil in the work of breaking
the power of Satan and redeeming mankind, is unmistakably stressed in the totally unexpected sequel to the
Presentation in the Temple, after the forty days of the

[9] St. Matt. ii. 13–23.

Purification had rolled by. These six weeks of bliss
were for Mary a pathetic preparation for what awaited
her when Joseph and herself had carried out the requirements of the Mosaic Law in regard to the child. The
devout Simeon, filled with the prophetic spirit, took the
Infant in his arms and said to *Mary His mother :* " Behold
this child is set for the fall and for the redemption of
many in Israel and for a sign which shall be contradicted. And thy own soul a sword shall pierce, that,
out of many hearts, thoughts may be revealed." [10] It
is not possible to read these words without being filled
with pity for the young mother, who was thus tragically
enlightened as to the fate that awaited the child. Yet
there was some comfort—even if a bitter comfort—for
the heart of a mother in the prophet's words. The fate
of the child was a tragic one : yet he would not be
alone in enduring it. It was unmistakably shown that
the mother herself should share the child's fate and be
caught up in the same tragic destiny. The logical
sequence of Simeon's phrases clearly reveals that an
indissoluble link bound Mary and Jesus together in the
great struggle which was to issue in the undoing of the
primeval curse. " Behold this child is set for a sign
which shall be contradicted . . . and thy own soul a
sword shall pierce." [11] The great contradiction was to
envelop them both. The Passion of the Child was to
have as its counterpart the compassion of the mother.
Here again Mary is the central and the tragic figure.
The light is turned full on her. There is not a word
addressed to St. Joseph nor is there any mention of his

[10] St. Luke ii. 34–35.
[11] St. Luke ii. 34–35.

name. He had no part to play in the great drama which the prophecy dimly and in outline foreshadowed. Again, when the days of childhood had passed and Jesus, for reasons that are for us inscrutable, but which certainly had a bearing on His Messianic mission, withdrew Himself from His parents for three days, it is Mary, not Joseph, who addresses Him a loving remonstrance after their agonising search had ended by finding the boy in the Temple conversing with the doctors of the law. " And seeing Him they wondered. And His mother said to Him : Son, why hast thou done so to us ? Behold Thy father and I have sought Thee sorrowing." [12] The reply and the actions of Jesus were enigmatic for both his parents. The actions appeared to contradict the words. He said to them : " How is it that you sought Me ? Did you not know that I must be about My Father's business ? " [13] By logical implication these words would seem to signify an intention on the part of Jesus to persevere in some course on which He had embarked and a denial of the right of His parents to seek Him out and withhold Him from it. On the other hand, He assents to Mary's implied request that He should return with herself and Joseph to the shelter of their home in Nazareth. He seems to oppose and yet to comply with her desires. " And he went down with them and came to Nazareth and was subject to them." [14] Mary not being given at this moment insight into the meaning of this mysterious occurrence, turned it over constantly, in all its details, in her mind, striving to probe its depths. " And His mother kept all these

[12] St. Luke ii. 48.
[13] St. Luke v. 49.
[14] St. Luke ii. 51.

words in her heart." [15]   Did the light dawn on her
eighteen years later when there took place another event
which constituted a close parallel to this one of the
Three Days' Loss and its sequel ?   *Did she understand
that, as it was in the plan of Divine Providence that her
prayer should inaugurate the public life of her Divine
Son, so also was it decided that her gentle pleading should
close the door on that mysterious hidden life* that was to
be the divinely ordained preparation for the Three
Years' Ministry ? It was at the prayer of " The Woman "
that were disposed the different parts of the scheme by
which the redemption was to be worked out, as it
was by the words and actions of " another woman "
that was determined the course of events that precipi-
tated the downfall of mankind.   The incident at Cana
is but an instance of the prevalent antithesis between
Mary and Eve.   Mary's Fiat, at the Annunciation, gave
Jesus to men : her gentle complaint secured the long
years of seclusion and preparation for combat : her
request at Cana inaugurates the life of conflict : and
finally, on Calvary the redemptive sacrifice was not
accomplished until she had signified her acceptance of
that sacrifice and surrendered her child to death on
behalf of mankind.

It is worthy of note that it was not, apparently, on
His own account but on account of His mother that
Jesus was present at the wedding festivities at Cana.
It is very likely that were her presence not looked for
by the bridal couple, He would not have been there.
It was to Mary that the invitation had been issued in
the first instance.   " And the third day there was a

15 St. Luke v. 52.

marriage in Cana of Galilee : *and the Mother of Jesus was there.*" [16]   Most probably she was asked to the feast because of some relationship between her and the wedded pair, and because her practical help and advice would be needed in the arrangements to be made for the festivities. A woman of her years, experience and capacity would be of invaluable assistance on an occasion of the kind. After having mentioned that the mother of Jesus was present, St. John continues, saying: *"And Jesus also* was invited and His disciples to the marriage." [17]   The logical sequence shows that the disciples were bidden to the feast out of compliment to their Master and the Master Himself out of compliment to His Mother. Mary is the door by which the Saviour enters on His public career. As the feasting progressed it began to appear that, as often happens in households when unusual numbers are gathered together, a miscalculation had been made. The supplies provided for the guests began to run short. Mary, who, most probably, had had a hand in the preparations and arrangements, was the first to perceive the menace of an awkward and, for the young spouses, a humiliating situation. Her woman's sympathy and solicitude were aroused. How was the danger, she asked herself, to be averted ?

We who read the narrative in the light of subsequent events, and are influenced by the knowledge thereby acquired, take it as being a very normal and natural thing that Mary should in her difficulty turn to her Son and ask for a miracle. The occasion seems to us to call for this. And yet a little reflection suffices to

[16] St. John ii. 1.
[17] St. John ii. 2.

show that her action was a complete departure from
what had been the customary in her relations with Jesus.
For thirty years she had lived with her Son and during
all that time nothing but everyday human means had
been taken to cope with the necessities that arose from
time to time. By daily toil the needs of the household
had been supplied. Frequently, at Nazareth, there
would be the usual interchange of good offices between
neighbours—the customary mutual borrowings and
lendings to meet special and transient necessities.
There had never been any manifestations of divine
power. In the present crisis the normal thing for Mary
would have been to enlist the services of kindly neighbours to save the situation. Yet she did not do this,
but turned to her Son, saying, " They have no wine." [18]

What moved Mary to take this step ? Did she look
to her Son to perform a miracle to save her friends from
the embarrassing situation in which they found themselves ? She had never seen her Son exercising any
miraculous power : she had never known Him to
apply anything but the obvious human means to meet
and solve the difficulties that life continually presents.
Nothing she had experienced during the thirty years
prepared her for a departure from what had been the
habitual mode of procedure. Yet, moved by an
instinct of the Holy Ghost, she addressed herself to
Jesus, confident that, somehow—very likely she was
not quite clear as to what steps would actually be taken—
Jesus would do something to meet the difficulty. She
expected that something would happen—she knew not
what. All that was definite was her perfect confidence

[18] St. John ii. 3.

that her anxiety on behalf of her friends would be relieved. It is not fanciful to detect a slight similarity between her state of mind and that of Andrew, the brother of Peter, on the occasion of the first multiplication of loaves. When Philip, in reply to a question of the Master, had stated that a very costly supply of bread was needed to satisfy the wants of the crowd that followed them, Andrew intervened, saying: " There is a boy here that hath five barley loaves and two fishes : *but* what are they among so many." [19] There is a great deal conveyed in that adversative conjunction, " *but* ". One can visualise the gesture of the hands and the expression of the countenance that accompanied it. In the light of the psychology of human intercourse, it is clear what was the state of mind of Andrew on this occasion. Whilst acknowledging the obvious fact that five barley loaves and two fishes could avail nothing towards satisfying the multitude, yet his making mention of them at all, and his drawing attention in the same breath to their insufficiency, manifested that in his secret soul he trusted that in some indefinable way the Master could with this small supply parry the situation that presented itself. In a somewhat similar fashion Mary on this occasion knew perfectly well that Jesus had neither money nor means to command an immediate supply of wine—yet she trusted Him to find a way out of the impasse. She does not ask for a miracle : she simply lays bare a pressing need, and leaves the rest to His discretion. This is an admirable way of praying. One merely exposes the wants of one's soul before the Lord and having unfolded them before Him, one

[19] St. John vi. 9.

expectantly and confidently fixes the gaze of the spirit
on the divine countenance. The unformed and
unphrased petition is more eloquent than the most
perfectly framed discourse.

Mary's touching and mute appeal is met, apparently,
with a rebuff. Jesus said to her : " *Woman*, what is it
to Me and to thee ? My hour is not yet come." [20] The
words are strange and mysterious, but not more mysterious than the ones pronounced eighteen years previously
in the Temple. At that time, as is expressly stated by
the inspired writer, the words of Jesus were not understood by His mother. They gave her food for deep
and constant thought. Now, on this occasion, there is
no hint given that she failed to grasp the meaning
underlying her Son's rejoinder. On the contrary,
everything that ensued demonstrates that she clearly
seized what the answer to her unspoken petition involved,
how it would be granted and *the principle of action*
behind Jesus' strange way of assenting to her request.

There is neither harshness nor disrespect in the words
of the Saviour. " Woman " is a title of honour and
reverence and has the same force as that mode of address
so frequent in Greek tragedies—Q Gynai, that is, Lady
or Mistress. " What is it to me and to thee " is an
expression that occurs frequently in Sacred Scripture
both in the Old and in the New Testament.[21] Whilst
having in all cases the same meaning substantially, this
meaning is invested with varied " nuances ", according
to circumstances, such as the tone of voice of the speaker,
the situation which calls forth the remark, the emotion

[20] St. John ii. 4.
[21] Judges xi. 12 ; 3 Kings xvii. 18 ; 4 Kings vii. 13 ; St. Luke viii. 28.

the speaker is suffering from and the rest. Taking the residue of meaning which is left, after abstracting from all these accidental differences the sense seems to be something like this. He who employs this peculiarly oriental locution wishes to convey to his interlocutor that the grounds on which the latter is basing or intends to base a certain course of action, and which, in his opinion, justify such a course, either do not exist at all or, if they exist, do not justify the action taken or intended to be taken. The party that utters the remonstrance says in effect to the other : " You are doing (or as the case may be, are about to do or have done) an action, and you judge yourself entitled to do so on certain grounds : in actual fact you are wrong in acting as you do, because the grounds do not exist or are not of such a nature as to leave you blameless if you take this course." The words have always a note of remonstrance. But the remonstrance bears on the principle of action primarily, and by way of consequence only on the action itself. Hence it is that it implies a refusal— though not necessarily. The words ordinarily imply a refusal, because, if the reasons which are thought to exist for taking certain steps do not really exist, then, of course, these steps should not be taken. But if the speaker insinuates that, though the grounds of action erroneously considered to be present are not really present, still there are other grounds discoverable which could justify the action in question, then the words do not intimate a refusal, but the necessity for a change in the principle of action. This is the situation at the feast of Cana. Mary, listening only to the promptings of her tender interest in, and pity for the awkward

situation in which her friends are placed, and accustomed
to the docility of her Son where her wishes are concerned,
approaches Him as she was wont to do during the
thirty years of the hidden life.   Without expressly
asking for a miracle, she implicitly does so.   For her
unspoken request could not be granted without a
miracle.   Up to that moment the *motive* that moved
Jesus in all the actions He did for His mother was
deference to that mother's wishes—deference to her,
who, as His Mother, had the right to direct and order
IIis doings.   But in the few days since He had emerged
from the obscurity of Nazareth a definite change in
their relations had taken place.   Obedience to His
Mother was the principle of the actions of His home life.
Miracles belonged to His public life.   In the public life
the controlling and directing influence—postulating
obedience on His part—belonged to His *Heavenly*
Father, not to His earthly Mother.   A miracle was part
of the " being about His Father's business " and could
be wrought only at the time, place, occasion and in the
circumstances determined from all eternity by God,
His Father.   " My hour is not yet come," He said.
He meant the hour marked in the eternal decrees.   The
shortage of wine had become acute.   It was the perception of that shortage that moved Mary to speak.   Jesus
perceived it on the instant it had become apparent to
the servants.   This knowledge of the acute want does
not stir Him to action.   The hour of need—that is, the
moment when the need was felt—was not the hour of
Divine Providence.   Some other circumstance distinct
from the need and over and above was required if Jesus
was to act.   *That circumstance was the intervention of*

Mary. When that intervention had taken place the hour decided on from all eternity had come.

A ray of divine light revealed all this to the Mother of the Saviour when His words ceased to sound in her ears. She grasped the change that had taken place. When she had begun to address Him, it had been in the old manner. *When His words ended she knew that her request was not refused but granted in entirely new conditions.* She realised that the words of her Son were not to her dishonour but to her exceeding great honour. It flashed on her in an instant that though she could not *command* a miracle as Mother, the miracle would, nevertheless, be conceded to her as all-powerful intercessor. She understood, in the instant, that the hour marked in the Divine Decree for the intervention of that all-powerful intercession of hers had now sounded. It stood revealed to her that the Almighty in His eternal regard for her linked indissolubly the inauguration of her Son's public career with her prayers. As the decree of the Incarnation hung on her Fiat, so the decree of the miracle that ushered in the life of power of the Incarnate God was suspended to her words of intercession. The "hour of Jesus" had not come, having regard to the mode in which Mary began her petition—that is, in regard to the ideas of things which were in her mind when she said : "They have no wine" —the hour had come if regard be had to the enlightenment as to her *rôle* in the economy of redemption, that was imparted to her at the words of Jesus. The hour had not come (to use a theological formula) "*in sensu composito*" with the idea which Mary had, at the outset, of the part that fell to her to play in saving the

situation at the feast : it had come " *in sensu composito* "
with the knowledge that was given her of the part of
tremendous import that was actually hers in this incident.[22] Her real part in this miracle was one that her
humility had hidden from her until the moment that,
with her Son's words, came the illumination of the
Holy Ghost, disclosing the inner meaning of things.
It stood revealed to her that the miracle was due to her
in her capacity of " Omnipotent Suppliant."

That Mary perfectly understood this time and was
not at a loss, as at the Finding in the Temple, is evidenced
by her prompt and decisive action. It is to be noted
that it is not Jesus but she that speaks to the servants,
in the first instance. She becomes the central figure—
always excepting, of course, her Divine Son. She
issues commands as being mistress of the situation.
She was perfectly instructed by the Holy Ghost as to
the fact that her request had been granted and as to the
grounds on which it was granted. She was enlightened,

[22] Regarded from the point of view of time, a scarcely measurable space
elapsed between the moment when the hour was not yet come, and that
when it had come. But there had taken place a considerable change in mora'
and spiritual relations. In Vol. II., p. 97, of the *Vie de N. S. Jésu Christ*,
by L. de Fillion, we read : " Only a very short space of time had elapsed
between Mary's order to the servants and the words of Jesus to her; but
according to a very profound remark a change in moral and spiritual conditions is not measured by lapse of time. At the moment that Jesus spoke to
His Mother the hour had not come. In the instant after, when her soul was
enlightened by His words as to the part she had to play in the miracle and
the attitude she should have towards Him in regard to His public life, the
hour had come. There is a parallel situation exposed in the 7th Chapter
of St. John's Gospel, when Jesus said to His brethren : ' Go you up to this
festival day : but I go not up to this festival day, because My time is not
accomplished.' But then immediately after we are told : ' After His brethren
were gone up, then He also went up to the feast, not openly, but as it were
in secret.' [23] He was not going up after the manner in which that going up

[23] St. John vii. 8, 10.

too, as to what should be done preparatory to the working of this great miracle.[24]

This changing of water into wine is the first of that long series of benefits that mankind has obtained from the providence of God through the intervention of the Blessed Virgin Mary. These benefits belong to the natural as well as to the supernatural order. She has a heart full of sympathy for all the sorrows and miseries that afflict the children of Adam. She is not one who is alive only to ills of a moral and spiritual nature, whilst remaining insensible to those which are of a purely

was linked, in the minds of His brethren, with a self-advertising display of power. He was going up, if regard be had to the manner of going up, *i.e.*, in an unostentatious way, that He contemplated in His own mind. He was not going in one sense : in another sense and after other principles than those which existed in the minds of His relatives, He was going."

[24] The Venerable F.M.P. Libermann, C.S.Sp., whose analysis of this incident in his commentary on the Gospel of St. John has been, with slight modifications, followed, writes : " The text may be explained in the following manner. The guests did not take Jesus for the Son of God but for a man inspired by God. . . . In His actions they saw the man only and believed that He acted out of love and obedience to His Mother, whereas in all that concerns His ministry and even during the whole time that He exercised it, He had no longer any relations of obedience to His Mother. For all that regarded His hidden life, it could be said of Him : He was subject to them, but for all that concerns His public life, He received orders only from His Heavenly Father directly and took action only in accordance with the eternal determinations that had been taken and decreed by His Father with regard to *all* His actions, and as to the time and manner in which they were to be done. . . . Therefore it is as if Jesus said to His Mother, ' To tell me, as being My Mother, that I ought to begin to work miracles, that does not enter into your function as Mother. You have not, as I have, read from all eternity in the bosom of the Father, His decrees on my works of grace. It is for Him to order and I ought to execute his orders directly. . . .' At the same time that Jesus spoke these words either to instruct His Mother at the beginning of His ministry or thereby to enlighten the attendants He addressed His Mother in different wise in the interior of her heart. He made her to understand the designs of God, showed her that her request had been granted, and taught her that God, having regard for her holy Prayers, had out of the great love He bore her inaugurated the hour of His miracles and His teaching. Mary, pierced through with the arrows of love that came from the heart of Jesus, made aware of her son's acquiescence to her pleading, *seeing clearly the greatness of God's designs on her* . . bade the servants do as her Son should tell them."

temporal kind.   She is ready to succour men even in
their temporal necessities, but in so doing she aims at
making her beneficent actions a means of drawing souls
to her Divine Son.   Her function is to distribute to
men the benefits of the redemption and thereby secure
their happiness.   It is for this she labours.   It is the part
in the work of salvation that has from all eternity been
assigned to her by God.   The Almighty having once
determined to give the Redeemer to man by the Immaculate Virgin, the plan of the imparting of the Divine
Gifts never undergoes a change.   Mankind having
obtained through her the inexhaustible fountain of all
grace, continues to receive through her intervention
all the different applications of that grace, as well in
the temporal realm as in the spiritual.   It is impossible
to use terms which exaggerate the power of the intercession of Mary on behalf of mankind.   She holds the
key of the Divine treasury—that treasury that is filled
to overflowing with the merits of her Divine Son.   To
her care is committed the distribution of the contents
of the treasury.   It is her prayer that unlocks it.   Her
Son cannot refuse her anything.   Her love for man, so
far from being diminished by her elevation to heaven,
acquires, on the contrary, a greater perfection.   To
secure men's welfare, temporal and spiritual, she will
leave nothing untried that lies within the vast limits of
the Divine Will concerning the children of Adam.
She never hesitates to demand any grace, whatsoever
it be, compatible with the known intentions of God.
These intentions as regards the human race are fully
revealed to her, as being Mother of the Redeemer
and called upon with Him to co-operate in the work of

redemption. Her power over the heart of God always remains a power of intercession. But she has in a certain sense a right that her intercession should be favourably received. " Because the Incarnate God is Son of Mary, and it is the duty of every son to cherish his mother, what is liberality on His part towards others becomes an obligation as regards the Virgin Mary." [25] The right that the Mother of Jesus has to be loved by Him involves a right to have her prayers heard and her desires fulfilled.

[25] Bossuet : 3rd Sermon on the Nativity of the B. V. M.

CHAPTER II

THE HUMILITY OF JESUS

" Learn of Me that I am meek and humble of heart."—St. Matt. xi. 29.

THE mysteries of Our Lord's life are ours and have in them a virtue of sanctification for us. If we wish " to put on Christ " in obedience to the injunction of the Apostle, we must study these mysteries lovingly; and by meditating on them, allow the spirit and disposition that animated Our Lord in each to penetrate our souls. Our Lord's life was eminently a human life and was meant to show us how man should comport himself before God and his fellow-men. " The whole life of Christ on earth," says St. Augustine, " was, through the humanity He assumed, an instruction in human conduct." [1] We shall have grasped the instruction fully when we shall have studied with faith and love each several mystery, for no single one of them reveals all the features of the character of Our Divine Lord. The different circumstances furnish occasions for the portrayal of different perfections. Contrast the charming candour and docility of the child of twelve, in presence of the learned and benevolent doctors of the law, with the majestic calm and manly fortitude exhibited by the Man-God, twenty-one years later, before the

---

[1] *De Vera Religione*, Cap. 16.

members of the Jewish Council, become His malignant
enemies and accusers ! The bearing of Jesus in both
circumstances is perfect, but how dissimilar the perfection
in each ! Our Lord has set before us the example of
every virtue and every grace ; there is no stage of life
of which He has not in His own presented a gracious
picture.

The Church, during the course of the Liturgical year,
in the Masses and Offices offers to our contemplation
different scenes from that life, inviting us to observe
and study the manner in which Jesus bore Himself in
each circumstance—in order that we may learn to
imitate, or better, to reproduce in ourselves His manner
of acting. The intention of the Spouse of Christ would,
however, be frustrated were we, by a kind of artificial
" morcelage," to fix our attention, on each occasion,
exclusively, in the particular virtue on which stress is,
for the moment, laid. Were we to devote all our efforts to
imitating now one feature, now another, of the character
of Our Lord, our endeavours would meet with little
success, for this would involve a dissipation of energy.
*The human mind naturally seeks to reduce variety to
unity;* and the law of simplification reveals itself in
the spiritual life as in the life of natural reason. Instinctively, we look for some unifying principle in the life
of Jesus, a principle which appears in the manifold
virtues in which His holiness finds its expression and
which will enable us to look upon all these virtues as
being the varying manifestations of one unique spirit.
Can we trace back these diverse streams, as it were, of
human activity to one human source from which they
take their rise and in which they are all found com-

mingled ? If this is possible, we shall be able to understand Our Lord's life as a whole, grasp the essential
unity reigning in the rich variety of that life, and shall
acquire a comprehension of Our Lord's human character
such as would not be yielded up by the most profound
study of the different mysteries taken separately and in
detail. *What is more, we shall have found the Key to
human existence* itself, and shall have discovered and
have had revealed to us the springs of human conduct,
if that conduct is to be conformable to what it is in the
intention of Almighty God.

What is this unifying and fundamental principle in
the human life of Our Lord ? He has not left us without
revealing it to us, for He knew that of ourselves we
should not have discovered it. He knew that even if we
did discover it, we should still be astray in our efforts
to imitate Him, for we should have looked upon it as
one principle amongst many, merely co-ordinate with
the rest, and not one which is the motive and inspiration
of, and which gives meaning to the others.[2]   " Learn
of Me," He said, " that I am meek and humble of
heart." It is as if He said : " My words, My works,
My virtues, My sufferings, My perfect endurance or
shame and humiliations are the direct consequence
of my humility. I am all that you see Me to be, I have
all the perfection that you admire in Me, because I
am humble. If you wish to be capable of imitating Me
in everything, in My virtues, in My words, in My actions,
in My attitude towards God and towards man, learn

[2] St. Thomas writes : " The pride of man is the great obstacle to his union
with God : that pride is put to shame and (as being the disease of human
nature) is banished by such great humility on the part of God."—*S. Th.* III.,
P. Q. 1., A. 2, C.

of Me to be humble of heart." *In a word, the perfection of Our Lord's human virtue is derived in a certain sense from the perfection of His Humility.* For though humility did not in Him usurp the place of the other virtues, yet it inspired and guided the mode in which these virtues found expression in the life and actions of the Saviour. This is especially true of those virtues which were called into play in His personal relations with God, with man and with the circumstances of His Life.[3]

On account of the vague and often incorrect notions that prevail as to the nature of this fundamental christian virtue, it is hard for us to realise how it can so colour the actions and character of Jesus. Wrongly judging certain practices, which are enjoined on us by asceticism with a view to the acquisition and to the development of humility and the curbing of pride, to be acts dictated

---

[3] In the hierarchy of the virtues, charity, of course, holds the pre-eminence. Hence all the saints without exception excelled in charity. Yet, as one beautiful human countenance differs from another, so one saint differs in moral beauty from another. Each has his own distinct spiritual traits, his own particular spiritual physiognomy : one is remarkable for apostolic zeal, another for tenderness towards the suffering, a third for a thirst for contemplation, and so on. Love of God finds inexhaustible variety of expression in them. Now what characterises the spiritual temperament of the Saviour is His humility. That is the " character " of His spirituality. A tender, tremulous, sensitive, childlike, reverent realisation of God's sovereignty and God's Fatherhood distinguishes the Saviour. His attitude towards God is a harmonious blending of profound awe and confident familiarity. Jesus was, in Himself, the perfect expression of the humility of childhood that He recommended to His followers, as the final and complete flowering of the christian spirit. He was eminently the " child of God " and hence eminently humble with the gracious and flawless humility of immaculate childhood. The more the christian captures the spirit of this perfect humility, the more *Christlike* he becomes. This is the Lord's own teaching. It is His own view of Himself. It is His express teaching on the " way of perfection ". Men will approximate to the charity of Christ when they approximate to the humility of Christ : hence it is that He expressly enjoined on men to imitate Him in His humility and did not bid them expressly imitate Him in His charity. He knows that the one will follow on the other, as the edifice rises on its foundations. Cf. *S. Th.* II., II., Q. 161, A. 5, Objection 4 and the reply to this objection.

by the virtue itself, the true nature of the latter escapes us.[4] What men are obliged to do to crush and repress their pride is wrongly taken to be the expression of the fundamental christian virtue. In this way we miss the meaning of Our Lord's life, because we consider Him as humble altogether on account of the lowly circumstances in which He decided that His life should move. This is a great error.

What is humility ? *It is a virtue that is derived from a profound reverence towards God. It lies in a recognition of our true position with respect to our Creator and fellow-creatures and in a disposition to shape our conduct in accordance with that position.* Humility is the true expression in thought and conduct of what we really are. Hence it is based on truth. It is primarily a disposition of our will to restrain that tendency which we all have to claim an esteem and consideration which is beyond our due and to assert an independence of judgment and of will that does not belong to us as creatures. The repression of this impulse of our unregenerated being to exalt itself, to exact consideration for itself as for itself, cannot be achieved by any self-analysis,

---

[4] " Humility, being a virtue, implies a praiseworthy self-abasement. This, however, may be only in the exterior and according to appearances. This is false humility. But when it has its origin in an inner movement of the soul, it is the true virtue of humility. Because Virtue lies not in what is exterior but rather in an inter or determination of the soul."—*S. Th.* II., II., Q. 161, Art. 1, ad. 2.

The Venerable Libermann writes in his turn in words that seem an echo of those of St. Thomas : " True humility does not consist . . . *in outward actions, or in the care which we take to seize upon everything that is outwardly humble* and to appear before the eyes of others in a lowly and humiliating posture or action. This may be, and often is, an effect *of true humility, which is a knowledge and intimate interior conviction,* by which we peacefully, meekly and lovingly *recognise before God* that we are nothing but misery, poverty, incapacity and detestable on account of the sins with which we are laden."—*Lettres Spirituelles,* Vol. I., N. 60.

no matter how thorough : it can have its source only in a deep sense of God's all-pervading sovereignty, and in a profound reverence arising from this ; for through that reverence man will not desire to assign to himself more than is due to him, by reason of the position given him by God. *To be humble, then, we must have a perfect understanding of what we are, and of the relations in which we stand to God.* When our conduct is directed and dictated by this true knowledge, and is in accordance with it, then we are humble.

Now, Our Lord at His Incarnation received the plenitude of human science ; that is, He had infused into His soul all that can be known of all created nature. He saw clearly with His human intelligence that His Own Humanity was something created and therefore absolutely nothing of Itself. He realised, as we cannot realise, the absolute nothingness of that Humanity when considered in Itself apart from God. He saw the full indebtedness of His Sacred Humanity to the Creator for every single instant of its existence, for every vital act and for every natural and supernatural perfection of which it stood possessed. Were there any dimness in that vision, His Humility would not have been perfect ; were there any weakness in His will or incapacity to make His actions perfectly conformable to this state of dependence, He would have failed, too, in the exercise of this fundamental virtue. But His will, being perfect and being unimpeded in its operations by any play of the passions, had no difficulty in commanding and executing conduct which was such as becomes a being that is nothing of itself and owes all to God. Hence the Will of His Father was the rule of conduct

to which He unswervingly conformed; His relations
with that Heavenly Father were characterised by the
most profound humility, because stamped with the
profoundest reverence.

This reverence towards his Creator is so essential
in the dealings of man with God that it was the great
passion of Our Lord's life—" Zelus domus tuae comedit
me "—for the zeal of thy house hath eaten me up. [5]
Whilst sin and ignorance found Him ever compassionate
and merciful, irreverence towards God roused Him to
stern and terrible anger, for He saw in it the subversion
of the order of truth and of justice. As reverence
begets humility, so irreverence nurtures pride—
" Humility is the just and truthful expression in our
thought, sense and conduct of our nature, our position
and our dependence as the subjects of God; it is the
order arising out of that subjection and dependence." [6]

*This reverence towards God demands submission not
only to God's Will but also to God's Providence.* And it
was in His submission to the Providence of God that
Jesus is for us the standard and exemplar of humility.
He has given the highest possible expression of this
virtue by accepting, without a murmur, all the consequences that followed for Him by His taking His place
amongst fallen creatures as one of them. Inspired by
a love of us reaching to the uttermost limits of sacrifice,
He made, in the interests of our salvation, a deliberate
choice on His entry into this world. What was that
choice ? *He chose, though perfectly just and holy, to be a
creature amongst fallen creatures in a fallen world, to be a*

---

[5] Ps. lxviii. 10; St. John ii. 17.
[6] Ullathorne: *Humility.*

*man amongst sinful men, and to submit to all the conse-
quences flowing from such a condition.* He could not
renounce His personal holiness, He could not commit sin,
but He could take all the life conditions that would be His,
were He a sinful man. This is what St. Paul meant by
saying : " Him that knew not sin, for us He hath made
sin, that we might be made the justice of God in Him." [7]
Christ though sinless chose to identify Himself with
and to espouse the lot of fallen and sinful man. St.
Paul dwells in another passage of great eloquence upon
this choice made by the Son of God when He became
man. The Apostle writes : " For let this mind be in
you which was also in Christ Jesus : *Who being in the
form of God* thought it not robbery to be equal to God :
but emptied Himself taking the form of a servant, being
made in the likeness of man and in habit found as a man.
He humbled Himself, becoming obedient unto death." [8]
This sentence with its close-packed thoughts may be
paraphrased thus : " Cultivate those dispositions which
were in the heart of Jesus. He, being of a divine nature,
might without injustice claim, even in this world, the
immunity that belongs to God. By His divine origin
He could claim to be treated as God ; by reason of His
sinless earthly origin He was not indebted to mortality
and its attendant evils.[9] But He chose to forego His
prerogatives as Son of God and Sinless Man and to
embrace the life conditions that are the lot of sinful
humanity. Having made this choice, He firmly abided
in it and claimed no exemptions from its consequences."
In this is His humility. This passage is all the more

[7] 2 Cor. v. 21.
[8] Philipp. ii. 5–8.
[9] Cf. *S. Th.,* III., P. Q. 35, A. 6, ad 1.

important as St. Paul cites this conduct of the Saviour as the example of and the motive for the humility He enjoins on His flock. But in humility let each esteem others better than themselves : for, " Let this mind be in you . . . etc." [10]

Christ accepted to endure the destiny that awaits every child of Adam in this world—a destiny fraught with pain by reason of the primeval sin—" God sending His Own Son in the likeness of sinful flesh and of sin ".[11] In other words, the Son of God, making Himself a child of Adam, submitted, uncomplainingly and without rebellion, to all the conditions of that state, just as if He were a sinful child of Adam. " Being made in *the likeness of man* and in habit found as a man." [12] St. Paul in this does not imply that Jesus was not really and truly man ; he asserts that He was man, and though holy and just, comported Himself, acted and suffered as though He were the same as other men—" one tempted (*i.e.,* tried) in all things like we are, without sin ".[13] Now Our Lord's humility did not consist in this choice of His— that was dictated by infinite love, not by humility ; neither did it consist in the poverty, obscurity and pain of His life on earth. A person may be in the most humble circumstances without being in the least humble. *It consisted entirely in the inner disposition of His will towards all these things.* Having chosen the condition of a sinful creature, recognising all that in the order of Providence might befall Him in consequence of that position, He did not rebel against it. *It consisted in*

[10] Philipp. ii. 3.
[11] Rom. viii. 3.
[12] Philipp. ii. 7.
[13] Heb. iv. 15.

His holding Himself in what was His true position—not by *nature but by choice.* By nature (in virtue both of his heavenly and His sinless earthly origin) He was not subject to mortality. By choice He made His own the lot of fallen humanity. It is important to understand this clearly.

What was the position ? God, when creating man as a being endowed with free will, contemplated in that creation the possibility of the perversion of that will. Man being free enjoys the power to use his free will rightly or perversely. God does not will such perversion ; His intention is that His creatures should attain greatness and happiness through the meritorious use of their freedom of choice. But it was in the order of His Providence that His creatures should have the power, if they so chose, not to respond to His designs in their regard, but on the contrary to bring disorder into creation by the perverse use of their faculties. *In other words, it is in the order of God's Providence that disorder would be in the universe, if men chose that it should be.* And man made this choice, thus throwing the whole creation out of harmony. God did not will this, but He permitted it, and therefore permits all the consequences that flow from it. With sin came strife and injustice. Whoever then is born of Adam comes into a world where the sinful passions of men determine many events. Every child of Adam at its birth is caught up by and dragged into a system where disorder reigns, and where it is bound to endure buffets and ill-treatment because of such disorder. Whoever makes himself one of our race, by the fact, enters into this system. And this Our Lord did. Once having chosen for Himself the condition of sinful creature amongst sinful and imperfect creatures, He never for one single instant sought to emancipate Himself from the consequences of that position.[14] Since that was His condition before God and man, He firmly abided in it and conducted Himself as became that condition. When His life was sought by a powerful prince He did not, as He might have done, use His Divine power to avoid the notice and escape the hatred of His enemy; He did simply what any child of the humble worldly condition that was His would do—namely, flee for shelter to a foreign country. The poverty, powerlessness, want of influence accompanying His station in life left Him without any other means of saving Himself from death, except flight and trust in the guiding protection of God. He did not repine or murmur at the cruelty and wickedness of His enemy. *In the actual order of things, wrongdoing, injustice, tyranny and persecution of the good are in the order of Providence. He submitted uncomplainingly to it all because all this was the consequence of the position He had assumed,* and in this lies His humility. And it is in this that He asks us to imitate Him, at the same time encouraging us by the thought that it is by this way that our souls can enjoy rest and peace.

We are by nature what Our Lord was by choice—namely,

[14] St. Thomas writes: " The original justice that Adam enjoyed empowered him to preserve himself from all that could work him harm. Christ could have assumed for Himself this power had He so wished. But as there are for men three states, viz., the state of innocence, the state of guilt, and the state of glory, Christ assumed something of each. . . . Of the state of glory, He enjoyed the Beatific Vision : of the state of innocence, He assumed the exemption from sin : and finally, of the fallen and sinful state, He took upon Himself that necessity in which we all are of submitting ourselves to the sufferings and disabilities of the present life."—*S. Th.*, III., P. Q. 13, A. 3, ad 2.

children of a fallen race in a fallen world and subject to the consequences of the fall.   All men are plunged in error—and the best among them are simply those who are forcing their way slowly and painfully out of the darkness of error into the light of truth.   *Where there is error* there are necessarily *mistakes, suffering, conflict and want of harmony.*   We are all sinners—" If we say we have no sin, we deceive ourselves and the truth is not in us." [15]   *Now God does not will sin ; but He willed that condition of things in which sin is possible ;* and *therefore the disorder* that arises if sin becomes a fact is in the order of His Providence.   *The reign of sin* means *the reign of injustice.*   Whoever exists under the reign of sin is necessarily involved in a system where wrongdoing predominates and where *each must suffer from the effects of that wrongdoing.   In other words, it is the law of things as they actually are that we must continually suffer from others ; it is the condition of our being that we shall be the victims of others' abuse of their free wills ; it belongs to our position that our desires and inclinations should be continually thwarted and that we should be at the mercy of circumstances.   And it is our duty to bear that without resentment and without rebellion.   To rebel is to assert practically that such things are not our due, that they do not belong to our position.   It is to refuse to recognise that we are fallen members of a fallen race. The moment that we feel resentment at anything painful that happens to us through the activity of MEN OR THINGS, at that moment we are resentful against God's Providence.*   We are in this really protesting against His eternal determination to create free beings ; for

[15] 1 St. John i. 8.

these sufferings which we endure are a consequence of
the carrying into effect of that free determination. If
we expect or look for a mode of existence in which we
shall not endure harshness, unkindness, misunderstanding and injustice, we are really rebelling against
God's Providence, we are claiming a position that *does
not belong to us as creatures.* This is to *sin against
humility.* It is pride.

Even if we ourselves are never unjust, if we never
hurt or pain others, if we never by a wrong act on our
part contribute to the existing disorder, we must not
on that account claim that we should be exempt from
the consequences of the disorder of others—it would
be to claim to be above, or beyond, or outside an order
of things permitted by Divine Providence—it would
mean a refusal to abide in our rightful position as
members of a fallen race ; and, as we have seen, *Humility
is nothing else than a practical determination to abide in
this position.* It is a refusal to learn of Jesus. St. Paul
bids us contemplate the mode of acting of the Christ
in order to find therein the stimulus to check the proud
uprisings in ourselves against the disabilities under which
we labour by reason of the Fall. " *For think diligently,*"
he says, " *upon Him that ' endureth' such opposition
from sinners against* Himself that you be not wearied
fainting in your minds." [16] Even if we ourselves were
free from guilt, we should, *without resentment,* after
the manner of Our Lord *suffer* contradiction and injustice. How much further should we be from resenting
anything that happens to us when we consider our own
sinfulness ! Anyone who looks into his own heart

[16] 1 Heb. xii. 2–3.

will discover there, if not actual sin, at least such vile tendencies towards sin, movements of pride, envy, jealousy, untruthfulness and meanness, that he ought not in justice to exact any consideration whatever from others. But still we do. *It is our very sinfulness that impels us to demand an exemption from the created consequence of sin* because in proportion as our sinfulness is great, is our humility little. We exact the most minute perfection on the part of others in their dealings with ourselves, whilst we readily excuse and even justify our own shortcomings in our dealings with them. We are indulgent to our own faults ; we are intolerant of those of others. *We, as it were, claim the privilege of being the only sinners in the world, and demand that all the world beside should be just.* This preposterous claim is involved in every deliberate movement of resentment indulged in, because others are wrongdoers and their wrongdoing affects us adversely. It is again an aiming at a condition that is not ours, and therefore a failure in humility. [17]

Our efforts after sanctity do not withdraw us from the operation of this law—quite the contrary. *The more just we are, the more injustice we are likely to endure*— as must be the case in an unjust, unbalanced world, that has swerved from the axis of truth. Our Lord's life has thoroughly exemplified this. Since the Fall, sin has invaded the world as a conqueror, and reigned there. The world was made by Original Sin an unsuper-

[17] This does not mean that we are not to do our best to correct the injustice of others and to protect ourselves legitimately against it. It is our duty to strive to establish the reign of justice in ourselves and in others. But it is wrong for us to cherish a spirit of sullen revolt against our condition as fallen creatures and to demand for ourselves the conditions of an unfallen world as being our due.

natural world, one from which the Divinity was banished. It had to be reconquered to the Divine, in detail, by Our Lord Jesus Christ. He came, therefore, into a moral order of which all the forces, without exception, were in irreconcilable opposition with Him. He stood for the Divine. The world stood for the anti-Divine. Therefore from the first instant of His earthly existence, He was involved in conflict. It was the conflict of light against darkness, of truth against falsehood, of the redeeming God against unredeemed men.[18] St. Paul speaks of the kingdom of sin arrayed against the kingdom of justice. St. John loves to contrast the two as darkness and light.[19] In the psalms, too, reference is made to this inevitable war—" Why have the Gentiles raged and the people desired vain things ? " [20]

There could be only one issue to this combat—Jesus conquered, but His Humanity was done to death in the struggle. The Divinity conquered through the moral annihilation of the Humanity. If that Humanity once yielded to impatience or irritation sin would have conquered ; but no, the Humanity stood firm unto death. Sin accomplished His death in so far as God could die, that is, in His Human nature. Our Lord's death was no accident. It was the consequence of His life and teaching. He stood in a world in which all was arrayed in hostility against Him. *He was the only Divine Being in a world which was undivine.* He was the only light in a world of darkness, and that world hated to be illuminated and therefore strove to extinguish the light. " And this is the judgment ; because the light

[18] Cf. St. Paul : Ep. Rom. v. vi.
[19] Cf. St. John's Gospel i. 5 ; iii. 19.   First Epistle i. 5 ; ii. 8.
[20] Ps. xi. 1–2.

has come into the world, and men have loved darkness rather than the light, for their works were evil." [21]

There was no truce possible : " What fellowship hath light with darkness ? " [22] Our Lord knew what was to be His fate, if He chose to live His life according to the actual conditions of existence. He resented nothing that happened to Him, accepting it all as the inevitable condition of His lot, *neither striving to lift Himself above it, nor to use His Divine power to escape it*. In this was His humility. And He thus achieved the victory and secured the supremacy of the Divine in the world, " blotting out the handwriting of the decree that was against us, which was contrary to us. And He hath taken the same out of the way—fastening it to the cross, and despoiling the principalities and powers. He had exposed them confidently in open show, triumphing over them in Himself." [23]

Now, what happened to Christ, happens to His followers. " All that will live Godly in Christ Jesus, shall suffer persecutions " [24]—and that, too, for the same

---

[21] St. John ii. 19.

[22] 2 Cor. vi. 14–15.

[23] Coloss. ii. 14–15. Jean Rivière writes : " Historically the sufferings of Jesus are the issue of the normal play of secondary causes. Having clothed Himself with our humanity, the Word of God could not but encounter suffering in the world, unless He protected Himself against it by miracle. His lot necessarily was bodily sufferings, because He was exposed to the ordinary miseries of earthly existence ; mental sufferings, because of the vulgar or brutal passions of His *milieu* roused against Him. His innocence, so far from protecting Him from this, was itself a source of more bitter and more numerous sufferings. All this is the logical outcome of the Incarnation, as arranged in the actual plan of God. This plan, with all its conditions, the soul of Jesus accepted in loving obedience. It is not a question of substitution for humanity but solidarity with humanity : this merciful solidarity, flowing from the charity of Christ, presupposes the freedom of choice of Christ Himself and of God."—*Le dogme de la Redemption* (1931), pp. 254–255.

[24] 2 Tim. ii. 13.

THE HUMILITY OF JESUS

reason. The godly life in Jesus is the development of the divine in their souls—and this straightway enters into conflict with the opposing elements. It is *in conflict with the undivine in others and with the undivine in oneself.* We have therefore to suffer from ourselves and also from others. The internal conflict ceases only when there is perfect conformity in our souls with Jesus by the entire sacrifice of self to God. Then the Divine has completely invaded and taken possession of our souls. This is the peace which is the crowning grace prayed for in the Mass. The external conflict will never cease until Jesus reigns in undisputed sway over the world. This will be attained only at the end of time. We are bound to suffer in our relations with others, *because, to the extent that God has not* possession of their souls, they will act through principles which St. Paul calls *carnal.* These are principles of self-love and, therefore, of injustice, and must wound. We ourselves to the extent that we are unregenerate will act in a similar manner. All this unsupernatural world is the kingdom of darkness and of Satan, and, therefore, of disorder, conflict and suffering.

To exist in the midst of this opposition is the condition of our fallen nature. It is irrational to rebel against it, it is irrational to expect that we shall not feel the effects of it every day and every hour of the day. It is the virtue of humility not to give way to bitterness; not to resent those wounds; and to maintain ourselves without repining or murmuring in that condition. It is thus the saints exercise humility, after the manner and example of the Divine Master. They look upon nothing that happens to them as being undeserved: they look upon it as being the logical outcome of things as they are. Pursuing order and justice themselves, they are not bitter when they encounter disorder and injustice in their *milieu*. Whilst they strive to remedy it they do not indulge in a passionate revolt against it. Their resistance to disorder is not a self-indulgent giving way to their own feelings of anger and bitterness. They do not allow the disorder they contend against to provoke disorder in themselves. Is there no truce to this disorder, no period or element of peace possible ? Yes, it is when the Divine in ourselves encounters the Divine in others— here there can be no conflict. God cannot be in opposition with Himself. Between those in whom charity reigns there can be no opposition, no conflict. This was St. Paul's ambition for his followers. " I . . . beseech you that you walk worthily of the vocation in which you are called, with all *humility* and mildness, with patience, supporting one another in charity, careful to keep the unity of the Spirit, in the bond of peace." [25]

Humility then has nothing to do with self-depreciation. It is not thinking little of oneself, it is rather not thinking of self at all. As long as we can feel humiliated we are not perfectly humble. For the feeling of humiliation arises from our conceiving ourselves to be in a state or situation inferior to what we consider suited to our dignity. And there is nothing in us belonging to ourselves for which we can claim esteem or consideration. " What have you that you have not received ? " [26]

All good comes from God, all evil has its source in the instability of the created will. To realise this is to

<hr>

[25] I Eph. iv. 1–3.
[26] I Cor. iv. 7

be in the truth; to have a disposition in conformity with such realisation is to be rightly disposed.   To make claims to consideration—not consonant with this position of ours—is to step outside the true order of things : it is to stand in error. Of Satan, the personification of pride, Our Lord uses these words : " He stood not in the truth." [27] There is a close affinity between truth and humility, as between pride and ignorance. Progress in real intelligence is always progress in humility. To be humble is to be in rectitude ; the Old Testament calls the perfect fulfilment of God's Will serving Him in truth.[28]

Since humility is allied with truth, it is possible to have the full perfection of the virtue and yet be perfectly cognisant of one's endowments whether in the order of grace or in the order of nature. Our Lord did not ignore His Own sanctity.   " Which of you," He said to His enemies, " shall convince (convict) me of sin ? " [29] Neither did the Blessed Virgin quarrel with the Angel's salutation when she was hailed " full of grace ".   Our Blessed Lady was perfectly aware of the fullness of her perfection, but she would have considered it absurd to take to herself any credit for her marvellous gifts, whilst esteeming those gifts at their proper worth. Hence the Magnificat. St. Thomas, too, asserted that what he conceived to be the greatest intellectual grace he received was the faculty of never reading anything without fully grasping its meaning as he read. And St. Teresa states that nothing can place such an obstacle in the way of our spiritual progress as the ignoring or striving to hide

[27] St. John viii. 44.
[28] 1 Kings xii. 24.
[29] St. John viii. 46.

from ourselves the graces we receive from God.

We find it hard to be humble if we are conscious of the possession of any gifts, because we have an inveterate tendency to identify them with ourselves and rob God of His title to them. We shall learn to hold them without hurt to ourselves if we come to look upon them *objectively*, if I might be permitted to use the term. What is the meaning of this? *To hold them objectively is to hold them as something independent of ourselves; and to regard them with the same esteem in others as in ourselves.* If they arouse in us the same emotions when seen in others as when they are in our own possession, then we have a correct attitude towards them. Without loss of humility we can prefer the gifts of God to us, either of nature or of grace, to those He has bestowed on our neighbours. We are not obliged to subject the divine in ourselves to the divine in others, though we may always subject what is of ourselves in us to what is divine in them—and thus fulfil the apostle's injunction, "but in humility, let each esteem others better than themselves ".[30] "Each one not considering the things that are his own, but those that are other men's " (v. 4). For we may also consider the divine gifts that are visible to us in our own souls inferior to the divine gifts which may be in our neighbour, though not apparent to us. This will enable us to practise easily the three grades of humility :—

(1) To subject oneself to one higher and not prefer oneself to one's equal in position.

(2) To subject oneself to one in the same position and not prefer oneself to an inferior.

[30] Philipp. ii. 2–8.

(3) To subject oneself to one's inferior.

But does not this seem to destroy our dignity ? By no means. For humility demands our subjection to God directly and subjection to man only on account of God. *Loss of dignity would be involved in submitting ourselves to man as such, by reason of his qualities, personality, or our own weakness.* This would be servility. Nothing is so opposed to servility as humility, and nothing is so protective of dignity. For by it we are prevented from aspiring after what is beyond us, and so making ourselves ridiculous, as well as saved from subjecting ourselves to that to which we should not be subject, and so degrading ourselves. Humility is based on reverence towards God, and it is through that sense of reverence that we submit ourselves to what is divine whether in persons or in the order of things prevailing. Our attitude of respect and submission is dictated by our sense of the presence of God in men and things— a presence either actual or possible. In this way we may maintain our independence of men and owe subjection only to God : in this consists perfect freedom and true dignity. Looking upon the authority exercised by superiors as being exercised for God and coming from Him, and executing its behests, influenced by this consideration solely, our obedience will be devoted, prompt and joyous, without trace of servility. And the superior who looks upon his authority in the same way can be firm in demanding unquestioning and absolute submission to it as such, without in the least degree being wanting in humility. We can and should always be dignified, through consciousness of the divine in ourselves, realising that nothing that can happen from outside can harm or impair that dignity that belongs to us as children of God. On the contrary all unjust ill-treatment serves but to enhance it, for it but serves to develop the divine in us. *Hence, if we are really humble, esteeming only what is of God, and not esteeming what is of self, we can never be humiliated.* Our Lord suffered untold humiliations but never felt humiliated ; in the midst of all He endured, He maintained His divine calm, dignity, and majesty.

It is only indirectly we submit ourselves to creatures. We *endure* them in their purely creature-activity as Our Lord did. We allow them to act on us, without per-mitting ourselves thereby to be moved from a true opinion of ourselves for what we are of ourselves and what we are of God. In this attitude of humility is found peace. " Learn of Me that I am meek and humble of heart, and you shall find *rest for your souls.*" In this wise we can possess ourselves in peace. Nothing from outside can affect or lower our dignity ; it is only from within that it can be lowered—by our descending through sin from our condition as children of God, that is, by acting as children of men. " And man not under-standing his own dignity, puts himself on a level with senseless beasts and is like unto them." [31] Esteeming only the divine in ourselves, looking only to what is divine in others, our relations with them will assume a character stamped by christian dignity, courtesy, charity and simplicity—to the complete exclusion of self-sufficiency and arrogance as well as of flattery and servility.

Humility imparts to us not only dignity, it also inspires us with boldness, enterprise and courage in the service

[31] Ps. lii. 13.

of God. Not being afraid to face the confusion and humiliation that attend on failure, we are always ready to undertake great enterprises for His glory; to attempt them through reliance on our own powers would be the height of folly; to set about them with confidence in the power of God is but the exercise of faith. Ignoring self and placing oneself entirely under the influence of what is divine, we can be perfect instruments in the hands of the Holy Spirit to effect His purposes in ourselves, in others or in the world of action. The more a man subjects himself to God, the more efficient can he become.

Humility, aiming at the extinction of self-exaltation, tends to obliterate self-love. It is, in a word, a constant sacrifice of self—in order that our souls may be free to receive the influence of God. " Humility is the spiritual element therefore in all sacrifice. It is the surrender of nature and life to God, that by His power they may be altogether changed into a better form." [32]

[32] Ullathorne: *Humility*, Lect. IV., pp. 105–106.

CHAPTER III

THE TENDERNESS OF JESUS TO THOSE WHO FAIL

" They that are whole need not the physician, but they that are sick."
—St. Luke v. 31.

JESUS is the way to God : " I am the way, and the truth, and the life. No man cometh to the Father but by Me." [1] The full meaning of these words escapes those who are at the beginning of the spiritual life. But according as progress is being made, and grace begins to shed a stronger and a less fitful light on the road along which those who are struggling towards perfection are painfully toiling, the inner sense of those mysterious words becomes plainer. It becomes clear that assimilation to the human character of Jesus is the essential condition of union with God, and that without this assimilation all our efforts to reach God and enter into union with Him are doomed to failure. After many fruitless efforts and after repeated disappointments, the soul begins to realise that all attempts to produce in itself by direct self-discipline and mortification that purity which permits the divinity to enter into free communication with the created spirit, meet with check and prove ineffective. Another path must be trodden. The attention of the soul has to be focussed on the

[1] St. John xiv. 6.

humanity of Our Divine Saviour, rather than on itself.
This does not mean that in the struggle towards spirituality self-examination has to be entirely laid aside. This
would run counter to the methods inculcated by all the
approved ascetical writers. But it means that the soul
shall see itself best by concentrating its attention on the
humanity of Jesus. In this way the soul does not
disappear out of the line of vision : it disappears only
out of the direct line of vision. It is seen and studied
not directly but indirectly. And it shows up more
clearly for what it is when it is bathed in the light that
radiates from the Sacred Humanity of Jesus. The study
of His human life, not, it is true, in its merely external
historical aspect, but in the inner workings of that life,
will quickly effect what an earnest, sustained and well-
meaning study of one's own interior has failed to achieve.
This study of Our Lord must be sustained by humble
prayer, by a real desire to become more intimate with
Him, and must be directed to acquiring a deep and
sympathetic understanding of the dispositions of His
Heart and of His soul.

When God's grace, which is always given in answer
to prayer, imparts the power to bring home to oneself
what Jesus felt, what thoughts traversed His mind,
what emotions stirred His soul—in a word, when it is
given one to realise in some measure how He humanly
reacted to all the circumstances of His life, then one
begins to walk with assured step on the road that leads
to holiness. This study reveals a wonderful similarity
and a still more striking dissimilarity between Him and
ourselves. We discover with delight that He was
affected by things much in the same way as we ourselves

are. He was hurt by misunderstanding; He was wounded by insult; He delighted in candour and innocence; He was revolted by hypocrisy; He was won by straightforwardness and simplicity; He hated lying and irreverence; He was fearless in the vindication of truth; His heart was deeply touched by those who showed faith and confidence in Him, and finally, He gave Himself without reserve to those who yielded Him their loyalty and their affection. But just as it dawns on us that in many things our experiences are very like what His must have been, we discover, too, a profound contrast between Him and us. There is a marked difference presented between the perfection of the manner in which He controlled the stirring of His feelings and guided their expression, and the imperfection and weakness exhibited by us at each moment in the direction of our thoughts, our feelings and our activities, *i.e.*, in the direction of our whole internal and external life. We see that His life was perfectly human and still humanly perfect : and we are obliged to confess that all the movements of our being, feelings, emotions, judgments, speech, attitude of mind and body, though bearing the stamp of humanity, are far short of the human perfection discernible in everything pertaining to the Sacred Humanity of Our Lord. The realisation of this contrast causes in us a pain and a sorrow which partakes more of the nature of love than grief.

The little knowledge we have acquired of the Heart of Jesus stimulates us to penetrate further into its depths, and is accompanied by the ardent desire to eliminate the unlikeness that exists between the movements of His Heart and those of our own. The study of Him excites in us the desire to become like Him as Man. And then when our life and our acts bear a resemblance to those of Jesus, God comes and pours His Divinity into our souls in abundance, lavishes on them the gifts of His Grace, and gradually breaking down the barriers that exist between creature and Creator, initiates souls into the happiness that accompanies union with the Divinity. Great happiness results from this union, even in the imperfect mode of it that belongs to the condition of our state of exile on earth. This is the whole theory of sanctity. The initiative in the giving of grace comes from God. He gives to all who do not present an obstacle to His giving. It is bestowed on children not yet capable of eliciting an act of choice. It is given to adults who wish for it and do not retain a deliberate affection for sin. But the initial grace is meant to be but the pledge of an ever increasing " largesse " of divine life. According as Our Heavenly Father sees the souls of His adopted children assuming the features of the soul of His Only-Begotten Son, He dispenses His treasures more freely. He gives in proportion to the degree of resemblance which He discerns us to bear to Jesus in the conduct of our life. This is the meaning of those mysterious words that were heard from Heaven on the occasion of the Transfiguration. " This is my beloved Son, in Whom I am well pleased, hear ye Him." [2] It is also the explanation of St. Paul's teaching, the whole burden of which was that the Christian should learn of Christ.

One desirous of holiness, therefore, cannot advance

[2] St. Matt. xvii. 5.

except by a constant, close and loving study of the human character of Our Lord Jesus Christ. To know Him is the end to which that exercise of the inner life, known as meditation, is primarily directed. This knowledge and this understanding of Our Lord's character comes from a contemplation of the events of His life and from a study of His teaching, as set forth by the Evangelists. But no efforts of our own can yield to us as perfect a portrait of Jesus as is given by His own occasional revelation of Himself. Our study would never venture to reveal Him so touchingly human as He reveals Himself to be. And we have this great consolation that He has not left to His disciples, but has taken on Himself the description of certain aspects of His character which most intimately concern us. These deal with that attribute in Him, which is most frequently called into exercise in His dealings with human souls—namely, His mercy.

With the exception of that comparatively small number of heroic men and women who have, from the dawn of consciousness, pursued unfalteringly the path of perfection, Christians as a rule belie the promises of their baptism and continually present obstacles to the increase of divine grace in their souls. Differing in many respects, we are alike in this, that we are all sinners, and that we have not only once, but perhaps several times in our lives disappointed God.[3]   " If we say that we have no sin we deceive ourselves and the truth is not in us "—says St. John.[4]   These words are true, not only of those whose lives are stained by

---

[3] Cf. " *Grieve not the Holy Spirit of God,*" Eph. IV. 30.
[4] 1 St. John i. 8.

frequent and grievous transgressions of the laws of God, but also, in a certain sense, of those who have been called by Our Saviour to live in close intimacy with Him, and whose lives, at least externally, appear good and devout. There are few religious persons who have not, at times, the depressing sense of being failures in the spiritual life. On occasions of retreat and recollection, and sometimes, too, in the midst of their occupations, there comes to them an agonising sense of having drifted away from God. There is a feeling that He and they move in different worlds with no point of contact. They feel very remote from Him, from His thoughts and His ways. The consideration of the barrenness of their lives and of the, apparently, wholly unsupernatural condition of their souls fills them with dismay. Their souls present a sorry sight when examined according to the principles of Christian perfection, and they have a sense of sinfulness which is more poignant than the actual consciousness of positive sin. Hateful to themselves, they judge that they must be an object of aversion for the Lord, Whose graces they have squandered and Whose hopes they have disappointed. Knowing His purity, His holiness, His utter devotedness to His Heavenly Father, they think that He can no longer care for beings so utterly different from Himself in all that appertains to holiness and rectitude of life. They are uneasy in His presence because they fear that He, so pure and so good, must shrink from creatures who are vile, mean and unworthy, as they know themselves to be. Seeing no good in their own souls, they are convinced that they can no longer be an object of regard to Jesus.

There comes to them at this juncture the subtle temptation to make their drifting away from the Lord a reason
for drifting still further from Him.

Now, this is totally to misunderstand Our Divine
Lord. It is true that He cannot but look with hatred
on sin, and that He cannot love us in so far as we are
sinners. But He can, and does love us for any little
good that remains in us, and above all He loves us
for what we can possibly become if we respond to
the pressing appeals of His grace. He does not love
sin, but He does love those who are sinners, and He
never shrinks from contact with us, or from our contact
with Him, as long as there remains the possibility of
our rejecting that which is displeasing in His sight.
It is to wrong Him to think otherwise; and the devil
has never got a fully decisive victory over a soul until
he has robbed it of full confidence in the inexhaustible
goodness of the Heart of Jesus to the wayward, the
faithless and the sinful. And not the very gravest
of our infidelities inflict so cruel a wound on that
Heart, as is that wound that is inflicted on It when
we doubt of Its tenderness and mercy. Those who came
in contact with Him whilst He lived on earth never
had this attitude of fear towards Him, even when they
recognised His awe-inspiring holiness. In spite of the
consciousness of grave sin that many who approached
Him must have had, we see no trace in their dealings
with Him of their having a tendency to shrink from
His presence or to dread His approach. " Now," says
St. Luke, " the publicans and sinners drew near unto
Him to hear Him." [5] So condescending did He show

* St. Luke xv. 1.

Himself to them on all occasions and such trust had they in Him that the charge of having a predilection for sinners and publicans was frequently levelled at Him, as He tells us Himself. His enemies were repelled by the life of austerity led by John the Baptist, and they pretended to be scandalised at the absence of rigid penance in the life of Jesus, and at His attitude of clemency towards sinners. They found fault with the one and with the other so that Our Lord was forced to call attention to the contradiction in their minds, saying : " John the Baptist came neither eating bread or drinking wine. And you say : He hath a devil. The Son of Man is come eating and drinking and you say : Behold a man that is a glutton and a drinker of wine, a friend of publicans and sinners." [6]

It is evident that not only did the Saviour show an habitual readiness to forgive sin, but He must have exhibited such graciousness, tenderness, sympathy and kindness towards sinners, that it caused comment and criticism amongst the " rigidly righteous ". The allusions to this subject are frequent in the Gospels. So constant did the murmurs of His enemies become, that one day Our Lord turned on them and in a series of parables, three in number, following one upon the other, He laid bare to an astonished world what passes through the human heart of God in regard to those who have left Him to seek for happiness in sin. The parables of the strayed sheep, the lost groat, and the prodigal son are a wonderful revelation of the tenderness of Jesus. It was as if Our Lord, stung to the quick at being required by those hard-hearted priests, the

[6] St. Luke vii. 33-34.

representatives of God on earth, and the ministers of
His covenant with men, to show Himself austere and
forbidding to those who have failed, was driven to
disclose the incomprehensible yearning of His great
Heart even towards the most unworthy of us. He is
forced, as it were, to reveal to the vulgar and the
uncomprehending, to the conventional and the narrow-
hearted, what looks like weakness where sinners are
concerned. He does not excuse His actions, He does
not even pause to justify them, He simply lays bare
the inner workings of His Heart—what the saints
have had the hardihood to call the folly of His love—
for us miserable failures in the way of holiness.

This Chapter in St. Luke [7] is remarkable and repays
study. It will be noticed that Jesus is not content with
one parable, but figure is added to figure, image to image,
detail heaped on detail, in order to give as complete
a picture as possible of the boundless mercy of the
God-Man. It would look as if all barriers of reserve
were broken down, and Jesus allowed men to penetrate
into the most mysterious recesses of His Heart. The
words follow rapidly one on another, the sentences
are vivid and eloquent, each parable succeeds the preceding one without a break, almost with an appearance
of breathlessness: and in all is observed the same
rapid movement, the same nervous phrasing, the same
vivid colouring. Jesus' defence of Himself is beautiful
in the extreme, beautiful in its simplicity, beautiful in
that eloquence which touches the innermost fibres of
our hearts. The story of the Lost Sheep might have
seemed sufficient in itself to bring consolation to the

[7] Chapter xv

repentant sinners for all time, and to inspire the most
obdurate with unbounded confidence in the Divine
Mercy, but Jesus was not satisfied with it. He supple-
ments this moving story by two others widely different,
but equally moving and, perhaps, more consoling.
It was as if Our Lord, as He was developing the first
parable, seeing all the other possible phases of human
waywardness, and fearing lest some sorrowing soul
in after time might find in the particularly heinous
circumstances of its sin a reason for doubting of the
mercy of God, laboured to forestall all such possible
objections by showing forth in the details of His instruction that no depths of wickedness and misery and failure
were too deep to be sounded by the plummet of His
Love. In the portraits of the Good Shepherd seeking
the stray sheep, the Anxious Householder looking for
the lost groat, and the Loving Father awaiting the
return of the Prodigal Son, He shows that the mercy
of God is multiform.[8] Though simple in its essence
it is many-sided and adaptable; able to meet every
emergency occasioned by wickedness. To every form
of sin it can oppose a new front; and wickedness will
more speedily exhaust the possibilities of crime than
it will exhaust the infinite resources of the Divine
Goodness. Nothing that we can do can find it at fault.
Our Lord has taken away from us every possible reason
that we might allege for not approaching Him with
confidence.

And as Our Lord was in those days so He is now.
He does not change with the passing years, neither can
our treatment of Him cause Him to alter. He is here

[8] Cf. " *The Hound of Heaven.*"

with us in our churches, the same in Heart and in Mind as He was in those days when He pronounced the parables of the Prodigal Son and the Good Shepherd. As He never then showed coldness, aloofness or displeasure towards those who approached Him, no matter how stained their souls were with sin, He does not do so now. Our badness cannot modify His goodness, nor can it rob Him of His interest in us. He looks out on us from the Tabernacle with the same yearning love, the same expectancy, the same hopefulness which no rebuff on our part can chill, as He exhibited to all those whom He encountered whilst on earth. He is concerned about us as He was about those He taught on the shores of the lake of Galilee, and those whom He compassionately fed in the desert. We are just as valuable in His eyes as they were. He will be at least as tender, as condescending, as kind towards us as He was towards them. They were probably no better than we are. No matter how frequently we may have failed in His service, there is no reason why we should not have an absolute, childlike confidence in Jesus. The great benefit that the little saint of Lisieux has conferred on mankind is to have revealed the spiritual reasonableness of this attitude. She writes : "If I draw nigh to God with love and trust, it is not because I have kept from mortal sin. Were my conscience laden with every imaginable crime, I should not have one whit less confidence ; heart-broken and repentant, I would throw myself into my Saviour's arms. He loves the prodigal son : I know His words to Magdalen, to the adulterous woman, to her of Samaria. Who would make me afraid if I know His mercy and His love ?

I know that all my numberless sins would disappear in an instant, like a drop of water cast into a furnace."

Our Lord's own choice is the basis on which this confidence is built. When cavilled at because He frequented the society of those who were not remarkable for the rectitude of their lives His answer was that "He was come not to call the just but sinners". Our sins, then, far from creating a barrier between us and Him, really constitute a reason and give us a title or right to come to Him, as they also constitute a reason for His coming to us. To the Pharisees He said equivalently: I frequent sinners because they need Me more than others—the physician passes his time with and gives all his attention and care to those that are ill, not to those that are in health. I am the Physician of souls. That is My work, and "They that are in health need not a physician but they that are ill." [9] Encouraging as is this simile for us, it does not fully exemplify the relations of Jesus to our souls. The doctor gives merely his services to his patients, places his skill at their disposal. Our Lord not only gives us His services, He lavishes on us His love as well.

That the Lord loves us is true, and it is incomprehensible. Why He is so devoted to us is not possible fully to explain, but one reason for it may be assigned. It is that we have cost Him so dear. It is for us as sinners that He has poured forth His Precious Blood. "Knowing," says St. Peter, "that you were not redeemed with corruptible things as gold or silver, but with the Precious Blood of Christ, as of a lamb unspotted and undefiled" [10]; and again we read in

[9] St. Matt. ix. 12.   [10] I Peter i. 18–19.

St. Paul : " For you are bought with a great price." [11]
The child is endeared to its mother by the very pain
it has cost her. Jesus values us because He has given
His all for us—every drop of His Heart's Blood. Is
it not an astonishing mystery that He appreciates us
so highly, and we, alas, so often so little appreciate
Him ? (" Appreciate " is to be taken in the etymological
sense, *i.e.*, to weigh, to set a price on.) Each of the
parables insinuates that what was lost was precious
in the eyes of the person who suffered the loss. To the
shepherd, the animal that he had seen grow up amidst
his flock had become dear. He had watched it as a
lamb, and he had cared for and pastured it with solicitude.
It had become an integral part of his possessions, and
he had looked to it to bring him an increase of wealth
in the shearing seasons. Anyone who is acquainted
with the life of the country knows how attached those
who tend domestic animals become to the objects of
their charge. Hence it was that the shepherd felt that
something had gone out of his life, when he observed
that one beast had strayed from the fold. In the second
parable the thrifty housekeeper had amassed, by diligent
toil, a modest fortune. Ten groats constituted her
hard-won savings—of considerable value to her as
representing the fruits of a life of industry. Her distress
was great then when she missed one groat from her
little hoard—it represented a tenth of her fortune.
Our Lord describes in sympathetic and tender detail
the anxious search she instituted for the missing coin
and her great satisfaction at its recovery. A kind of
climax is reached in the third parable. In this, it is no

[11] 1 Cor. vi. 20 ; and vii. 23.

longer an animal of the flock, or a relatively large portion of worldly possessions, but a dearly beloved son that, by his desertion, wrings with anguish the heart of a loving father. There is infinite pathos in the description of the sense of loss and abandonment felt by the bereaved parent. The deprivation of land and goods and household treasures counted as nothing with him when weighed in the balance against the loss of his youngest and his dearest son. All those details are purposely accumulated by Our Divine Lord, in order to bring home to us that consoling truth, which we find so difficult to accept—that we mean very much to Him, that we are very precious in His sight, and that He is ready to go to any lengths to keep us close to Himself.

And yet, the history of most souls is a history of blind and heedless straying from the company of our beloved Redeemer. Some, in a rash desire to taste to satiety the pleasures that an existence given to self-indulgence promises, barter, like the prodigal son, the peace and calm and purity of the Father's house for the excitement, the dissipation and the carnal satisfactions of what is called a fast life. Others, bereft of all Christian ideals, incapable of relishing spiritual things and all engrossed in the sordid details of the money market, are, like the lost groat, drawn down to earth and stained with its mire. But the story of the lost sheep is the story of many who aim at living a more perfect Christian life. In the early days of their conversion they were invited into the pastures of the Lord and they enjoyed the pleasures of His intimacy. They tasted and experienced that the Lord is sweet.[12] In the time of

[12] 1 Peter ii. 3.

the first beginnings, and again on those occasions when the force of Divine Grace stirred up fervour, they became illuminated, tasted the heavenly gift, were made partakers of the Holy Spirit and, moreover, tasted " the good word of God " [13] ; and then gradually, little by little, they strayed from the Saviour's enclosure, allured by seemingly fair pastures elsewhere. They begin well and for a time enjoy and desire only the intimacy of the Good Shepherd. His care, His attention and His caresses satisfy the longings of their nature. These are given as a bait to allure souls and to wean them away from other attractions. They were also a feeble image or a slight foretaste of the happiness that would be theirs later when the process of purification should be gone through. These first delights are never meant to endure; they belong too much to the world of sense to be adequate for spiritual beings. Touching as is the relation that is shown as existing between the shepherd and his flock, it is not adequate to express the bond that binds Jesus to the human soul.

There is little in common, in reality, between the shepherd and the beast he tends; the gulf that lies between the rational and the irrational can never be bridged. There may be devotedness and care on the part of the guardian of the flock to the animals committed to his charge. But there cannot be love, where there is not community of nature. But in the Lord's sheepfold this gulf is not impassable. He has given us that Divine Life which makes us partakers in His Own Divine Nature, and by putting us through a process of purifica-

[13] Heb. vi. 4–5.

tion, He can gradually cause us to cease living according
to that sensual animal nature that is at first so strong
within us, and to replace it by one that is more spiritual
and more akin to His own.[14] That this process should
be gone through, it is necessary that the delights we
first experience in the Lord's friendship be withdrawn
from us. Although good in themselves, they tend to
nourish and keep alive that life of fallen nature which
must yield place to the supernatural. We miss and
pine for the gratifications that have been withdrawn.
What happens then, is that in our eager desire for
satisfaction we seek it elsewhere than in the Lord's
pastures. We allow ourselves to be absorbed by our
work, to seek after success, to select that form of occupation which appeals to us, to give a loose rein to our
natural tendencies, to renounce, in a word, the process
of purification through which every soul that aspires
to be spiritual must pass. We drift imperceptibly.
At first, we just graze outside the gates of the sheep
pen ; a fairer tuft at a little distance excites our appetite ;
the sun glints pleasantly on a stretch of sward further
afield, and we are attracted thither. We do not intend
to wander too far from the fold, we have the desire to
keep always in the neighbourhood ; but we stray
farther and farther each day, until finally, we lose contact
altogether with the Lord and realise with anguish that
we are lost. A sense of utter loneliness and abandonment
descends on us, piercing our souls with anguish.

This is a picture of the tragedies that are taking place
daily in the spiritual life. A moment comes for every
soul when a decisive sacrifice is asked of it. It may

[14] Cf. Romans viii. 8, 9 ; and 1 Cor. xv. 46.

be a mere nothing, but it involves a deliberate choice. The soul's spiritual destiny (not necessarily its salvation) hangs in the balance, and it does not realise that it is so. Friendship with Jesus demands a certain renouncement and the soul pauses, hesitates and then—refuses. It reasons that it can be saved without foregoing this thing—it is not a sin to cleave to it. Conscience pleads that though it is not a sin to cling to the object desired, the delicate demands of friendship with the Lord call for its surrender. The soul replies that—what it is pressed by grace to forego cannot be of such consequence and to cleave to it is not positively forbidden by God's law. The decision is taken against the Lord. Instantly the ideal of life is lowered. It is no longer the love of Jesus which is its inspiring principle, but a selfish determination to secure salvation at the least cost to nature and to self. The gradual decline continues. Faults multiply. Satisfaction after satisfaction is pursued. Every gratification that is not incompatible with God's positive will is sought. There is less and less effort made to struggle against deliberate venial sins. The externals of a life of piety remain. There is nothing outstanding in the way of guilt—but the habitual disposition of the soul is one of estrangement from God. Examinations of conscience do not disclose anything very seriously wrong—and yet, one feels that everything is wrong. And then comes over the soul a sense of isolation, of loneliness, of dereliction, and of powerlessness to move hand or foot to escape from the miserable impasse to which it has come. Its efforts at release, like those of the poor ensnared sheep, only serve to entangle it more securely in the thorns and briers.

The soul lives under a haunting fear and is continually pricked by the thorns of remorse.

In its state of utter helplessness it can do nothing but cry piteously to the Master it has abandoned. Its cries do not fall on deaf ears. The Good Shepherd is not far off and His approach is guided by the piteous bleating of the poor lost thing. And then there is the last delicate touch to this exquisite sketch. The sheep is not led or driven home. The Lord assumes for Himself the toil of the return as He has of the search : " And when He hath found it, doth He not lay it upon His shoulders rejoicing," [15] forgetting in this joy all that this long pursuit has cost Him ? No matter how selfish and perverse we are, the Lord will never relinquish His pursuit of us, as long as life lasts. He is ever hopeful of our return—always expectant that sooner or later our souls will yield to the solicitations of grace. He is unwearied in His efforts. There is a depth of meaning in the words, " doth He not go after that which was lost until He finds it ".[16] The Latin text corresponding has " vadit " for the English " go after ". It signifies a long, toilsome journey in which much fatigue is undergone, difficult spaces traversed and many dangerous obstacles overcome. Our Lord wishes us to understand that nothing can oppose an insurmountable barrier to His love, except one thing alone—which He has given us Himself, and which He will not do violence to, even by His grace—that is, our free will. He looks anxiously for the first stirrings of that will, its first feeble attempts

[15] St. Luke xv. 5.
[16] St. Luke xv. 4.

to respond to grace, and as He notices them, His Heart throbs with pleasure. He craves our love, but He is too delicate to force it. It has no value for Him unless freely given.

No matter how sinful we have been, at the first word of repentance, at the first indication that our heart has turned away from created things and turned again towards Him, He forgets all that has passed and like the father in the parable, He clasps the soul to His embrace, clothes it with the robe of sanctifying grace, bestows on it those actual helps that it needs to walk once more in the ways of holiness, and gives it the ring which is the pledge of affection and union. And even when the soul cannot utter words of sorrow like the prodigal, and when it cannot send up its cries for help like the lost sheep, the Lord does not abandon it. Like the thrifty woman of the story, He seeks out the erring creature amidst the refuse and the sweepings of the earth to which it has been dragged down, and in which it lies helpless and motionless. It cannot stir or cry out ; it lies helpless, powerless even to desire to escape from its wretched surroundings. Even so, the soul at times has not the spirit to wish to break the chains which bind it and keep it enslaved to the earth. But even then, it is not left to its fate. A Mind is anxious about it—thinks of it day and night. A Heart is longing for it and sending its rays of grace hither and thither in the dark corners where it lurks and hides. Eyes rendered keen and sharp by love and anxiety peer for it through the gloom and light up with joy when, in the darkness, the soul sends back a faint glimmer of light, as the rays of grace fall on it. " Or what woman having ten groats, if she lose one groat doth she not light a candle, and sweep the house and seek diligently until she find it ? "

There is only one thing that can frustrate Our Lord's search and cause it to end in failure—it is the resistance of our free will. " Turn to the Lord, for He is gracious and merciful, patient and rich in mercy, and ready to repent of the evil." If, doubting of His care for us, of His love, of the infinite riches of His mercy—if, setting limits to His powers of forbearance with our repeated lapses into forgetfulness of divine things, we give way to hopelessness and do not look to Him for succour, then His efforts on our behalf are in vain. His effective action on our souls is dependent on our will. " He," says St. Augustine, " Who made us without ourselves, cannot save us without ourselves." But once He discerns in us the first, faint stirrings of good will, He stoops immediately to our souls to lift them out of the morass in which they are plunged. We cannot form an idea of the great lengths He will go in the endeavour to win a soul to sanctification. He wrestled with death, and suspended His own most rigorous laws to console the heart of a sorrowing father and to wipe away the tears from the eyes of a bereaved mother—in each case to assuage a merely human suffering.[17] But when it is a question of the soul and the soul's life—of its nearness to or remoteness from God, there are no limits to be placed to the extent of His anxious tenderness. Hence His almost extravagant joy when the sinful or the lukewarm, surrendering to the assaults of His grace, turn to Him appealingly

[17] The Daughter of Jairus and the Son of the Widow of Naim.

and cast themselves at His feet with a sincere confession of their helplessness and a humble appeal for help. The acknowledgment of our powerlessness leaves Him, as it were, powerless to resist our entreaties. It was His own feelings He was revealing when He said: " I say to you, that even so there shall be joy in Heaven upon one sinner that doth penance, more than upon ninety-nine just who need not penance." [18] This we cannot understand unless we realise that though it is the God in Jesus that gives grace, it is the Human Heart in Him that seeks us out, and makes Itself the channel through which this grace is transmitted to us. It is a Human Heart that pities our misery, a Human Heart that passionately desires to save us, and an eminently Human Heart that beats with pleasure when we accept Its advances. And when His enemies take exception to Our Lord's lavishing attention and affection on sin-stained creatures, He could reply to them in words used in another connection : " Is thy eye evil because I am good ? " [19] Jesus is good. In that lies the explanation of His attitude towards the weak, the erring and the helpless. Not all created goodness taken together could give even a feeble image of the goodness of the Heart of Jesus—for It is Itself a perfect reflection of the Uncreated Goodness of God.

[18] St. Luke xv. 7.
[19] St. Matt. xx. 15.

CHAPTER IV

THE TRIUMPH OF FAILURE

" Think diligently upon Him that endured such opposition from sinners against Himself."—HEB. xii. 3.

EVERY life which leaves the christian, who has lived it, a mediocrity from a spiritual point of view is a life that to a large extent has belied its promise. Since each earthly existence, its successes and its defeats, its doings and its sufferings, has been planned by God's Providence, for, in a certain sense, one sole purpose, namely, that of working out the perfection of the individual soul, one is obliged to confess, as life draws to its meridian, that in the case of too many christians, God's designs are to a large extent frustrated.

We are, most of us, disappointments to Almighty God—and *this need not be so.* For, many, perhaps all, who have received the call to a fervent christian life, enter on the pursuit of perfection animated by the greatest good will. They begin their spiritual course with the sincere and earnest desire of arriving at, or at least approximating to the ideal of sanctity that is set before them by the approved spiritual guides. And yet there are amongst the multitudes, that through divine grace succeed in saving their souls, very few that arrive at the sanctity destined for them by God. One can be certain that *this is not a necessary consequence of*

*human conditions, nor is it an issue of human endeavour
in which we must acquiesce, and accept as inevitable.*
Otherwise, Our Lord, Who knows as no one else does
the possibilities of human souls, their capacities, their
powers and their limitations, when sustained by the
grace He never refuses for the asking, would not have
so insistently called upon all, indiscriminately, to model
their lives upon His, to walk in His footsteps, to take
on their own shoulders the cross He carried, and to
face life, its trials, its problems, its dark issues, in the
same spirit as He faced His. Our Lord could not ask
of men what is impossible, unreasonable, or even
exceptionally difficult. It is repugnant to His Wisdom,
to His Goodness, and to the depths of His insight into
the human heart, that He should do so. The knowledge
that Our Lord has of each one must give Him a right to
expect of us, in the way of sanctity, *far more than the
vast majority ever give.* It is not that He is mistaken,
but that we fail to bring our own powers to fruition.

When a certain time of life has been reached the
tragedy of this universal failure is felt with an extraordinary poignancy. The sense of it chills the heart,
damps the spirit and takes away the colourfulness from
life. Positive sin does not cause such an acute sense
of despondency, of helplessness and hopelessness.
Whether this sin exists in ourselves or in others, somehow it is something tangible towards which we can
direct our spiritual energies, something with regard
to which we can make strong appeals for grace, something, which in its defeat, gives us the sense of doing
something to please God, and of drawing nearer to
Him. But there is no such exhilaration derived from

the contemplation of a spiritual mediocrity which one feels powerless to grapple with, or to amend. When middle age is reached, when the enthusiasms of youth are cooled, when its hopes have been more or less imperfectly realised, and when above all, the tasks to which life's energies have been consecrated, and the execution of which was regarded as life's purpose, no longer claim the forces of mind and body, one perchance awakens to the fact that nothing has been done, no progress has been made—that in spite of all the activity put forth little seems to have been achieved and life appears to have been, from a spiritual point of view, a mere marking time. Around us we find our own contemporaries, those who started with us in pursuit of the same lofty ideals, awakening to the same bitter consciousness. For them, and for us, the years, apparently, have brought little or nothing. A certain amount of work may have been got through—a few bricks, as it were, may have been heaped together, a few lessons taught, a few acres ploughed, a few material comforts conferred, a few kindnesses, perhaps, bestowed —*but nothing lasting, abiding, eternal, left to perpetuate our existence.* Looking into ourselves we find that the years have brought us little but the decline of the powers and energies on which we relied so much.

We look at others, and we see in them no growth in wisdom, in power, in sanctity, in depth of soul. They reveal the same faults, they display the same tendencies, they manifest the same superficiality or worldliness of judgment and sentiments that they did in the very beginning of their career. If any change has come, it lies only in that, with the passage of the years, all the unamiable traits of character have deepened, the fair promises of youth have been blighted, the generous impulses of early days, and the virtues that began to appear under the first influence of grace have shrivelled up. This is accompanied by the uneasy feeling that the spectacle we present to others is much the same. We should have left the point where we started and gone forward with the years, and there is forced on us the consciousness that it has not been so. We see that the years have passed over us, as water flows over the stones in the river bed, and left us where we were. We *find that having put forward much activity, we have done nothing, because nothing has been done to us.* Life has not transformed us; day has succeeded day, and the years have followed the years; *we have been alive all the time, but we have not lived.* And now we know that the greater part of our earthly existence has slipped from us, and we look to the end that is approaching swiftly, surely, and we do not know how to make the time that remains yield results different from those of the time that has gone by. If we spend our remaining days as we have those which have passed, we know they will be just as meaningless, as barren of result. Besides this there is no longer the possibility of using the years that are to come even as well as the years that have gone—poor as that " well " is now seen to be. For the energies of mind and body have slackened with the passage of time. We do not know how to put meaning and purpose into the years that remain to us, because our experience has shown *that we were mistaken in what we thought to be the meaning and purpose of life in the past.*

There is nothing so sad as the sight of those who once pressed forward to the goal of perfection frittering away the days and the hours in silly preoccupation about things that are futile, transient and unsubstantial. It is a ghastly thing to be playing with trifles on the verge of the grave and finally, to stumble into it, in the very midst of idle concerns, and without speculation on the existence that opens out beyond the tomb. There is an awful bitterness in the realisation that comes to the moderately good, that their whole life has been a great wastage of opportunity. And yet such lives, when regarded in their external aspect, seem to have been spent in useful activity and the faithful accomplishment of duty. To ourselves, as we go through the years, we may appear to be discharging with fidelity the tasks that Providence has laid upon us. But when we look back over the years, we know deep down in our hearts *that nothing of good has been done for others, for we find that no good has been wrought in ourselves.* We realise that something has been missing —and we cannot tell what it is. We know that as a result of our activity we should be other than we are —and we do not know how that change could have been brought about. Death might have been faced with courage in our younger years, for then we felt that we had it in us to rise to the grandeur of the crisis, and fling ourselves with faith and confidence and charity at the feet of our God. No matter how little we had done, we had at least not gone far enough in life to make evident to Him and ourselves that our trial on earth issued in nothing but the betrayal of His trust, and the disappointment of His hopes. In other words, if we had died then we had not lived to the consciousness of having largely failed in realising God's plan.

As the vitality of youth diminishes, as the wheels of life slow down, as the powerlessness to put forth incessant activity comes on, one is forced to reflect on the ultimate meaning of things. In these periods of reflection it becomes clear that life has not been lived as the christian in his baptismal promises implicitly engages himself to live it—namely, as a novitiate for eternity. It comes home to one that apart from the formally religious acts, the doings of life were, for the most part, accomplished out of all relation to an eternity of whose activities they should have been a reflection. Little attempt has been made to secure that the doings of time should be in principle the doings of eternity. In a dim way it is realised that time ought to have been, as it were, eternity in embryo—and that it has not been this, whatever else of seeming good there may have been in it. And now we feel, in an agonising way, the sands of time slipping away beneath our feet and the span of life approaching its inevitable term, and we feel powerless to be at death what we know a christian, one who has been trusted by God, ought to be.

This is an analysis of what many a soul experiences in the later years of its earthly existence. It is an experience that novices in the spiritual life should never have to undergo. These failures do not come because of the inherent weakness in human nature, nor are they due to the sins into which men have fallen. God's grace can remedy the worst effects of human weakness—and positive crimes have not prevented many souls from attaining to the heights of sanctity. *We fail, not because* our wills are irresolute, or our passions strong—but because we allow our intelligence to be obscured as to the meaning and purpose of life. It is not our will that is at fault so much as our intelligence. Very many souls embark on the spiritual enterprise, and knowing that Christ is the Way, have been willing to tread that path, but at some point or other have made a false turning and directed their steps towards a mistaken objective.

To understand our own life, it is necessary for us to make a study of the life of Christ. And here again we must be careful not to allow ourselves to be arrested at the external imaginative features, and *fancy we are following in Christ's footsteps, when we are given to some practices of virtue, which bear some resemblance exteriorly to those which He exhibited.* It is true that to imitate Christ is to act as He acted, but it is equally true that this is impossible unless we are trained to think as He thought—particularly as regards the purpose of our life, in its relation to our own soul and to God. Hence it is that St. Paul, in his exhortations to the christians, urges on them the necessity of having the *same mind as Christ in regard to the ultimate issues of life.* " Let this mind be in you, which was also in Christ Jesus " [1] he tells them. To make our efforts after sanctity issue in some real transformation of our souls, *we should make a study of the interior dispositions of our Lord, and grasp the broad principle according to which He worked out His life's task.* Of course some progress can be made by striving, through careful study of His virtues, and through the use of the means by which these virtues are developed in us, to make our

[1] Philipp. ii. 5.

lives conformable to His. But no attention to details can give such valuable results as *the apprehending and accepting His whole mental attitude towards life itself.* If we *seize His mental outlook, and if we try, steadily, to adjust our own to it, we shall,* in spite of, perhaps, constant lapses in practice and of repeated falls, *still secure ourselves against that agonising sense of failure* which torments so many at the close of life.

Our Lord's life was a bitter cross that He had to carry day by day : in carrying it He was called on to display constantly the most heroic fortitude. To understand this, we must know what *He considered his life's work, and how the execution of this work affected the interior dispositions of His soul.* In all things He felt as we should feel were we placed in similar circumstances. Life's experiences called forth in Him reactions similar to those they provoke in us, if we exclude what savours of sin and imperfection.[2] The consideration of the varying moods produced in our own interior by the daily conflict enables us to understand in some measure what the Saviour went through in heart and soul. Even when we bear ourselves wrongly towards things, we have, as a rule, a fairly clear perception of the way in which we ought to act if we were not swayed by passion and if we were shaping our conduct according to the rules of human perfection. This perception aids us to enter into the interior dispositions of the Saviour. There is one striking feature of His mode of handling existence which shows in every page of the

---

[2] Cf. Heb. iv. 15. "For we have not a high priest who cannot have compassion on our infirmities : but one tempted in all things like as we are without sin."

Gospel and in which He presents a marked contrast
to us. We are prone to assign, practically if not theoretically, but a relative importance to the task we are actually
engaged on. That to which we shall unreservedly give
our attention is generally something that is yet to be.
Even those who set perfection in their several acts
before them as an ideal are prone to defer careful
attention to perfect execution (according to the requirements of spirituality) to a future date and allow imperfection to insinuate itself into the task of the moment.

Now Our Lord's way of acting was not vitiated by
this habit of thinking the future always of more moment
than the present. He may be said, in a certain sense,
to have lived for the instant in which He was acting.
It is true, that, in a certain sense, He looked forward
in all His doings to the Passion, as the hour of His life.[3]
But that is to be understood only in this sense, that it
was ever before His mind that in the decree of Almighty
God it was only by the Passion that the redemption
was to be achieved. It is not to be understood as if
He attached importance only to that act in His life
and regarded all the others as ones that did not call
for all the attention of His soul in the doing of them.
His looking forwards to the Passion did not cause Him
as it were to slur the execution of all the tasks that
presented themselves before that decisive event came
on. Each thing that Christ had to do called into play
the full moral and spiritual perfection of His soul as
if it were the only thing He had to do. In this point of
view each several task had for Him an absolute value.
His attention was wholly given to the particular work

[3] Cf. St. John xii. 27.

that lay ready to His hand to accomplish. The doing
of the thing, as being something appointed Him by
His Eternal Father's Will, was all-important in His
eyes. He did that particular thing His Father enjoined
on Him to do, and He spoke those words that were
prompted to Him by the Holy Ghost and those only.
In the explanation vouchsafed by Him, from time to
time, of His life's activities, He returns on this point
with peculiar insistence. On the eve of His death,
giving a retrospective glance over the years that had
passed, He said : " As the Father hath given Me commandment, so I act." [4] Forceful and eloquent as His speech
must have been, it was evidently marked by a superhuman restraint. He was never carried away by the
interest of His subject, by the tide of His own eloquence
nor even by over-eagerness to win the souls of His
audience. He seemed intent on keeping to the exact
words of the message He understood it to be His mission
to deliver. "I have not spoken of Myself, but the
Father Who sent Me, He gave Me commandment
what I should speak." [5] His attention seems to be
wholly riveted to the accomplishment, in the *most
perfect disposition, of the task that lay ready to His hand
to do*. He seemed to be contented with doing rightly
what He had to do, and not to look beyond that to
the issue of His acts. That is to say, that it was not
the happy result that was to flow from His actions that
motived and inspired them, but the filial desire to do
as His Father bade Him act, and so please that Heavenly
Father. His first recorded utterance was, that He should

[4] St. John xiv. 35.
[5] St. John xii. 49.

be about His Father's business—His last was: "It is consummated." And the Evangelist allows us to penetrate into the train of thought that preceded these final words. He shows us Jesus, in full possession of His faculties, going over in spirit all the recorded will of His Heavenly Father, and assuring Himself that He had carried out that will to the last detail. "Afterwards Jesus, knowing that all things were now accomplished, that the Scripture might be fulfilled, said: I thirst." [6] Jesus' life, and His attitude towards that life, is framed in between and illuminated by these texts.

It is clear, then, that Our Lord saw, in His life, a series of events appointed for Him by Divine Providence. He saw that God's designs were wrought out rather by the perfection of His attitude towards these events than through His being concerned with what He actually achieved through His activity. He saw, as it were, that if life was to be re-fashioned by Him, this could be brought about by His reacting in a certain perfect way to events rather than by positively determining a train of events. It was by His perfect docility to circumstance that He revolutionised circumstance. He allowed events to determine His actions rather than aimed at determining events by His actions. All that He does and endures seems to be called forth from Him by the circumstances in which He found Himself. If He moulded events, it was rather by His lending Himself to circumstance than by positively imposing Himself on circumstance. If He were not what He was, it could be said of Him that He was shaped by events, rather than shaped them to His will. His life was rather,

[6] St. John xxx. 20.

a passion than an action, partook more of the nature of an enduring than a doing. It was a giving of Himself and not an imposing of Himself. Everything He had to do in His relations with men and with life made a tremendous demand on His human sensibility. For it was a difficult, toilsome and ungrateful work—physically and mentally. His apostolic labours meant fatigue of body and still greater fatigue of mind. He could be but little understood in the world in which He moved. He met with little understanding and sympathy even from those most intimate with Him—what must it have been with others ! There was a constant and wearing opposition to His thoughts and His acts. But he knew that in a mysterious manner God's purpose was fulfilled in His maintaining Himself in the purest disposition in His work, in spite of all that would tend to disturb the balance of His soul. Like all human agents He could not but seek the end of the work on hand. He could not teach but to persuade —reason but to convince—show love but to win affection and confidence in return. *But He did not find in this the motive or inspiration of His work.* It was as if He really were indifferent to results—as if, even though His activities could not possibly have their natural intrinsic consequence, He would not have accomplished them with any less intensity and force. Hence it took nothing from the value of His act, in his eyes, that it failed in its immediate purpose—that which of its own nature it tended to effect. He saw the highest good in the doing of a thing, as His Father wanted it to be done—apart altogether from consequences ; even if no successful issue were possible. *To do things*

*rightly—to act as God wanted Him to act, was the object
of His life. Though He flung Himself into His tasks
with all the mighty energy of His superb nature, He yet
stood strangely aloof from them.* He undertook each
task as if it were all-important, and yet He assigned
that supreme importance, not to what it was in itself,
but to the mere right execution of it.[7]

There is a peculiar evenness and balance in Our Lord's
life. He is not more wonderful in act than in repose
—in speech than in silence. In itself, especially
with Our Lord, Whose nature was so perfect, there
must needs be an immeasurable distance between the
intrinsic value of a word fallen from His lips, and the
same word withheld. Something of much value would
have been lost to the world—a treasure never brought
to light. Yet it is not so. Christ expressed Himself
fully in His life. All His greatness seems to be in the
perfection with which He endured each succeeding
circumstance—whether that demanded the putting
forth of or the cessation from activity. The bending
of Himself to things—His perfect pliability to things—
His power of maintaining His disposition perfect in
every conjuncture, seems to be the aim and purpose of
His life, rather than something positive to achieve.
He seems to have left achievement to us, taking endurance
(or passion) to be His. He knows full well that it is
thus the world is saved by Him, and that it is by following

---

[7] Cf. the following passage from Newman : " Christian zeal looks for
no essential improvements or permanent reformations, in the dispensation
of those precious gifts which are ever pure in their origin, ever corrupted in
man's use of them. It acts according to God's will, this time or that, as it
comes, boldly and promptly, yet letting each act stand by itself, as a sufficient
service to Him, not connecting them in one, or working them into a system,
further than He commands."—Newman : *P. and P. Sermons.*

His example in this that each individual soul is to be forged to perfection. In the establishment of the Kingdom of God He assumes to Himself the function of the Sower. He went through the world sowing in tears : others follow in His footsteps reaping in gladness.[8] His activities seemed to be regarded rather for what they effected in Himself than what they effected outside of Himself. His life, in a word, intensely active as it was, was rather a perfect subjugation to things rather than a radical conquest of things. In this lies the sublimity of our Lord's life, and its grandeur.

Richly endowed by nature and by grace with every quality that could assure success in His dealings with men and with human affairs—majestic presence, charm of manner, persuasiveness of speech, profound insight, limpidity of soul, infinite wealth of grace—His life, nevertheless, as men judge things, was a complete failure. " The pattern of all human perfection achieves His triumphs, His kingship in hearts by a pilgrimage of which failure and continued agonising effort under failure, is the beginning, the middle and the end." Those He healed were ungrateful ; those He taught remained ignorant ; and the hearts which He laboured to soften and convert remained obdurate. Neither His eloquence nor His kindness won for Him the loyalty of His people. The few whom He did win to His side abandoned Him in the crisis of His life. We miss the real pathos of Our Lord's life when we read the Gospel, because we have the vague half-formed idea

[8] St. John iv. 37, 38. "For in this is the saying true : that it is one man that soweth, and it is another that reapeth. I have sent you to reap that in which you did not labour : others have laboured and you have entered into their labours."

that in all He went through, He was buoyed up by the view He had of ultimate success. This would have taken from the absolute perfection of Our Lord's Fortitude. It did not take one whit from the sharpness and harshness of the trials of His life, that He foresaw that the salvation of men would be ultimately effected through that life. Just as the bliss of the Beatific Vision which He enjoyed did not detract in the least from the intensity of His sufferings, so the salvation of the world ultimately achieved did not minimise the pain of the actual positive failure of the moment in which He lived. As the knowledge of the Resurrection that was to follow Calvary could not blunt the sharp sword of grief that transfixed the heart of Mary, so the vision of a world ultimately to be transformed by His Sacrifice did not minister any natural support to our Lord's fortitude. Jesus' feelings were habitually determined by His experimental knowledge and He experienced daily scarcely anything but reverses and disappointment. Our Lord had constantly to drink to the dregs the cup of bitter and abject failure. He knew He would succeed in practically nothing, regard being had to the immediate object of His personal action. And yet He did not for all that put any less firmness, force and intensity into His acts. He laboured with as much assiduity and heart as if He hoped to succeed, though with His vision of the immediate future He knew He could not. And even if we abstract from the certitude of this fore-knowledge, He read His failure in the signs of the times as they revealed themselves to His penetrating gaze. As he stood before the multitudes, and set before them in gracious and eloquent, though simple and picturesque language, doctrines consoling as well as sublime, He could read the positive resistance to truth in the frozen glances of some, the dullness begotten of vice in the looks of others, and absolute incomprehension in the eyes of most. He knew that He possessed the Truth, and He knew, too, that He expressed it in the way best adapted to the human intelligence. He knew how these truths, if accepted, would, for His hearers, solve the riddle of existence, satisfy the restless yearnings of their souls, and banish all unhappiness, if not all pain from their lives. He knew what the acceptance of these thoughts of His mind, which He clothed in such persuasive language, would mean of happiness for his fellow-men, what loss would be involved for them in their rejection, and He used all the vast resources of His mind and soul to succeed—and He failed.

And yet His ill-success did not upset the calm serenity of His action ; opposition to His principles did not rouse Him to indignation, and powerlessness to persuade did not cause Him to desist from His efforts in despair, or renounce these efforts in petulance. He was not moved, either to over-eagerness in manner, or to excess of vehemence in words. Each day, unmoved from His earnestness, or His dignity, or His calm, by the previous day's failure, He resumed His work with the same force, the same courage, the same unimpaired energy of mind and will as before, exactly *as if the disappointments of the past were not to be expected in the future.* The heart-breaking wilfulness of men caused Him pain, but no indignation. He was not irritated by, though He wondered at their incredulity. Their persistence in error in the light of Truth so clearly, vividly and persuasively presented to them, stirred Him neither to bitterness, nor to anger, caused Him neither to be piqued nor disheartened, though it weighed like lead on His heart.

Nothing that He had to contend with wrought in Him the least change in the perfection of the dispositions—the interior dispositions—with which He faced each new circumstances of His life. Ingratitude and forgetfulness on the part of those whom He healed and comforted produced no diminution of tenderness and mercy in regard of those, who, anew, presented themselves for His ministrations. With what looked like unconquerable optimism He worked miracle after miracle to prove His Divine mission, and when the powerful reasoning with which He adduced these miracles to support His claims broke in vain on the adamantine prejudices of His countrymen, *He recommenced once more with unabated courage.* And it was not as if His passing triumphs kept alive His hopefulness. He was well aware that these triumphs were superficial and ephemeral, and more apparent than real. The Evangelist relates somewhat sadly: " Now many believed in His name, seeing His signs which He did, but Jesus did not trust Himself to them, for that He knew all men." [9] Even in the narrow circle of His intimate friends, Our Lord failed to excite a sympathetic understanding with Himself. That He should have been misunderstood by His enemies would have been tolerable, if only He had not been so misunderstood by His friends.

<hr>

[9] St. John ii. 24.

Amongst the keen sufferings that marked each stage of the Saviour's life, the loneliness of soul which was His habitual experience must rank as one of the most bitter. The minds even of those who formed a devoted band around Him were poles apart from His : men, of the earth, earthly, could not enter into His views. One who reads the Gospel with some little attention cannot but remark that Jesus is, at times, deeply affected by this loneliness and that His Heart aches to be understood. There are pathetic manifestations of a desire on His part to nestle, as it were, in the understanding of His followers, when He is smarting under the prevailing incomprehension. Now and again He throws out a thought and looks with a kind of wistful expectancy to see if His apostles follow the trend of His mind. Almost invariably He is disappointed and chilled by their want of mental receptivity. He said to them one day : " Beware of the leaven of the Pharisees." The dull literalness of the interpretation that they gave to His words must have wounded His own quick perceptions and delicate sensibility like a blow. They understood Him to chide them for having forgotten to provide bread for the journey over the lake. One who has clothed a profound thought in figurative language and finds his hearers taking his words in their literal sense, and, therefore, completely misunderstanding him, experiences a feeling of hopelessness in face of such stupidity. Our Lord could not feel hopeless but must have felt baffled by the obtuseness of understanding shown by the Apostles. There is sharp pain and almost a sob of the heart in His words pronounced on this occasion as on, probably, many another : " Do you not yet understand ? " [10]   And sadly He turns to pursue His lonely way through life. He was the teacher *par excellence*, and He had unrivalled opportunities for forming the intelligences of His disciples to apprehend reality as He apprehended it Himself. When He tests the success of His teaching, He meets with scarcely anything but disappointment—one would be tempted to say disillusionment. During His lifetime His endeavours to form the mind of His apostles to His own met with but a scanty reward. There is something deeply pathetic in the loneliness of Our Saviour. *He met with much opposition, a little loyalty but scarcely any understanding.* Apart from His Blessed Mother, St. Joseph, and to a certain extent, Mary Magdalen and St. John, nobody understood Him, and nobody was capable of sharing the thoughts or aspirations of His mind. The desertion of His followers at the great crowning event of His life (which He looked upon as His great triumph, and they regarded as absolute failure), and the fact that on the day of the Ascension they still had their minds filled with anticipations of the satisfaction of their worldly ambitions in the new earthly kingdom to be established by the Risen Lord, proves that up to the day of Pentecost His teaching had met with nothing but dull incomprehension on their part.

Yet, in spite of all this, Our Lord did not repine nor did He think His work idle or useless. Unsuccessful it might be in producing the immediate effect He aimed at ; it had, nevertheless, the fullness that belongs to a task done in the most perfect dispositions and in fulfil-

---

[10] St. Matt. xv. 16 ; xvi. 9.

ment of God's will. Each day He took up life's burden in the same calm way, and went straight on through its round of tasks, content with doing each rightly, and never allowing His interior dispositions to be altered or disturbed by the immediate fruitlessness of His labours. It is true that He felt keenly His repeated failures, but He never was tempted by the pain He suffered in His sensitive nature to renounce His enterprise, and to take refuge in inactivity, or in the execution of things which should meet with a better measure of success. *He did each day the right thing, because it was the right thing to do, and He never shirked life's responsibility through fear of the humiliation of failure.* Though His actions failed in their effects on others, He knew that they did not fail in the eyes of God. He was well aware that by His manner of dealing with life God's purposes were mysteriously fulfilled, and the glorification of His Humanity secured : " Ought not Christ to have suffered these things and *so* to enter into His Glory ? " [11] That He was not speaking merely of the last week of His life is proved by His adducing in support of His words all the details of His career, as foretold in the Sacred Scriptures. Strong in His resolve to tread the path marked out for Him by Divine Providence, *He did not use His life, His energies or His talents to minister to His own satisfaction, or to gratify His egoism.* Though His sensitive nature was wounded through and through by hostility, unkindness, ingratitude, and want of understanding, He allowed nothing that He suffered from others to modify in the least the perfection of His attitude towards them. At all

[11] St. Luke xxiv. 26.

times He bore Himself with the same calm, unchanging, unbroken, undeviating fortitude. *He wasted no valuable time in repining or in self-pity;* He wasted no energy in rebellion against circumstances; *and He did not passively acquiesce to the inevitable with a gesture of indifference or despair.* The whole attention of His great Soul was concentrated on the doing of the task that the occasion offered, never once reflecting on what it should mean to Himself in the eyes of men, satisfied that He, in the doing of it, should be approved of in the sight of God.[12]

The followers of Christ, all who wish to walk in His footsteps and press towards the goal of sanctity, must cultivate the same attitude towards life that He had. They must be prepared to face the tasks that Providence assigns to them regardless of success or failure. If they shrink from the work God imposes on them, and take up only that in which they foresee success, in order to enjoy the satisfaction of feeling themselves efficient, and being thought so by others, they miss the whole meaning and purpose of life, and

---

[12] The following words from Newman find an application here. " I call resignation a more blessed frame of mind than sanguine hope of present success, because it is the truer and the more consistent with our fallen state of being and the more improving to our hearts, and because it is that for which the most eminent servants of God have been conspicuous. *To expect great effects from our exertions for religious objects is natural, indeed, and innocent, but it arises from inexperience of the kind of work we have to do— to change the heart and will of men.* It is a far nobler frame of mind to labour, not with hope of seeing the fruit of our labour, but for conscience's sake, as a matter of duty, and again, in faith, trusting good will be done, though we see it not. Look through the Bible and you will find God's servants, even though they begin with success, end with disappointment—not that God's purpose or His instruments fail, but the time for reaping what we have sown is hereafter, not here ; that here *there is no great visible fruit in any one man's lifetime.*"—(Newman) *P. and P. Sermons,* Vol. VIII., p. 129. In all this the Saviour willed to be a pattern for His followers.

arrive at old age with empty hands. Our existence on earth, with its enterprises and its toils, is given us by God to be used for the transforming of our souls, and not for the flattering of our inordinate desires of excellence. The true disciple of the Divine Master does not desist from his efforts to create in himself and around himself the reign of justice, because he is thwarted and cannot have his own way in dealing with circumstances. He realises that things are all wrong not when *he* cannot have his way with things, but when God cannot have His way with *him*. We are not meant to mould persons and events to our will, but rather to be moulded by life's contacts to the form preordained for us by God. If we achieve great things outside of ourselves, and the achieving of them does not effect any change or development in ourselves, we have done nothing. *Life's purpose is to purify us, not gratify us.* It is not a theatre where we are called upon to play a brilliant part with a view to gaining the applause of the audience, nor an arena in which to achieve a success to be greeted by the acclamations of the onlookers, *but a process, by which our souls are to be made strong with the strength of supernatural life.* Existence is not a toy that we can use or abuse at our caprice, but a mill of God, in which everything in our souls that proves an obstacle to the supernatural life is ground into dust. Rightly used, as its events are planned by God's Providence, it should work to crush to atoms all the perverse egoism of our fallen nature. This cannot be accomplished without pain and bitterness to nature— a pain and bitterness from which it necessarily shrinks. Existence for the Christian is not a cosy fireside by

which to sit and warm himself, but a furnace in which
he is to be plunged in order to be refined as silver or
annealed as steel.   Ill-success or failure to realise the
ideal in things is the characteristic mode which this
process takes, especially in the case of those who are
called by God to influence the lives of others.   The
soul instinctively desires and promises itself that kind
of life-work which it feels to be within the compass
of its powers, in order that its excellence, its efficiency
and its force may be acknowledged by others.   It seeks
for itself the contentment that arises from the sense of
being equal to the calls that are made on its resources,
at being able to acquit itself with credit of all that it
is called upon to execute.   But sooner or later events
bring it about that each person is confronted with a
situation, which if accepted holds forth no prospect
but the humiliation of failure and ill-success.   The trial
will present itself in different ways following the temperament of each individual.   But this is common to all—
that a generous response to the will of God manifested
through the ordinary working of Providence, or communicated by the voice of authority, will be foreseen
to be likely to end in nothing but discredit.   Nature
shrinks from and struggles desperately against this
humiliation ; it will seek every avenue of escape from
it, and do anything to throw up a shelter for its self-love.
In a word, when life in its complexity threatens to become
too complex to allow of the soul's continuing undisturbed
in the enjoyment of its own sense of excellence and
superiority, it is tempted to refuse, through fear of
failure and humiliation, to make the sacrifice God asks
of it.   *Very few have the fortitude to face that life or*

that action in life, in which they foresee that nothing awaits them but to be regarded by their fellows as failures. Very few can accept to be finally judged by those with whom they live as men whose career has belied the promise held forth by their talents. They shrink from being spoken of, as Our Lord was spoken of by the two disciples after His death, as " one whom they had hoped should have redeemed Israel "—but who had tragically disappointed their hopes. " And one of them whose name was Cleophas, answering, said to him : Art thou a stranger in Jerusalem, and hast not known the things that have been done there in these days ? . . . concerning Jesus of Nazareth, who was a prophet, mighty in work and word before God and all the people : and how our chief priests and princes delivered him to be condemned to death and crucified him : but *we hoped* that it was he that should have redeemed Israel." [13]

It is only if we take up our cross daily, that is, face each task that each day brings with courage, intent only on doing it *rightly and well, striving to succeed, but not making success the condition of our efforts, doing it because it is God's bidding, and not because it holds out a prospect of ministering to our egoism—it is only on this condition that our life will produce its transforming effect on us, and make us like to Jesus Christ, Who " having joy set before him endured the cross, despising the shame ".*[14] We must regard ourselves as so many grains of corn that the Lord takes and grinds in the mill of life, in order that our souls may be made into a pure white flour which is capable, under the trans-

[13] St. Luke xxiv. 18–21.
[14] Heb. xii. 2.

forming influence of Grace, of being changed into another Christ. God designs the circumstances of life with a view to making them His instrument in effecting this change. *If our will rebels against the dispositions of Providence, and betrays us into anger, irritation, repining, or cowardice in face of these dispositions, then we frustrate God's action.* Oftentimes we do this; we give way under opposition; we relinquish the struggle; we refuse to endure being thwarted, on the vain plea that this " opposition of sinners to us " makes us incapable of fulfilling God's work. This is to deceive ourselves grossly. In the order of God's decrees of predestination, it is ourselves, our spiritual transformation, that is primarily intended, not what work He may effect through us. God is more interested in ourselves than in our work. The work serves as a means to us rather than we as a means to the work. God knows full well that if we become what He intends we should, through the action of life's events on us, then our passage through this world will become in a mysterious way a most potent influence in the diffusion of God's Kingdom on earth, and in the extension of the reign of Jesus Christ in the souls of men.

CHAPTER V

THE SUPREME GIFT OF JESUS

THE BLESSED EUCHARIST

" He that eateth Me, the same shall live by Me."—St. John vi. 58.

" Before the festival day of the pasch ; Jesus knowing that His hour was come, that He should pass out of this world to His Father ; having loved His own who were in the world, He loved them unto the end." [1] These are the solemn and weighty words, words instinct with deep feeling and emotion, with which St. John opens the narration of the Passion of the Divine Master and of the events that immediately preceded it in time. There is an intimate and vital bond, linking together in a close and necessary unity the Passion of Our Lord and the institution of the Blessed Eucharist. The connection was very clear to the mind of the Apostle at the time, towards the end of his life, when he penned the words just quoted. Jesus knowing that His death was at hand prepared to give Himself to His friends in order to communicate to them that life, of which He enjoyed the plenitude, before He surrendered Himself into the hands of His enemies, to undergo His death. Paradoxical as it might seem, His death at the hands of His enemies was that which prepared the way for and

---

[1] St. John xiii. 1.

made possible the communicating of Himself to His
friends, though the events on Calvary were subsequent
to those that took place in the Supper Room. Death
lies between us and God. We have to pass through its
portals to enjoy the vision face to face. Hence it was
that St. Paul longed to be dissolved in order to be with
Christ.[2] By divine decree it was ordained that Christ
should, as it were, pass by death to reach us and to enter
into supernatural union with our souls. The Passion
was divinely appointed to be the means to that contact.
Jesus had said : " This is eternal life : that they may
know Thee, the only true God, and Jesus Christ Whom
Thou hast sent." [3] The Passion is the source of that
knowledge. It reveals God to man as nothing else does.
Without it man would have remained eternally a stranger
to God, without any life-giving knowledge of Him.
By another strange paradox, our life springs from the
death of the Son of God and has its beginning in that
death. Jesus, the Author and Source of all life, had to
die in order to impart life to us. The surrender to death
of the Son of God was the supreme proof of the devoted
love of the Three Divine Persons for man, the apparently
insignificant work of their hands. Whilst the Angels,
that sinned, were left to their doom, God the Son gave
Himself to death in His human nature on behalf of men
that were sinners. God the Father surrendered to the
Passion on their behalf the Beloved Son, Who was the
object of all His complacency. God the Holy Ghost
in His turn took upon Himself the communication to
men of that life that had been purchased for them at

[2] Philipp. i. 23.
[3] St. John xvii. 3.

such a great price—at the price of the Blood of God. "Knowing that you were not redeemed," writes St. Peter, " with corruptible things as gold or silver . . . but with the precious blood of Christ, as of a lamb unspotted and undefiled." [4]

In His last discourse to His disciples, Jesus let fall a statement which the instinct of mankind has seized upon as being the most perfect and most appropriate rendering in words of the devotedness of the highest friendship : " Greater love than this," He said, "no man hath, that a man lay down his life for his friends." [5] There is a profound pathos attaching to these words on His lips at the moment of their utterance, for He knew as He said them that in a few hours they were to find their most complete exemplification in His own case. He would die and His death would be the *supreme proof* of His love for His hearers and for all mankind. Before it should come to pass, however, He has still to give them the *supreme expression* of that love He bore towards all. His charity for the sons of Adam called upon the Omnipotence of God to express that love, not in words merely, but in a *fact* which should be worthy of the exercise of that Omnipotence. The response of the Omnipotence was the Blessed Eucharist. These two facts, the laying down of His life for His friends as testimony of His love for them, and His giving Himself to them in the Blessed Eucharist as the most perfect mode of expressing that love, are as it were but two aspects of one complex reality. The Passion is directed towards the Blessed Eucharist:

[4] 1 Peter i. 19.
[5] St. John xv. 13.

it leads up to it, in the order of causality, and makes it possible. It is only because the Body of Jesus has been broken and mangled on the Cross that it can become our spiritual food ; it is only in virtue of the fact that His veins have been exhausted to the last drop of His Precious Blood, that It in turn can become our spiritual drink. Hence Our Lord said : " Take ye and eat, this is My Body which is given for you " ; " This is the chalice, the new testament in my blood, shed for you." [6] It is to be noted that the body that the apostles are given to eat is a body described as " given " or " offered in sacrifice ", or, as another reading has it, " broken ", that is, in sacrificial death : likewise the blood that is handed them to drink is blood that is poured out in death. It is a body and blood that has been sacrificed that the apostles are bidden to consume. At the Last Supper, and at every Communion table since, the disciples of Christ are gathering the fruits of Calvary : their banquet is on the Body and Blood of their God, offered in sacrifice on their behalf. In that supper chamber for the first time are verified the words He had spoken to them long before : " Except you eat the flesh of the Son of Man, and drink His blood, you shall not have life in you." [7] As the apostles took the divine gift from the hands of the Master they scarcely realised that their access to this life-giving food was through the death of Him Who was giving them Himself to eat at that moment. With what tenderness their hearts must have melted later on when they looked back and understood the full significance of

---

[6] St. Luke xxii. 19 ; 1 Cor. xi. 24.
[7] St. John vi. 23.

the phrase so mysterious and incomprehensible to them
at the time. There is in all these texts a strange conjunction of life and death. The death of " Life " Itself
was the life of those who were dead. Christ's death is
the life of His followers, because it is only by His Cross
and Passion that their spiritual death is taken away and
that they are restored to supernatural life. To administer
spiritual food to the spiritually dead would be vain
and useless ; one must be living with the life of grace
before it becomes possible to partake of and to profit
by the heavenly nourishment. It is in Christ's death
we are baptised to the newness of that life which is
nourished by the Eucharist. The Blessed Sacrament is
indissolubly linked with the death of Jesus. Hence the
joy with which the Church celebrates the memory of
this act, which has left her in unending possession of her
Spouse on earth, is deeply tinged with sadness. The
chants of Holy Thursday are sombre and full of pathos.
The Church cannot but exult in the stupendous act of
love, but its exultation does not allow it to lose sight
of what that act of love cost to Jesus. The same thought
haunts St. Paul, and for him another element of sorrow
is added to the memory of the great event. There is
deep feeling in the words with which he prefaces the
history of the Last Supper : " The Lord Jesus the
same night in which He was betrayed . . .".[8] The night
on which was given His greatest gift to men was the
night also which witnessed His betrayal to death by
His own. The same note of intense though restrained
emotion is discernible in the narrative of the Evangelists

[8] 1 Cor. xi. 23.

as they unfold the wonderful events that took place in the Supper Room on Jesus' last night on earth.

The Pasch had been consumed according to the ancient rite; the table was cleared of the remains of the Feast of the Passover; and thus disappeared for ever the figures of the Old Law. Some loaves of unleavened bread were then placed before the Saviour. All eyes were fixed on Him. A sense of impending disaster weighed on the minds of the apostles. They were filled with a vague foreboding, for their Master's words had become more and more explicit and signified all too clearly that a crisis that augured ill for their earthly aspirations was swiftly approaching. At the same time they were filled with an eager expectancy. Everything pointed to the accomplishment of the promise He had made months before that He would give them His flesh to eat. Their hopes had been stirred to the highest pitch by the assurance that had been vouchsafed them that this divine nourishment would impart to them everlasting life—a life wholly different from that ministered by that other heavenly food which their fathers had eaten in the desert, and which nourished only for a time. Their souls were awakening to a sense of the supernatural; the extraordinary and elaborate preparations that they had made under the directions of the Divine Master, had betokened that the Pasch that was about to take place was one which was to be carried out on a plane infinitely higher than that in which the old rite was to be accomplished in the other houses in Jerusalem that night.

As for Our Lord Himself, His eyes glowed with a strange light. In spite of a certain air of sadness, His features bore an expression such as wear those who are at last within sight of a longed-for goal. The moment had come when He was about to perform that great act which was to perpetuate His presence amongst men until the end of time. "With desire," He said to them, "I have desired to eat this pasch with you, before I suffer." [9] As other men pursue pleasures and satisfactions, Our Lord sought for sacrifice, not, indeed, for its own sake, but as the price of the salvation of men. "I have a baptism," He had said previously, "wherewith I am to be baptised: and how am I straitened until it be accomplished." [10] That hour of His baptism in blood was eagerly sought for, because His death was the condition of His being able to give His Great Gift to men—the Gift of Himself. That moment to which He had looked forward with such ardent longing had now come, and He raised His eyes, shining with happiness, the happiness that shows in the eyes of those who make their sacrifice complete and unreserved. He raised His Divine eyes towards Heaven and thanked His Father for the power that was given Him to do what He was about to do. He took the unleavened loaf in His hands, blessed it, pronounced those words which, instinct with the Omnipotence of God, effect what they signify: "This is My Body." And at once the most wondrous thing which creation had ever witnessed took place in the awe-stricken silence of that upper room. Only the words of God broke that tingling silence, and as their sounds died away one substance had become another. The substance of bread had

---

[9] St. Luke xxii. 15.
[10] St. Luke xii. 50.

become another substance—and that, the substance of the Body of Jesus Christ—united with His Soul and Divinity ! Similarly He took the chalice. Again the silence was broken : " This is My Blood of the New Testament "—and where there had been wine, there was now the Blood that was to flow so profusely from His veins a few hours later.

In this dual consecration, in which there is a seeming separation of Body and Blood, was set forth in vivid symbol the death to which He had submitted Himself and which was to take place on the following morning. The institution of the Blessed Eucharist is intimately bound up with the sacrificial death of Christ. The mysterious change having taken place, Our Lord said : " Take ye and eat," and the wondering apostles, one after the other, communicated at the Hands of their Divine Master. It was their first communion. They received with a childlike faith and simplicity, realising that now there was accomplished in a mysterious manner that saying of His which had so scandalised His incredulous followers some months previously. The apostles had not trusted to their own human views according to which it would be impossible for Jesus to give them His Flesh to eat ; they had trusted in His Omnipotence and now that trust was rewarded ; though as yet they understood but little, for the Holy Ghost had not yet descended upon them. Jesus had wrought a wonder surpassing the wonders of creation. It is a greater exercise of Omnipotence to make one thing be another than to draw something out of nothing. And yet in the bringing forth of the universe out of nothingness no creature could fulfil an instrumental or ministerial *rôle.* Creation is an act in which no creature can play a part. Whereas in the still greater wonder of Transsubstantiation God wrought through the instrumentality of human words pronounced by human lips. But the inventions of Divine Love are inexhaustible. Again Our Lord raised His Hands over the apostles, His lips moved in prayer, and He then said : " Do this in commemoration of Me " ; and the great mystery that He had just accomplished is perpetuated, is made possible to the end of time. The Holy Ghost descended invisibly upon the followers of Jesus, and they received the stupendous power to do as He Himself had done, and to transmit to others that same power. The Catholic Priesthood was inaugurated. By this act Our Lord made possible for all time His stay on earth amongst men, whom He loved to such an excess. And yet He knew with His Divine foresight what that meant for Him. Though He saw that His Body and Blood would be treated with reverence by a multitude of devout souls, yet He realised full well that in many and many an instance in the course of ages He would be placing Himself at the mercy of unworthy and sinful priests who would treat Him with irreverence and sacrilege. He saw in vision all the profanations, outrages and, what was more painful still to His loving heart, the cold indifference that He was to endure from tepid and careless Christians. Nothing of that was unknown to Him, but He willed to submit Himself to all in the interests of those who were to profit by His Divine Condescension and meet His advances of love. Love, especially Divine Love, does not halt to calculate and weigh advantage and disadvantage in the balance.

He risked all to serve some, whom He aimed at drawing into close intimacy with Himself.

This brings us to the final object of this supreme effect of the Charity of Christ, that surpasseth, St. Paul tells us, all we can imagine or conceive it to be.[11] This love of His for us compels Him to enter into ever closer union with human souls, to be ever nearer to them than He was when He moved on earth and conversed with those about Him. During His mortal life He spoke and His words sank into His hearers' hearts and stirred them strangely. But in Holy Communion His contact with us is much more intimate and vital than it then was with those who thronged His footsteps along the Galilean highways. It is also much more active and life-giving.[12] Our Lord's love is of a Divine Purity, and it is therefore divinely disinterested. It is solely in view of our interest that He desires to enter into this close relation with us in which His soul is united with ours. It is we, not He, that derive advantage from this spiritual union. On two distinct occasions God His Father in Heaven proclaimed that the Child of Mary was His beloved Son in Whom He was well pleased.[13] The significance of this testimony lies in this : there is no being in whom God can find His pleasure, and to whom therefore He can extend His love, unless it be Jesus Christ or one who bears a resemblance to Him. No other form of human life can please God except His, or one that takes its pattern from His. Hence

---

[11] Eph. iii. 19.
[12] " The love of God is not idle. When it is present it effects great things," as St. Gregory says in his homily on Pentecost. Hence, by this Sacrament, at least, as far as regards its own virtue, not only are habitual grace and the virtues conferred, but acts of charity are also provoked.
[13] St. Matt. iii. 17 ; xvii. 5.

St. Peter says : " Be it known to you all, and to all the people of Israel, that by the name of Our Lord Jesus Christ of Nazareth, whom you crucified . . . this man standeth here whole : Neither is there salvation in any other. For there is no other name under heaven given to men, whereby we must be saved." [14] Unless we are pleasing to God we cannot be saved, we cannot realise the purpose of our divine adoption. We cannot please God unless we resemble Jesus Christ, and the Blessed Sacrament is instituted for the very object of perfecting in us this likeness.[15] Bodily food is transformed into the flesh of him that receives it ; this heavenly food, the food of our souls, which is the Body and Blood of Jesus Christ, has the directly opposite effect : it changes him who receives it into Itself. It must not be forgotten that the presence in us which follows the reception of Holy Communion is a living active presence. Our Lord is more present with us than is a person with whom we are speaking. As He influenced whilst on earth those who allowed themselves to fall under the charm of His Personality, so He exercises a profound effect on the soul of the communicant, if that soul wishes to submit to His action. We cannot be in the society of one who is good without being incited to goodness ; we cannot be with Our Lord—and we are as close to Him as our desires extend—without receiving the effects of His virtue and without being stirred to become as He was, without being drawn, in a mystical sense to become one with Him, to become " *Christified* ".

---

[14] Acts iv. 10.
[15] " Hence, no salvation without Communion *in re vel in voto* though in a different way from Baptism."—*S. Th.*, III., P. Q. 73, C. d.

He lived through human life in all its stages and conditions. In this He accumulated a vast store of merits and graces for His Mystical members. As Head of the Mystical Body He can communicate to each cell of the body the graces appropriate, and the activities proper to its state. No matter what be the age, function or condition in life of any of His members, He can communicate to that member a holiness which works in it a resemblance to Jesus Himself. Priests, religious, school children, all receive the same spiritual food. To the priest it imparts the grace to comport himself as Our Lord Himself did in His work of teaching and sanctifying men. At the Holy Table the religious sister draws from the fountain of all grace the Christlike prudence, wisdom and patience that she needs to train and instruct in truth the youth committed to her care. Children, in their turn, learn from contact with Our Lord that candour, docility and supernatural obedience that distinguished Him during the period of His boyhood. In short, each receives from Holy Communion that form of sanctity that his life requires in order to have that life formed on the pattern of the corresponding stage in the life of Jesus. As with the manna in the desert, each finds in it the savour that he relishes, desires and needs.

In a word, the Holy Communion has as its distinct effect to form in us the mind and heart of Christ. The motive force of His Life was Divine Charity, that is, love of God, zeal for His Glory and an ardent desire to translate that Love into the activity of His daily life. The Blessed Sacrament is called the Sacrament of Love. It was the extreme expression of the love of

Jesus for us. It was the uttermost point to which love could go, even having omnipotence at its service. Its virtue is to *provoke on our part* a corresponding charity. St. Thomas tells us that It does not merely give us the habit of charity, It gives us charity in act— It excites to the act of charity. Every action on the part of Jesus as boy, as youth, as man was inspired, animated and informed by love of God. Holy Communion has its direct, special and connatural effect to enable us to perform the acts of the state of life in which we are, in a similar disposition of charity.

But if the Holy Eucharist produces such wonderful things in our souls, why is it that so frequently those who communicate show so few signs of becoming better ? This is a common objection. Men are always prone to judge by what appears. The Saviour Himself commented on this tendency on more than one occasion.[16] The subtle effects of transformation that take place in the depths of a christian's soul are visible only to God. That the changes effected by the Holy Communion are imperceptible does not mean that they are not real. The operation of the Blessed Sacrament may be likened to the invisible, slow and mysterious working of the seedling in the earth, of which the Lord speaks on another occasion.[17] What a great revolution by slow and imperceptible stages has been worked in the manners and morals of the young since the worthy Pontiff Pius X. promulgated his decree on frequent Communion ! How few there are that do not show themselves in better dispositions during the moments that follow

---

[16] St. John vii. 24 ; viii. 15.
[17] St. Mark iv. 26–30.

closely on the reception of the Blessed Eucharist than they do at other times of the day ! But in spite of the hiddenness of the working of the Holy Eucharist in souls, " there are moments when we get transient glimpses within us of what the habitual nearness of the Blessed Sacrament has done for us. We perceive that it has not only done something to each virtue and grace God may have given us, but it has changed us, it has done a work in our nature ; we perceive that it has impregnated us with feelings and instincts which are not of this world and that it has called up or created new faculties to which we cannot give a name or divine their functions ".[18] We think the effect of each communion is small because we do not understand what immense opposition to His transforming charity Our Lord finds in the soul of each one of us. The less opposition to Him, the greater the effect—hence the efficacy of the Holy Eucharist, normally speaking, is proportioned to the perfection of the dispositions we bring to Its reception. The more perfect our dispositions, the greater the benefit we shall ordinarily derive from our communions.

What are these dispositions ? The first is Faith. We should approach the Holy Table with a firm belief that under these appearances of bread and quite close to us is the same Jesus Christ Who was born of Mary, lived on earth, and died on the Cross to expiate our sins. We should stir up our minds and hearts to a vivid realisation that when we receive Jesus Christ we are receiving God the Son, the Second Person of the Blessed Trinity, Who comes to us hypostatically united with the Sacred Humanity and prepared to use it as an instru-

[18] Faber : *At the Foot of the Cross*, p. 168.

ment of His Divine Power to effect a wonderful change in us. And we should ardently desire that the same God and Saviour would by His presence penetrate into our souls, sanctify them, expel from them everything impure, and fashion them to the resemblance of His Own. Since this is the Sacrament of Charity we should excite ourselves to a great love of Him Who gives Himself to us. And since this love would be false, did we not include in it those who are His members, those who partake with us of the same spiritual food, those who receive the same supernatural life as ourselves, we must bring to the Holy Table a spirit of forbearance and love, free from all deliberate feelings of jealousy, envy, or dislike of our fellow christians. And finally, since there are only two loves which can dispute the possession of our hearts—the love of God and the love of ourselves—and as it is this latter that alone is an obstacle to the Creator's taking complete possession of our souls, let us give up all self-love. If our communions are to produce a deep, transforming effect on our souls, we must aim at desiring God as our only Good, and not the satisfaction of our own desires. We should yearn to be made, through the Bread of Life, more and more like to God and more and more removed from the form of our evil self. The final disposition, and perhaps the most practically important, is that we should long to have developed in us through an intimate contact with the Saviour in the Holy Communion a docility of mind and heart like to His. Life presents great difficulties to all. Some Christians, when faced with them, approach the Lord to expostulate with Him about them. Others, more enlightened, come to Him

for light, encouragement and strength to bear up against
their difficulties after the example of the Saviour. These
latter necessarily derive more benefit from their Communions than the former. It is much better to use our
contact with the Lord for the purpose of drawing
spiritual development out of our trials than of seeking
to evade them. We take our natural food in order
to be able to live and work, not to evade life's burdens.
We should nourish ourselves supernaturally with a
view to acquiring strength to bear the Cross—that is,
the life-work that is ours, as elevated to the supernatural
order. If we should bring these dispositions to the
Holy Table what a great transformation would take
place in our lives ! And what peace and happiness should
possess our souls ! And not only our souls but our
bodies should also benefit. At the contact of the garment
of Jesus virtue went forth from Him and healed diseases.
How much greater virtue must flow out to us from the
contact of the Sacred Species ! The Holy Liturgy
speaks of the Blessed Sacrament as " a sacred banquet
in which is given us a pledge of future glory ".[19] St.
Thomas tells us [20] that It, indirectly, diminishes the
force of the concupiscence of the flesh and gives us
power to resist the corrupt desires of our senses and is a
most powerful aid to the cultivation of Holy Purity.
The Fathers love to call It the Seed of Virgins.[21] It
is a heavenly medicine that heals the wounds caused in
nature by the primeval sin, and restores to us, in some

---

[19] Antiphon : *O Sacrum Convivium.*
[20] " (The Eucharist) is not indeed directly ordained to diminishing the fire
of concupiscence. It, nevertheless, diminishes it, by way of consequence,
inasmuch as it increases Charity."—*S. Th.,* III., Q. 79, A. 6 ad 3.
[21] " Vinum germinans virgines." Zach. ix. 17.

measure, the preternatural gifts of immortality and integrity we lost in the Fall.

There is one important respect in which the Blessed Eucharist differs from the other sacraments. These latter are signs of a supernatural effect on the soul; the Blessed Eucharist is a sign of an abiding presence under the Sacred Species of the Source of all grace— of Jesus Christ Himself. Wherever is the white Host, there is present Our Lord in all His reality, with the same understanding, the same affection, the same divine power and the same profound sympathy with everything human as He had during those days on earth. It is the Sacrament of the Real Presence of Emmanuel, of God with us, of God made man, dwelling with men and rendering Himself easy of access to them. For He is there in our tabernacles, not solely as the object of our worship, but as the intensely human Friend that looks forward to our visits and awaits our communications. He is always ready to receive us, with an infinite sympathy and tenderness; we can pour all our confidence into His Sacred Heart and entrust all our anxieties to Him. He will listen to everything and will impart to us all the strength and grace we need. He is not at all indifferent to our human cares and anxieties and will give a patient hearing to them. He will always administer comfort and occasionally help where that does not militate against the supernatural good that He aims at for us. For, above all our bodily needs, the welfare of our souls is His chief concern. That He is ever unwaveringly ready to promote.

Of course all these communications take place in a way superior to the operation of our senses and our reason. It is only by Faith that we see and hear. But the going to visit Our Lord is just as real and just as effective, or rather more real and effective than it would be were we living with Him when He passed His days at Nazareth. We think that were we alive then we should never have wearied of returning to the Holy House to converse with Him and His Mother and Joseph. Perhaps ! If we had a very strong and deep faith—yes. But if we had only the faith that we actually possess, our visits would have had that measure of frequency and spontaneity that they now have—that, and no more. To be attracted and drawn to the side of Jesus in a way that affects our spiritualisation is to be drawn by the divinity that is in Him. Other attractions will not transform us. That divinity is just as " visible " now as it was then, when He stood by His carpenter's bench. If we " sense " it now, we would have " sensed " it then. If we are not attracted now we could not have been attracted then. It is always " the same Jesus Christ, yesterday and to-day, and the same for ever ".[22] All vital contact with the Reality that He is is on a supernatural level. To sense and reason He is always hidden. If we were to enter Joseph's workshop and look on Jesus we should see with our eyes only a man like ourselves, simple and upright, and a painstaking workman. Nothing more ; that is what all his fellow-townsmen saw. Their gaze could not penetrate deeper because of the imperfection of the dispositions of their hearts. I suspect that the visits of the ordinary good people of the village, drawn to the Holy House by supernatural interests, were just as occasional as those

[22] Heb. xiii. 8.

of ordinary good people in the present day to the Blessed Sacrament. No more than that.

One who thinks that were he at Nazareth he would desire to go very often to see Our Lord, and who does not desire to go often to the church where the same Lord dwells, is labouring under a delusion. He is simply wanting in faith. It is the same loving Saviour, with the same kind heart, the same benignity, the same majesty, the same holiness and the same zeal for our good, who once abode in Nazareth and now abides in the tabernacle. He will receive us now as He would then. He would not have shown Himself cold to us simply because we had proved ourselves weak, imperfect, wayward or even forgetful. All He looks for is that we should desire to approach Him and turn away from what displeases Him. He is of unwearied kindness, and has only one ambition—if I might use the word— and that is, to do us good and make us supernatural. That is the sole reason of His Presence in our tabernacles. That was the story of His life—" transiit benefaciendo ". He passes distributing kindness. But we must never forget that with all the infinite tenderness of His Human Heart, He is yet God. He is as truly the Son of the Eternal Father as He is the Son of Mary : He is great as well as humble, holy as well as simple, just as well as merciful. The consideration of the human must not lead us to forget the divine attributes in Him. We must always approach with a profound sense of reverence as well as with an unbounded confidence. If this be our ordinary attitude, we can, with joyous expectation, look forward, when our life draws to its close, to meet as our Judge Him with Whom we have dealt during our life as with a friend.

CHAPTER VI

THE PASSION OF JESUS

" He humbled Himself becoming obedient unto death ; even to the death of the Cross."—PHILIPP. ii. 8.

THE whole life on earth of God made man is profoundly mysterious : it is as full of mysteries as it is of days. In spite of assiduous meditation on that life and the light shed on it by the virtue of faith, one always has a sense of being baffled by its mysteriousness and of being but just able to penetrate slightly beneath the surface of what the Evangelists present for contemplation to the christian soul. It is as if one were unable to penetrate beyond the vestibule of a vast edifice which is known to contain many beautiful apartments filled with all kinds of the rarest and most exquisite treasures. The few glimpses that sometimes, in the course of absorbed prayer, are vouchsafed to the soul, of the inner sanctuary of the life of Christ, stir up an eager desire to know more and see further. One becomes, as it were, impatient of the limitations of one's own faith and longs for the piercing intensity and far-seeing power it has in the case of the saints. One would be glad to grasp Christ's life as they grasped it, to have it mean as much to oneself as it meant to them. The meditative christian who is but at the beginnings of his spiritual course cannot but feel a pang at realising that to the penetrating gaze of the intimate friends of God are revealed depths in the mysteries of the life of Christ which are completely hidden from him. The pain is all the more bitter because of understanding, that the difficulty of vision arises, not because God deliberately, as it were, veils off these things from the common gaze, but because one's own power of seeing is feeble through the imperfection of one's faith. It is not to the God-Man's unwillingness to be seen and understood, but to the imperfect christian's spiritual short-sightedness, that the inability to see little more than the surface of the mysteries of Christ is to be attributed. But if at any time one envies the saints their penetrating vision it is when one approaches the contemplation of the Passion of the Son of God. For there the mystery which envelops all the other incidents of the life of Jesus deepens to such an extent that it is almost impossible not to be seized with a sense of utter powerlessness in face of it. " What," exclaims the great Pope, St. Leo, " amongst all the works of God that tax even to fatigue the efforts of human contemplation, so attracts *and yet overmasters* the mental gaze of man, as the Passion of the Saviour ? " [1] The other scenes and incidents in the life of Christ offer a hold to the imagination. It is not difficult to find for them, at least in their outward historical aspect, some faint parallel in what comes within the range of average human experience. This parallelism is clearer for those who, leading an interior life, draw from what they go through within and without themselves an understanding not only of the exterior

---

[1] Eleventh Sermon of St. Leo the Great on the Passion of Jesus. Lectio of the 2nd Nocturn in the Matins of Palm Sunday.

incidents of the life of Jesus, but also of the supernatural
realities of which these incidents were the sensible
expression. But when one penetrates into the obscurity
of the great week of the final Pasch all familiar landmarks
disappear. All the ordinary laws of the sequence o
cause and effect seem to suffer violation—as in a sense
they really do. There is nothing in what precedes in
the life of the Saviour—if we except His own enigmatic
hints and warnings—that prepares the mind for the
terrible events to take place in the week of the triumphal
entry into Jerusalem. The hatred and jealousy of the
conventional priests and princes of the people, and their
disappointment as they saw the crumbling of their
Messianic dreams in the predication of Jesus, foreshadow
their resolve to bring about His death and thus destroy
His influence. The plot against Jesus' life was to be
expected; but expected as one that would take a long
time to mature before there would be a chance of success.
Nothing pointed to such a sudden and catastrophic
dénouement in the life of Jesus of Nazareth. Up to the
time of, and even in the very preparation for the Last
Supper, Jesus always showed Himself as being with the
utmost ease master of the situations in which He found
Himself. He met with much hatred and antagonism;
He yielded to it at times and retired before it. But
whenever He chose to face the conflict, the opposition
melted away before Him. As He sat at table at the Last
Supper with an unbroken series of triumphs behind
Him, nothing indicated to human prevision that before
the sun should set on the following afternoon He would
be a mangled corpse hanging on the Cross. And even
if one could possibly surmise, from the machinations

in the camp of the priests and princes of the people, that death would come to Him with a stride ere the festival should close, who could possibly dream of the accumulated horrors and cruelties that should be packed into those few short hours ? If death were to come, who could expect it to be attended with such fiendish brutality ? Who could believe that the world would ever present such a scene of tragic irony as that of the pagan procurator, the worshipper of idols, pleading with the chosen people for the life of their God—the One true God, Who had led them out of the bondage of Egypt and had showered favours on them ? What is it that caused the insane choice of this people, in which, for their king, they preferred Cæsar to God, rejected the beneficent Christ in favour of the murderer, Barabbas ? Pilate clearly was kindly disposed to the inoffensive Nazarene and meant the scourging to be but an excuse for setting Him free. He thought that a disgraceful chastisement would appease the fury of the Jews. He had no desire to inflict any undue suffering. How then came it about that the Roman soldiers, who had nothing whatsoever to stir them up against the Christ, should indulge in such an orgy of brutality in the scourging and crowning with thorns and in the gibes and mocking that accompanied these sufferings ? Why should the scourging have taken place at all, since it availed nothing towards the purpose intended by Pilate ? What could be the reason of this apparently meaningless and yet appalling suffering ? As has been said, no ordinary moral laws of cause and effect explain these things : one feels one's mind crushed and over-whelmed in their presence. What is contemplated attains

proportions that indefinitely transcend the human. In
the darkness in which the reason gropes, aided by the
faint light of faith, it is dimly perceived that one is in
close contact with the ultimate in things, that is, the
ineffable sanctity of the Divinity and the awful horror
of its opposite, Sin. It is felt that the titanic happenings
of the Passion are the supreme effort to present sensibly
to man these ultimate and stupendous realities. It is
felt that nothing but the interplay of these " ultimates "
could explain events on a scale of such magnitude. It is
not astonishing that the soul falters somewhat as it
brings itself to the contemplation of the tragic horrors
of Holy Thursday and Good Friday. Yet, as can be
learned from the revelations made to the saints from time
to time, Jesus earnestly desires that the faithful should,
not occasionally, but constantly, place themselves in
presence of this overpowering mystery to contemplate
it. His own words, as given to us in Scripture, reveal
that He recognises that the contemplation of His Passion
carries with it a divine efficacy to move souls. " And
I," He said, " if I be lifted up from the earth will draw
all things to Myself." [2] And St. Paul, always the faithful
echo of his Divine Master, when urging on the
faithful Philippians the perfect practice of the true
christian spirit, sets before them no more powerful
incitement to the exercise of all the christian virtues
than the consideration of the sufferings and death of the
Saviour. He bids them find in the study of the inner
spirit of Jesus in His Passion the force to carry his
exhortations into effect. " For," he says to them,
" let this mind be in you, which was also in Christ

[2] St. John xii. 32.

Jesus, Who being in the form of God, thought it not robbery to be equal with God ; but emptied Himself, taking the form of a servant, being made in the likeness of men, and in habit found as a man. *He humbled Himself, becoming obedient unto death : even to the death of the Cross.*" [3] It is evident that in the mind of Christ the baffling nature of this great mystery of faith does not dispense the Christian from a steady contemplation of it. Of course, if it is only the intellect alone that is brought to bear on the mystery, no fruitful results will be obtained. The heart and the will, as well as and even more than the intelligence, have their part to play in this work. The study of the Passion must be approached in a spirit of compunction, of humility and of earnest prayer to the Saviour Himself to vouchsafe to us the great grace of being able to penetrate to some little extent into the secret of His sufferings, so incomprehensible to human reason. The proper attitude of the soul during those solemn days which the Church consecrates to the contemplation of the last hours of the mortal life of Jesus is one of deep interior abasement, accompanied by a sustained inner silence and quiet attention of soul. If the Christian places himself deliberately in these dispositions, he will be bound to experience in the depths of his being the faint stirrings of emotions and thoughts which are not of this world and are certainly not the fruit of what the ascetical writers are accustomed to call human industry. It matters little that these emotions and thoughts defy exact formulation, and still more, outward expression. They are none the less real

[3] Philipp. ii. 5-8

for all that and produce secret and salutary effects upon
a man's supernatural life.

Yet numerous are the christians who experience a
sense of relief as the liturgical cycle of the Passiontide
and Holy Week passes away and they can turn to what
they would call less sombre spiritual thoughts. This
half-conscious shrinking from a sustained and attentive
contemplation of the passion of the Saviour is not
confined to the worldly and pleasure-loving amongst
the faithful. It is, perhaps, a more pronounced characteristic in the case of the less superficial and the more
thoughtful and reflective christians who have a consciousness that their lives are unworthy of their profession. These experience a certain discomfort—better
expressed by the French word *malaise*, when the fulfilment of their religious duties obliges them to give their
minds to a consideration of the final sufferings and death
of Jesus. In the realisation of their sinfulness they find
themselves a prey to that same sense of shame which a
criminal would suffer from were he forced to look on
at tortures inflicted on an innocent man for crimes of
which the onlooker was himself culpable. What man,
not bereft of all feeling, would not undergo an inner
conflict and agony of soul at the contemplation of
another enduring the extreme of torture for crimes that
were his, not the sufferer's ? Literature occasionally
endeavours to portray the agonising feelings of men
placed in this predicament. The description is, as a
rule, harrowing—the state of mind revealed, pitiful in
the extreme—and this, too, where it is a question of
men of criminal character and instincts. How much
more poignant must necessarily be the pain of soul

experienced by the average reflective christian who
knows full well that it is for the expiation of his sins
that the Innocent Saviour is being treated with such
barbarity ! Any soul not devoid of generosity should
feel all this with keen pain. But the discomfort and
indefinable uneasiness that such persons feel, who are
high-minded but whose lives are not what they ought
to be, is not wholly to be explained by the spectacle
presented by the innocent suffering in the place of the
guilty. There is another and more profound cause.
One who does not stop at the surface of things is obliged
to sense in an unmistakable though dim manner that
the Passion implies something more than a tragic ending
that befell Jesus through the rage of the Jews and the
vacillation of Pilate. It is felt in a vague manner that
Jesus saw in the cross not something that came to Him
through an unexpected conjuncture of circumstances,
but something that perfectly harmonised with and was
appropriate to the scheme of reality as He saw it. In a
word, one shrinks from the conviction that is forced
on one by the Passion, that the cross is not a mere
accident in the life of one man but the forcible, vivid
and compelling expression of a theory of life for all
men—as things now are. The thoughtful christian
realises that a mere sentimental sympathy for the sufferings of the Saviour—a sympathy that costs nothing
to the sympathiser—is a very hollow and futile thing.
He knows, though he may not formulate his knowledge
expressly, that a practical and effective sympathy with
the Passion means an embracing of that theory of life
of which the Passion is the expression. He knows that
it calls for a rejection of that philosophy of life after

which he lives, though it be not the one that he professes, namely, that " the world is made for the enjoyment of such a being as man and that man is put into it for the purpose of extracting as much enjoyment out of it as possible."

As has been pointed out, if events be regarded from the point of view of the sequence of natural causes and their effects, it is very disconcerting to human reason that a man who lived with the perfection with which Christ lived should die condemned as a criminal and amidst unheard-of tortures. It is all the more disconcerting if it be taken into account that His judge declared Him innocent and that those who clamoured for his execution had received nothing but benefits at His hands. Yet when the story of Christ is unfolded to the minds of christians as yet unspoiled by worldliness or sophistry, the ending of the tale is not looked upon as incredible, considering what preceded it. Normally speaking, the first movement of the mind should be one of disbelief or, at least, doubt. It is truly remarkable that such a movement, in ordinary christian souls, is never experienced. There is in the depths of the christian consciousness some secret instinct which, running counter to all the natural laws of cause and effect, recognises in the Passion a strange and mysterious harmony with the rest of the life of Jesus. This is not due merely to the psychological factor that one is born into the christian tradition, and that the human mind has become, in the course of ages, habituated to the sequence of events set forth in the Gospels. This is not so. The spontaneous and unquestioning acceptance of what in itself should prove bewildering to the reason is not a new thing. It has existed from the very beginning of christianity. It does not spring from such a superficial and material cause as heredity. Its source lies much deeper. It is found in the supernatural instincts generated in the soul by its incorporation with Christ through baptism. It is rooted in supernatural faith. The soul, enlightened by this divine virtue, recognises an indefinable fitness, an inevitableness, as it were, in Christ's dying on the cross. With this sense of the fitness of things in the case of Jesus is conjoined a secret conviction that if one's own life is to approximate to the christian ideal it will necessarily retrace in some measure the features of the divine tragedy. It is dimly felt that though the cross came to Christ only because He permitted it, the cross must come to the christian of a necessity and the christian is not free to evade it if his life is to reflect, in some degree, the perfection of the life of the Son of God on earth. Christ had perfection of soul without the cross : there is a secret instinct which tells the christian that he cannot have perfection of soul without the cross. St. Paul knew full well that he would not be preaching Christ unless it were Christ crucified he preached. It was perfectly clear to him that " in the cross and Him Who hung upon it, all things meet—that the cross is the centre and interpretation of all things ".[4] *It is this obscure but intimate realisation that the Passion is not a mere historical contingent fact, affecting one man, but a theory of life applicable to all men, that stirs uneasiness and a species of discomfort in the heart of the thoughtful and honest christian in face of the Passion and death of Christ.* In language of stark and compelling simplicity

---

[4] Newman : *P. and P. Sermons*, Vol. VI., p. 86.

the cross expresses the christian theory of life on earth, *namely, that life here below is not a satisfaction but a purification.* Every instinct of fallen human nature revolts against this theory. To it " the world seems made for the enjoyment of such a being as man, and man is put into it. He has the capacity of enjoyment, and the world supplies the means ".[5] This is the philosophy of the natural man ; it is utterly different from the philosophy of the cross. Few there are who embrace wholeheartedly, at least in practice, the austere teaching of the crucifix. And yet the christian consciousness, in spite of the specious pleadings and reasonings of fallen nature, assents to its truth. The honest christian whose life is at variance with the philosophy of Christ must sense in the crucifix a reproach. He feels his life stands condemned in its presence. He knows that the Passion is not an isolated and accidental occurrence standing in violent contrast with all the rest of the life of Christ, but rather completely of a piece with it. He is well aware that it is Christ's most forcible expression of His view of human existence, if human existence in the actual order of things is to issue in what God has planned that it should issue. In his christian consciousness the follower of Christ knows full well that suffering and conflict did not await the last days of the Saviour's mortal life in order to cross His path : it is borne in on him with a force that is irresistible, with a certitude that admits not even the shadow of a doubt, that hardship and pain dogged the Saviour's footsteps from the moment He set foot in His creation, and that, in very

---

[5] Newman : *P. and P. Sermons*, Vol. VI., p. 86.

truth, as the author of the *Imitation* says, " the whole life of Christ was a cross and a martyrdom ".[6]

In spite of the perfection with which Jesus bore Himself towards God and towards men, sacrifice and pain formed, so to speak, the warp and woof of His earthly career. Far from exempting Him from trials, His perfection was the occasion that called them forth. It was because He was so good that He was called on to endure so much. He has scarcely made His appearance on earth when His life is aimed at. He is only a few months old when He and His parents are forced to endure the rigours of a painful exile. At the age of twelve, He burned with the ardour to be about the business with which He was entrusted by His Heavenly Father and yet, at the word of His Mother, He forced Himself to curb that eagerness and hold it in check for eighteen long years.[7] In spite of His wisdom He

---

[6] *Imitation of Christ*, Book II., Chap. XII.

[7] This is an instance of the distinction between those two wills, or rather modes of willing, in Christ which the theologians name *voluntas ut natura* and *voluntas ut ratio*. Christ's human will, as being in Him the faculty which is attracted by what is good in itself, was naturally captivated by the appeal of God's business to be embarked on and the redemption of mankind to be undertaken. This was an eminently desirable object for Jesus and drew Him strongly. In this there was the connatural appeal of a true good to a will perfectly attuned to good. On the other hand there was the movement of the same will as following upon the consideration of reason, divinely enlightened, manifesting that the enterprise for God's glory was to be engaged in only at the time and in the circumstances foreordained by God. According to this will Jesus checked his ardour until He should have reached man's estate. By His *voluntas ut natura* He was all eagerness to be forthwith about His Father's business : by His *voluntas ut ratio* He would not take a step in this direction until the eighteen more years should have rolled by, for so God willed. By the former will He willed ardently that object which God willed : by the latter will He willed the attainment of it in the manner willed by God, just as in the Garden of Gethsemane, Jesus, with His *voluntas ut natura*, shrank from and pleaded against the death on the Cross and yet with His *voluntas ut ratio* embraced that same death, saying : " Not My will but Thine be done," Cf. Billot : *De Verbo Incarnato*, Thesis XXVIII., pp. 309–311, Ed. V.

submitted the direction of His conduct wholly to two of His own creatures during thirty years. He Who nourished the birds of the air procured for Himself the necessaries of life by hard and unremitting toil during the greater part of those long years of secluded life. He laid claim to none of the prerogatives that were His by right of His divine parentage. Eight days after His birth He underwent the painful rite of circumcision just as if He were a sinner like all the other children of Abraham. At the outset of His public career He submitted to baptism at the hands of John as one of the multitude that came confessing their sins. Though the true Son of God, He, as is evident from the Gospels, enjoyed no special prestige amongst his townsmen at Nazareth. He made no claims on His own behalf. He conformed to everything, submitted to everything, surrendered Himself to all the exigencies of life. No privilege of any kind was laid hold of by Him. He did not live to please Himself; He lived to satisfy God and God's creatures because of God.

The self-oblation, characteristic of the hidden life, continued when He made His appearance before men and mingled with their social doings. He worked miracles to smooth life's path for others, never to make His own an easier one. He would not cause the stones to be made bread when He was hungry, nor would He bid the angels bear Him onward when He was tired. Any miracles that might appear to be worked for His own interest, as for instance when He made Himself invisible to escape the hands of the Nazarenes, were wrought not to save Him from pain but to preserve Him for the painful mission He had been sent to accomplish.

His every action was dictated wholly by the interests of God, not by His own. Even His ardent love for mankind was subordinated to the divine interests. If He allowed Himself to be moved with compassion and to exercise His healing power on behalf of suffering mankind, He did so only as He saw that the divine will demanded it. And when He did perform miracles He disclaimed all credit for them. His works, He stated, were done under the direction and at the dictation of His heavenly Father. "The Father Who abideth in Me, He doth the works." [8] In a similar way He strove to direct to God the esteem that He won by the originality of His doctrine and the force with which it was presented. The satellites of the Pharisees were paralysed in their purpose when they allowed themselves to fall under the spell of His eloquence. To their masters they excused their failure to arrest Jesus, saying: "Never did man speak like this man." [9] The Saviour is careful to assign all the virtue of His teaching, both as to its content and to the mode of its presentation, to His heavenly Father: "For I have not spoken of Myself, but the Father Who sent Me, He gave Me commandment what I should say, and what I should speak. . . . The things therefore that I speak, even as the Father said unto Me, so do I speak." [10]

If sacrifice is to be taken to mean the surrender of what one has to further the interest of another, then the life of Jesus was one of complete and unbroken sacrifice, because both Himself and all that was His were utterly

[8] St. John xiv. 10.
[9] St. John vii. 46.
[10] St. John xii. 49–50.

and uniquely devoted to further the interests of God. He avowed this Himself, saying : " I do always the things that please Him " [11] ; and again : " My meat is to do the will of Him that sent me." [12]   The life of Jesus was one of perfect religion : it was literally a life " all for God ".

Now although in itself, because of the great love Jesus bore His heavenly Father, this surrender of Himself and the use of all His powers and faculties to promote the good of God was a surrender that was made joyously, yet it was not unattended by pain.   There is in fallen nature a deep-seated jealousy of God and resentment of His claims.   Men brook ill that what is of themselves should become consecrated to God.   Jesus was a man amongst men, was of man's race and blood and could not be wholly given to God without drawing on Himself correspondingly the hostility of men.   He was one of them and yet did not belong to them, but openly manifested that He belonged wholly to God.   His attitude of soul was profoundly resented by every instinct in fallen human nature and, at every step, He was made to feel the effects of that resentment.   The intensity of the antagonism was proportioned to the completeness of His sacrifice to God, and that sacrifice, as has been said, was absolute.   This was not the only element of bitterness that was mingled with the cup of Jesus.   In His devotedness to God He was called upon to forego many of the consolations that ordinarily, in the case of His disciples, attend on such devotedness.   The saints of God who, by penance and labour and hard

[11] St. John viii. 29.
[12] St. John iv. 34.

study, prepare themselves for the sacred ministry, are usually accorded the satisfaction of seeing great numbers swayed by their words and won over to a renouncement of sin and the practice of virtue. God's saints regularly draw crowds after them and have the happiness of seeing their labours crowned with success. There is a touching pathos discernible in the words which Jesus, half in soliloquy, half directly, murmured in the hearing of His apostles one day as the vision of the harvest of souls was suggested to Him by the sight of the fields ripening for the sickle : " for in this, is the saying true, that it is one man that soweth, and it is another that reapeth. *I have sent you to reap that in which you did not labour :* others have laboured, and you have entered into their labour ".[13] Never was there eloquence and persuasiveness like to His in any servant of God, and yet His mortal eyes beheld little fruit for His toil—nothing more than the little group that huddled together at the foot of the Cross. And yet His labours, though so fruitless as to their immediate results, were intensely absorbing. They demanded of Him a continued and rude renouncement : His apostolic toil made large inroads not only on the working hours of His day, but on the time sorely needed for refreshment and repose. St. Mark on more than one occasion refers to this *surménage* in the life of Jesus. " And they came to a house, and the multitude cometh together again, so that they could not so much as eat bread." [14]   And in another place, speaking of this same thing, he shows how much Jesus felt it : " And He said to them : ' Come apart

---

[13] St. John iv. 37–38.
[14] St. Mark iii. 20.

into a desert place and rest a while '. For there were
many coming and going, and they had not so much as
time to eat." [15] Twice the Evangelists reveal Him as
completely overwhelmed with fatigue, when He sat
down by the roadside on the verge of Jacob's well,[16]
and when in the midst of the storm He slumbered in
the boat.[17] The service of the ignorant and of the
suffering demanded of Jesus a still greater sacrifice than
was involved in the loss of food and rest. He loved
solitude and it was an intense satisfaction to Him to be
alone and to be able to fix all the powers of His soul in
undisturbed communing with His heavenly Father.
The pages of the Gospel render clear evidence that silence
and prayer had an immense attraction for the Saviour.
Few were the occasions in His public life in which He
could surrender Himself undisturbed to these attractions. He was surrounded by the crowds by day and
by His apostles during the watches of the night. Rarely
did He enjoy the pleasure of being alone. It must have
cost Him much to be obliged to tear Himself from the
quiet communings with His heavenly Father that
were occasionally possible for Him, to return to His
instruction of the multitude so dull of understanding
and so devoid of sympathy. In His thankless task there
was little compensation. His adherents gradually fell
away from Him. He failed to bind His followers to
Himself. It would have been some consolation had He
been able to retain, at least, the personal fidelity of His
intimates. This, too, was denied Him. Only a few

[15] St. Mark vi. 31.
[16] St. John iv. 6.
[17] St. Luke viii. 23.

women, with their natural loyalty to the person even
when the cause is lost, clung to Him to the end, to the
everlasting honour of their sex. What a dark picture of
utter isolation is suggested by the words: " *Then* the
disciples *all leaving Him*, fled ! " [18] There was not an
aspect of failure which Jesus was not called on to experience. He was a teacher of unsurpassed power of mind
and enjoyed unique opportunities for forming the minds
of His apostles, yet after three years of continuous
instruction, they remained dull and unenlightened.
" Philip saith to Him: ' Lord, shew us the Father,
and it is enough for us.' Jesus saith to him : ' *So long
a time have I been with you*, and you have not known
Me ? Philip, he that seeth Me, seeth the Father also.
How sayest thou, show us the Father ? ' " [19] In these
words one can detect the intonation of mingled surprise,
disappointment and gentle remonstrance such as
insinuates itself into the teacher's voice when his questions elicit the proof that the pupil has understood
nothing of what has been painstakingly explained to
him and what he might reasonably be expected to have
firmly grasped. The same evening on which these
words were spoken was destined to witness the closing
stage of a still more heartrending failure on the part of
the Saviour. Jesus had employed every means, short
of such as would do violence to the human power of
free choice, to save the soul of Judas from perdition.
He exhausted in this effort all the rich resources of His
nature. His attitude, His words, His gestures to this
unhappy soul on that fatal night, when one takes account
of the knowledge He had of the actual stage which

[18] St. Matt. xxvi. 56.   [19] St. John xiv. 8 and 9.

events had reached, fill the reader with astonishment. The forbearance, the restraint, the tenderness, the yearning, the varied modes of entreaty—all these reveal the heart of the Saviour as scarcely anything else in the Gospel does. He continues His assaults on the hardened soul long after all hope of success might have been reasonably abandoned. And although with inventive and tireless love Jesus multiplied and varied the terms of appeal to His erring apostle, His efforts resulted in abject failure. This failure must have been one of the most bitter drops mingled in the Saviour's cup of sorrow. The zealous priest who has laboured long and earnestly but in vain to save a soul from the clutches of Satan can have a dim perception of the anguish which wrung the Saviour's heart when the soul of Judas escaped Him.

From the point of view of suffering, renouncement, self-effacement and complete devotion of Himself and all His powers to the glory of God and to the good of men, there is a perfect continuity between the Passion and all that precedes it in the life of Jesus. The Passion but expresses more intensely and emphatically what all the years that went before it expressed. " Catholic theology does not isolate the life and the death of the Saviour as if they were two measures of different value. When it speaks of the death on the cross as the source of our salvation, this is but a compendious or abridged statement in which is understood that the supreme sacrifice of Jesus is linked up with the sacrifices of His whole life, constituting but the term and the apogee of these sacrifices." [20]

[20] Rivière: *Le Dogme de la Rédemption*, pp. 188–189.

Nevertheless there is a profound difference between the incidents that followed the arrest of the Saviour and all those that went before. It is true that the whole life of Jesus was one long tissue of sacrifice. But sacrifice in this connection must be understood in the purely moral and spiritual sense. Sacrifice in the formal, technical, liturgical and ritualistic sense is applicable only to the passion and death. The doings and sufferings of the Saviour from the evening of Thursday to the afternoon of Good Friday are invested with a character and a formality with which previously they were not clothed. This difference is strongly marked. It was not on the night of Thursday that Jesus became for the first time a prey to the hostility and the persecutions of His enemies. He had suffered from them already. They had before plotted against His life : His death had been more than once actually attempted : as far as they were concerned they set no limits to their violence. But Jesus on His side set a limit to that violence—a limit beyond which it would not pass. He allowed them to cause Him to suffer, but only up to a certain point. He remained master of the situation. His power controlled and limited theirs. When they tried to stone Him [21] He hid Himself : when His fellow-townsmen tried to cast Him from a precipice He made Himself invisible.[22] They could persecute but could not lay hands on Him.[23] In the Passion events undergo a profound change. In obedience to the injunction of His heavenly Father, Jesus renounced the exercise of His

[21] St. John viii. 59 and x. 39.
[22] St. Luke iv. 29.
[23] St. John vii. 30 and 44.

power to control the activity of men and of other creatures in His regard. He was to be passive in their hands. They could treat Him as they would until they should have compassed His destruction. This is the sense in which it was the hour of creatures. " When I was daily with you in the temple," Jesus said to His captors, " you did not stretch forth your hand against Me : *but this is your hour and the power of darkness.*" [24] The passivity of Jesus was voluntary. It was divinely decreed and He freely submitted Himself to that decree. If He was powerless in their hands it was because He so willed it. " He was offered because it was His own will, and He opened not his mouth. He shall be led as a sheep to the slaughter and shall be dumb as a lamb before his shearer, and He shall not open His mouth." [25] All the incidents of the Passion are but steps in the unfolding of a ritual that had been fixed by divine authority. It was carefully and accurately determined in all its parts and by the same authority as had fixed the ceremonial of the sacrifices of the Old Law. The Passion was the real liturgical sacrifice of which those of the Mosaic ordinance were but shadows. A sacrifice in the technical, ritualistic sense is a symbolic rite in which, by means of actions and words exercised about an object destined for man's use, a priest expresses the absolute dependence of himself, and the people on whose behalf he acts, on God as absolute sovereign and supreme arbiter of life and death. It is a public act accomplished in presence of the multitude of God's people by an official ordained for the purpose and speaking in their name.

[24] St. Luke xxii. 53.
[25] Isaias liii. 7.

The object about which the priest exercises the ceremonial rites is technically termed the victim. Sacrifice in its most perfect and complete expression involves the destruction of the victim. By that destruction is expressed most forcibly and vividly the utter surrender and submission of the people to God. Christ in His Humanity was the Victim in the Sacrifice of the Passion. In it, as far as human instruments could effect, His Humanity was utterly crushed and consumed. " He was wounded for our iniquities, He was bruised for our sins." [26] It was permitted to men and creatures to proceed to this destruction of Christ in the Passion, because Jesus in all these scenes fulfilled the *rôle* of victim for sins. As a victim it was necessary that He should be completely passive. He did not, however, play a uniquely passive *rôle* in this ceremonial arranged by God in His eternal designs of mercy. Jesus, as well as being victim, was also priest in this ritual act or series of acts. In the whole Passion Jesus as priest played an intensely active part. He was there as the High Priest of all mankind offering up in the face of the whole world His own victimised Humanity to God in a sacrifice of reconciliation. As priest He actually set before God His sufferings, His wounds and His death, as expressive token of His unreserved submission—and in that, the unreserved submission of mankind, hitherto rebellious, to the Will of God. The Passion and Death was on Christ's part a magnificent gesture expressive of the submission of man to God and of the recognition of God's absolute Sovereignty. In all the obediences of Christ's life prior to the Passion there was demanded

[26] Isaias liii. 5.

merely that conformity to God's Will which is required
if man's actions, freely determined by himself, are to
come up to the standard of Divine perfection. Obedience
to God in these cases consisted in acting with perfection
and in a spirit of filial love. The obedience of Christ
in the Passion involved His undergoing a veritable
immolation, which He was free to accept or to reject.
In obedience to God He underwent the Passion which
He was perfectly free not to undergo if He so wished.[27]
"Therefore," He said, "doth the Father love Me,
because I lay down My life, that I may take it up again.
*No man taketh it away from Me : but I lay it down of
Myself*, and I have power to lay it down ; and I have
power to take it up again. *This Commandment have I
received of My Father*."[28] The Passion was something
more than the crowning act of obedience in the life of
Christ. It stood apart and alone in the category of acts
of obedience. It was in an altogether exceptional manner
a conclusive and triumphant expression—a final, adequate
and complete expression, admitting of none more
perfect, of the utter obedience of the Sacred Head of
mankind to God. It was a complete reversal and
annihilation of the primeval act of disobedience. The
voluntary endurance of the terrible sufferings of the
Passion culminating in the awful dereliction of soul
which is rung from the lips of the dying Saviour the
mysterious and terrifying cry : "My God, My God,
why hast Thou forsaken Me ?"[29] was in some inscrutable
fashion a testification, such as nothing else in the life

[27] For the freedom of Christ in undergoing the Passion, see Mattiussi,
de Verbo Incarnato, p. 222.
[28] St. John x. 17–18.
[29] St. Matt. xxvii. 46.

of the Saviour was, of the unqualified allegiance of Jesus to His God. Nothing could express so perfectly and adequately as the cross the obedience of the creature to the Creator. Were it permitted us to see into the depths of the mystery of Jesus' freedom in undergoing the Passion and Death, we should see how this is so. It was clear before His own mind, when towards the close of the Last Supper He turned to His apostles, saying, in reference to the Passion about to commence : *" But that the world may know that I love the Father,* and as the Father hath given Me commandment, so do I : *' Arise, let us go hence.' "* [30] Hence it is that the Church with divine intuition repeats over and over with loving iteration during the days of Holy Week : " Christ became for us obedient—obedient even unto death— yea, even unto the death of the Cross." [31]

[30] St. John xiv. 31.
[31] In the Office of the last days of Holy Week.

PART III

THE HARVEST OF VICTORY

" If you be risen with Christ, seek the things that are above.
. . . Mind the things that are above, not the things that are upon
the earth."—Coloss. iii. 1, 2.

CHAPTER I

THE RESURRECTION

" Know ye not that all we, who are baptised in Christ Jesus, are baptised in His death ? For we are buried together with Him by Baptism into death : that as Christ is risen from the dead by the glory of the Father so we also may walk in newness of life."—Rom. vi. 3–4.

THE Resurrection is the central dogma of Catholicism —and it is not obvious why it should be so. The Acts of the Apostles show it to be the fact in the history of Christ that is the most energetically proposed to the belief of those to whom the Apostles preached. This insistence on the resurrection in the apostolic preaching strikes us with some surprise. It is true that its value from an apologetic point of view might be sufficient explanation of its importance in the eyes of the first preachers of the Gospel. In rising from the dead, Christ proved Himself God and therefore could claim the subjection of every human intelligence to all the religious and moral truths that He had propounded to men during the three years of His public life. His Resurrection stamped all that teaching with the approval of God. It was proved true with the truth of God. It established the validity of His claim to be truly God. This reason, though it is true as far as it goes, is not quite satisfying. And it is because we see no other explanation for this passionate and reiterated proclamation of Christ's life after having been crucified, that the instructions of the first heralds of Christianity, such as they have come down to us in the sacred writings, strike us as being singularly cold and ineffective. They stir us scarcely at all. To us, accustomed to a different line of approach to the life of Christ, the preaching of the pioneers of the Gospel message appears to miss or, at least, to stress very insufficiently what is the chief appeal in the life of the Saviour. We instinctively look for a more eloquent and enthusiastic predication of the truths that Jesus came to reveal to men, especially as the Apostles had, by the light from on high received at Pentecost, obtained a vast and deep comprehension of these truths. To their minds, enlightened by the " Spirit of Jesus," what they had dimly and imperfectly understood as it had been spoken to them by the Lord became clear and luminous. After the descent of the Holy Ghost they acquired a grasp of the whole of Christ's revelation in all its truths, in the details of these truths, and in the marvellous unity which bound all these dogmas into one vast, harmonious and dazzling system. Many a Catholic student feels a thrill which is akin to ecstasy, when, having mastered in detail the different treatises of Catholic theology, the perfect unity and the inexhaustible riches of the whole system are presented for the first time to his intelligence, in one comprehensive synthetic view. Such light is but darkness compared to the effulgence that irradiated the minds of the Apostles. Is it possible that under the first ecstasy of that effulgence, their preaching could be coldly apologetic ? Scarcely. Their boldness, their fire, their enthusiasm was such that those who heard them believed that they

were beside themselves owing to the fumes of strong
wine. They were, of a truth, delirious—but delirious
with the intoxication of the new understanding of things
that they had received. They were drunk, not with
wine, but with wisdom and knowledge. They flung
themselves forth from the upper room, under the violent
impulse of the Holy Spirit, to preach Catholicity—and
they proclaimed the Resurrection. This being so, it
needs must be that in some way or other this dogma
must embrace the whole economy of redemption—must
be a compendium of the Faith. St. Paul, indeed, in his
words to the Corinthians implies that for him it is such.
" If Christ," he says, " be not risen again, then is our
preaching vain and your faith is also vain." [1] If we
understood that mystery as did the Apostles, if we could
see it in the light in which it was revealed to them and
in which they must have set it before their hearers in
their instructions, we would realise that this must needs
be so.

The mysteries of Christ's life are something more
than mere historical events. If we consider these
mysteries exclusively in their historical aspect, the life
of Our Lord, as related to us by the Evangelists, will
be to us much the same as would be the meagre record
of the acts and words of a great and good man, whose
fate excites our pity and whose heroism stirs our admiration. It would be that and nothing more. But the
incidents narrated by the Evangelists are something
more than the lifeless facts of history. They have a
life-giving potency that does not and cannot belong to
the ordinary contingent incidents committed to the

[1] 1 Cor. xv. 17.

pages of human records. They are not something transient, having no other reality than an aptitude to furnish materials on which to build up an argument or from which to construct a theory.

The events which make up the history of Christ's mortal life are much more than all this. Far from being " dead " facts they are a perpetually energising force in the world. They are, as it were, a typical and dramatic representation of the experiences that the christian soul must go through in the process of " divinisation ". To be for us what it was for the Evangelists, the life of Christ must not be solely an external objective event which we contemplate, but an internal experience which we undergo. The phases of that life are to be reproduced in our personal experiences if we are to be faithful to our christian vocation—that is, if we are to correspond to God's designs in our regard and follow the spiritual path that He has traced out for us. This is the constant theme of St. Paul's teaching.[2]

As the Church is ever re-enacting, during all the ages, the life story of her Divine Spouse—undergoing in the Mystical Body what He suffered in His Natural Body, so it must be, too, in some measure, for every individual christian that lives in real unity with Christ. It was thus that the saints understood the life of the Divine Master. *They not merely contemplated it, they lived it.* This was the source of the immense sympathy they were capable of experiencing for Him in His different states. They felt in a certain measure what He felt, and what is true of Our Lord's life considered as a whole must be true

---

[2] Cf. St. Paul, *passim*, Cor., Romans, Eph., Heb., especially Philipp. ii. 5–18.

in no imperfect or limited manner of that which was the
supreme and crowning mystery in that life—namely,
the Resurrection. *This must be, not merely a fact in
christian history, but a phase of christian experience.*

And yet it is not easy to establish the vital connection
between Christ's Resurrection from the dead and our
inner spiritual life. The mode of application is not
readily discovered : the relation is far from being
obvious. This is the reason that meditation on the
Resurrection is somewhat vague and unsatisfactory,
and to ordinary souls not helpful. It does not yield as
fruitful results in imparting spiritual impulse as does
meditation on any of the other mysteries of the life of
Jesus up to and including the death on the Cross. We
know that the contemplation proper to Easter Morning
should give us something of great and special import
spiritually, and we have a secret feeling that it has *not*
been for us what the Church evidently means it to be.
We do experience a certain kind of joy—but the emotion
that brushes the surface of our soul is in no way comparable in depth or in intensity to the gladness we
experience as we bend over the manger in the stable
of Bethlehem and gaze on the face of the newly born
Babe. There is something inspiriting, too, in the
ascetic discipline of Lent. Conscious of our sinfulness
we recognise the necessity of expiating our faults and
reducing our rebellious flesh to subjection. The Offices
of Lent give us courage to undergo these voluntary
sufferings, and in the thrill of combat with ourselves
we feel that we are doing something definite towards
the sanctification of our souls. The tragedy of the Passion, the terrific drama of Calvary, cannot fail to inspire

us with horror of sin, which has been the cause of it, and with love of the Incarnate God, whose tenderness for us has driven Him to undergo the torments of the Cross for our sake. This compunction for sin and gratitude to Him Who saved us from it and expiated our guilt are a sustaining force for us in our struggles with our nature. We should, therefore, reasonably expect to find, in the crowning mystery of Our Lord's life, a vigorous impetus towards perfection—and ordinarily speaking, we fail to find it. For many— even spiritual persons—the Paschal time is not one of progress, but rather the contrary. The efforts maintained during Lent are relaxed with a corresponding decline in fervour and interior recollection. During the Infancy, the Hidden Life, the Public Life and the Passion one feels near to Our Lord. His risen life seems to make Him somewhat remote from us. The " Noli me tangere ",[3] addressed by Our Risen Lord to Magdalen, haunts our minds and seems to imply an aloofness on the part of Jesus that was not exhibited before His death. We cannot enter into union with Him in His impassible condition as readily as we can do so in His passible condition. The Resurrection is for us, effectively, a withdrawal of Jesus from us; whereas according to everything in the words of Jesus on the eve of His death, it ought to be a more perfect approach of Him to us.

There is certainly something amiss in this somewhat common spiritual attitude. Things should surely not be so. If Our Lord continued to dwell on earth for some time after He triumphed over death, that portion

---

[3] " Do not touch Me," St. John xx. 17.

of His life must be meant to have its own purpose and its own meaning for the spiritual life of all those who aim at assimilating themselves to Christ. It is significant that this strange but quite common mental disarray experienced by even pious souls, in their efforts to derive from the mystery of Easter its appropriate spiritual effects, is a reflection of the confusion of mind shown by the disciples when the Risen Lord appeared to them. They simply failed to adjust themselves to the situation. They could not reconcile the thoughts of their mind with the evidence of their senses. They doubted, they feared, they did not know what to believe. We should expect them to be overwhelmed with joy, but we find their joy strongly tempered by fear and perplexity. The reason is found in this, that their understanding of the significance and purpose of the life that Christ led amongst them in His passible state was extremely inadequate. Their dullness of comprehension was due to this, that they shared with their compatriots a very imperfect concept of the spiritual life and consequently of the relations that were meant to exist between them and the Saviour. They were tainted with the prevailing formalism and were probably only just a little less puzzled than Nicodemus as to what the inner transformation and rebirth mentioned by Jesus Christ could signify. They had enjoyed a close union and intimacy with Jesus during the three years together : they had little idea of a kind of union with Him other than that. Hence the Resurrection found them somewhat at a loss. They experienced great difficulty in adjusting themselves to a situation and to a mode of contact with Jesus that was both new to them and unexpected.

Their view of what a spiritual life really meant had to undergo a profound modification.

The death of Christ had come as a dolorous surprise and a cruel disappointment to them; it upset all the hopes they had built on Him. So now, although the fact of the Resurrection established conclusively His claims to the Divinity, it brought them little comfort and less enlightenment. It threw no light, for them, on their own interior or exterior life. The circumstances and manner of the risen life left them little room for hope that the Resurrection would prepare the way for the reconstruction of their shattered earthly dreams. Their dreams had not been entirely dispelled by what should have been the rude awakening of the Crucifixion![4] But, nevertheless, with a certain sinking of the heart they vaguely surmised that the return from the tomb, though a work of such astonishing power, could not mean the undoing of what they regarded as the great defeat of the Passion. It had not yet clearly dawned on them that there was no defeat to reverse—that, in fact, what appeared to be a defeat was a final and crushing victory. Not as yet having been able to see the forces that were actually locked in combat on Calvary's hill, they did not behold the rout. Hence it was that their joy at seeing Jesus again was tempered by a certain bewilderment and disappointment. They felt that it would not mean all for them that they desired. Presuming that His life's purpose was the restoration of the temporal kingdom of Israel—and they presumed that

---

[4] This is clear from the question the apostles tentatively put the Lord at one of the meetings that preceded the Ascension. " They therefore who were gathered together asked Him, saying : Lord, wilt Thou at this time restore again the kingdom to Israel ? "—Acts i. 6.

this was His object—why, if He were able to come back
from the dead, had He allowed Himself to be done to
death ? Had He escaped dying, a thing which was much
easier in itself than coming back to life, He would,
they reflected, have prevented that utter overthrow of
their hopes that, for them, necessarily followed the
catastrophe of Calvary. It was incomprehensible to
them that He should be able to come back to life and
yet that He should permit Himself to be slain. They
rejoiced to see Him again, for they loved Him. The
Resurrection was a stupendous and wholly unexpected
event, but remained in some sense unsatisfactory. It
led nowhere as far as they could see. It did not make
possible the realisation of the hopes and ambitions they
had based on His leadership. It left the main problems
of existence apparently unsolved.

Now all that was due to the fact that their whole
outlook on the life of Christ was imperfect—which is
another way of saying that their theory of the spiritual
life was found wanting. They thought that union with
Christ would end in a certain manner : when it did not
so end they were utterly at a loss. They judged that
His leaving them through death was the greatest mis-
fortune that could befall them, although He had told
them that it was expedient for them that He should go.
Union with Christ was understood by them in a purely
physical and material sense ; they did not grasp that it
was union of a mystical and spiritual kind that would
bring them the advantages that Christ destined for them.
They persisted in regarding His life as an epoch in the
political and national history of their people ; they did
not understand that it was the central event in the

religious and spiritual life of the race. They were very
slow to realise that the life of the Master that they loved
was meant to be a force in the spiritual and not in the
temporal order. This realisation began to dawn on
them only by degrees as they saw that the days following
the Resurrection were spent by Our Lord *not in bringing
about a political revolution amongst the people, but a
mental revolution in themselves.* The last shadows were
dispelled from their mind only on the day of Pentecost.
It was only then for the first time that they understood
the place of Calvary in the scheme of things.

We also have our Messianic dream when we launch
forth into the adventure of close intimacy with Jesus.
At first we follow Him eagerly : we look to Him expectantly to realise for us the ideal of life on earth. We
outline that life for ourselves in imagination. We
picture a state of things in which we shall live close
by His side and in the enjoyment of a happy existence
in a world bathed in sunshine—a world which He will
create for us by action on men and things. Then,
when He begins to drop dark hints of a cross to be
endured as a means to the realisation of our ideal,
doubts and hesitations arise within. The cross, far
from being a stepping stone to the ideal, appears to
us to bar all access to it. We cannot get the cross into
our dreams of a happy existence with Christ. The
cross seems to us to lie across the path to happiness,
like an insurmountable obstacle. To the apostles a
progress, development and improvement in the conditions of life they enjoyed with the Master prior to
the crucifixion seemed something much to be preferred
to the conditions of a life conditioned by death. The

life they knew and enjoyed had much more appeal to them than the Risen Life with its strange and somewhat unearthly conditions. As in the case of the apostles, our difficulties with regard to a proper spiritual apprehension of the Resurrection arise from a failure to understand Calvary. We miss the true import of the Resurrection and fail in consequence to assign to it its proper place in the world of spiritual realities. For us, as for the apostles, the Cross has a certain finality, though the finality assigned to it in each case is somewhat different. For them it meant the death-knell of all their political hopes : for us it is something ultimate in the spiritual life, with nothing beyond or behind it in the present world. Absorbed in the contemplation of the Passion as an expiatory sacrifice, we see in it the destruction of our sins, and our rescue from eternal death. If our meditations on the Passion have as their effect to inspire us with a great hatred of sin, which demanded that cruel expiation ; to give us the consoling realisation of the Saviour's love which constrained Him to endure such agony for our sake ; to excite in our hearts an affection which should be some response to this great love of God for us, and finally, to give us the strength to bear our crosses with the courage of which Our Lord has given us the example, it would seem that there is nothing else that we should look for in these meditations. If there is anything else that we should look for from the Cross it is to be found—so we judge—in the world beyond the grave—in the happiness of heaven whose gates it has opened for us. And the Resurrection means little else to us than a pledge of our own future rising from the dead when the soul shall be united to a glorified body, to enjoy, in union with it, the happiness God has prepared for His elect. The Cross has its meaning for us in this life, the Resurrection in the life to come. We do not readily perceive that, in God's plan, not only the Cross, but the Risen Life that followed it, is meant to be part of our terrestrial existence. Christ did not pass from the Cross straight to heaven : the christian is not meant to do so either. In the case of Jesus the cross preceded, prepared and prefaced a risen life on earth : in the case of the christian the cross is meant to play a somewhat similar *rôle*—that is, to be the prelude to a risen life, even here below. The cross cannot be completely understood except it is viewed in the full light of the splendour of the Resurrection. It is the latter, not the former, that is the ultimate mystery for us. God is a God of the Living, not of the Dead. He is a God of Life, not of Death. In any order of things, therefore, established by Him, Life, not Death, must be ultimate. So it is that it is the Resurrection, not the Crucifixion, which must be made the object of christian endeavour. Our rising from the dead must, in a spiritual sense, be accomplished after the pattern of Christ's whilst we are still on earth. And it is to this that we must direct all our efforts. The Cross is a means, not an end ; it finds its explanation only in the empty tomb ; it is an entrance into life, not a mode of death. Any death that enters into God's plan must necessarily issue forth in life. If He lays upon us the necessity of dying it is in order that we may live. In God's plan death cannot, even in a modified form, be ultimate. What is or appears to be death in the scheme of things must be,

with God, nothing else than a necessary stage in the
evolution of life. Life is the end of death, and not death
the end of life. With Him death must issue in life.
In the spiritual order of things, which is the one towards
which are directed all the operations of God's eternal
plan regarding creatures, it is from our dead selves
that we must rise to newness of life. This newness of
life is the resurrection that is consequent on the death
of revolted nature in us, that is, of that life in us which
seeks its expression and development at the expense
of the divine life of the soul. There is a death which
is nothing else but death—and there is a death which
leads to a free untrammelled existence. It is to this
latter species of mortality that we are united by the
Saviour on the Cross, in order that we may rise with
Him to the perfect freedom of the life of Easter Morn.
What in us is opposed to God must die, in order that
God's life, being free from the bonds of mortality that
impede it in us, may develop itself without restraint.
" Know you not," says St. Paul, " that all we who are
baptised in Christ Jesus are baptised in His death ?
For we are buried together with Him by baptism unto
death : that as Christ is risen from the dead by the
glory of the Father so we also may walk in newness of
life." [5]

We rise to this newness of life when we are no longer
under the domination of our concupiscences. When we
move at the behest of our sinful inclinations we are
developing in ourselves the seeds of spiritual mortality.
The action of the Cross is to destroy the vitality not of
the soul but of the concupiscences which constitute the

[5] Rom. vi. 3.

dangerous disease of the soul. In order that we may live as we ought, our rebellious nature must be crucified. Crucifixion always remains the only mode of salvation.

God sends trials and crosses simply to deaden in us the activity of the forces that make for the decay of the spiritual life, in order that that spiritual life may develop and expand unimpeded. According as the life of perverse nature ebbs away from us on our Cross united with Christ's, the Divine Life that God has placed in all whom He has called begins to make itself more manifest and to display increased vigour and vitality. Our Resurrection to the newness of life, the life wholly controlled by the impulses of God's graces, comes, without any interval, straight on our death to self. It is to that Resurrection, that life in death, that God directs all the circumstances of our life—it is the object He aims at in His dealing with us. We, in our blindness, in our utter incomprehension of that rising from the dead which Our Lord speaks of to us, oppose His designs, thwart His purposes, and cling desperately to the life of self which knows no Resurrection. It is strange how history does repeat itself. Frequently, without our being aware of it, we shall be found re-echoing the words of St. Peter in which he dared to expostulate with Our Lord. The Saviour spoke to him of His death and of the restoration to life that was to follow hard upon it. Peter, seeing nothing in the sufferings foretold but something abhorrent; discerning no connection whatsoever between them and the state of glory to which Christ referred; and feeling no attraction for a condition of life which, however good in itself, did not seem to hold out any prospect of

greatness in the world where his ambitions were centred,
quarrelled with his Master's freely chosen destiny.
The risen joys to follow the passion and death had for
the apostle but a very cold appeal and did not seem to
him a compensation for the sufferings and ignominy
and rejection which paved the way for these joys.

The difficulties which the apostles experienced on
Easter Morn in adjusting their minds to the fact that
the Christ Whom they knew, with Whom they had
lived, and Who had died by a death that was made
unmistakable by the soldier's lance, was actually before
them in flesh and blood, with life coursing through the
Body still showing all the marks of the terrible crucifixion, point to the conclusion that, when our Lord
had spoken to them of His Rising from the dead, they
always understood His words in an eschatological
sense. They deemed that the Resurrection had reference
to a post-terrestrial life : in a vague kind of a way
they assumed it to be something that was to take place
when the present world should be at an end. They
had not grasped that it had a bearing on man's earthly
destiny. Their beliefs in this connection were, very
likely, those voiced by Martha, the sister of Lazarus,
when on receiving the assurance from the Lord that
her brother would rise again she immediately understood
Him to refer to the resurrection at the last day. They
had scarcely a conception of any other rising from the
dead—still less had their minds entertained any idea of
a newness of life to be attained through suffering.

And yet it is to lead us to this newness of life that
God orders all the sufferings and trials He sends us in
our earthly pilgrimage. Our Lord draws us towards

this risen life by His example after having merited it for us by His Passion. He teaches us that to arrive at the term it is necessary that the concupiscences in us be crucified, and that it is God's love for us that orders and directs the execution. That tendency in us which makes us cleave to the creature to the prejudice of the Creator, which makes us elect perishable things in preference to eternal, must die. To reach the perfect freedom of this life that is all for God, there must be effected in us a detachment from all that is not of God. Pain and sorrow are the instruments of this detachment. It is through them that sinful desires are dulled and concupiscence reduced to a state of quiescence.

The attraction to evil that is in us, in consequence of original sin, cannot be made to disappear completely in this life. It continues to exist even in the saints. The repugnance we experience in ourselves to what God's laws desire of us, and to what our own will aspires to, retains us in humility and allows us to distinguish clearly between what we can do of ourselves and what God can accomplish in us by His Holy Spirit. The experience of our own powerlessness in the fight against the evil tendencies in our nature teaches us not to attribute to our own strength, but to God's grace, the victories we may achieve in the struggle. The ever-renewed conflict in us convinces us of the necessity of the crucifixion of our wicked nature in order that we may be able to serve God without offending Him.

To live to God we must die to sin, and this death to sin cannot be achieved without its own passion. It was through the Cross that the world was redeemed— it remains that by the Cross and the Cross only, per-

sonally borne and endured, each individual enters fully
into the redemption and is sanctified. Self must die in
order that God may reign in undisputed sway in us.
In that lies the whole explanation of suffering in life.
It is only over the hilltop of Calvary that we make our
way into the brightness and splendour and glowing life
of the Garden of the Resurrection. The beauty of a
body, free from the corruption of sin, and the radiance
of a soul filled with God's life is that in which our
Calvary finds its explanation and the term in which it
issues. The Cross is the way or the means to the
Resurrection. Without the one we cannot have the
other. If God makes the path of our life converge on
Calvary it is only in order that it may lead us into the
calm and peace and light of the Resurrection—of a life
in which the germ of mortality, namely, concupiscence,
has been successfully combated by the healing virtue
of the grace of Christ, working through sufferings
patiently accepted.

But, of course, not all sufferings effect in us this
wonderful transformation, which is at once an image of
Christ's glorious life, and a pledge of future immortality. There were three who underwent crucifixion
together on the Hill of Calvary. One of them suffered
and blasphemed. Guilty though he was, he rebelled
against his fate. He dared to abuse God for the tortures
he had brought on himself by his own misdeeds. He
railed at and cursed Divine Providence for the evil
that had come upon him. "And one of those robbers
who were hanged blasphemed Him, saying : ' If Thou
be Christ, save Thyself and us.' " [6] So there are many,

6 St. Luke xxiii. 39.

who, when crushed upon the cross of life, instead of entering into themselves, acknowledging their sinfulness and humbling themselves under the Hand of God, revile their Maker for allowing suffering to exist, or at least, for allowing it to befall them. Such men, far from being purified by their passion, plunge themselves into a worse death than that of the body. They sink from one death into one yet more profound.

There are those who when they suffer accept what comes to them in a spirit of expiation. They recognise their sinfulness and acknowledge that by reason of it they deserve chastisement at the Hands of God. Like the good thief, they cast their eyes upon Jesus and consider the fearful tortures that He endured—though sinless. Contrasting His Innocence with their own guilt, they strive not to repine at the cross to which they are nailed ; they simply humble themselves under the powerful Hand of God, appeal for mercy and pardon, and beg their offended Master to accept their sufferings as an expiation of their guilt. They ask the suffering Christ to sanctify their crucifixion by applying to it the virtue of His, and they thus merit to hear from the Saviour's lips the promise that from the Cross they shall ascend into the Kingdom of Heaven. In the Cross they find that detachment from earth, that unworldliness by which their salvation is secured. Were it not for the Cross they could never have been severed from the life of earth and brought to the side of Christ.

There is still another class of sufferers. They are those who enter into a voluntary participation in the Passion of Christ—through love of Him and zeal for souls. They have passed the stage where the Cross has

been active in promoting in them the love of Christ;
it is now that very love which creates the Cross for them.
These souls do not merely support with patience such
trials as befall them; they will to suffer in order to
be more like their Divine Master. They aspire to be
united with Christ on the Cross not only that His life
may reign in them, but also that, by their own sufferings
united with those of the Saviour, effects of salvation
may flow out on others. This is the highest and most
sublime mode of suffering, and it is only the chosen few
that enter on it.

Death implies the cessation of activity. The death
through which we are to reach newness of life is the
cessation of the activity of the principles of sin in us.
Though, as a penalty of the First Transgression, the
roots of sin itself cannot be torn out from our being,
the vitality of sin can be destroyed. The apostle does
not ask us not to be sinners, but he commands us not
to be the slaves of sin. He requires that its domination
over us should cease: " Let not sin *reign* in your
mortal bodies." [7] The christian who has passed through
the crucible of suffering to a purification of soul is
not exempt from the assaults of sin. The newness of
life which he has reached cannot be retained without
effort. Even the saints are not free from solicitude and
anxiety. In spite of their sanctity they remain sinners,
but they are not the slaves of sin. The reign of sin has
ceased in them, in that they have ceased to obey its lusts.
They maintain a constant struggle against their concupiscences, and when they suffer a momentary defeat
they do not acquiesce in or take pleasure in the evil to

[7] Rom. vi. 12.

which they have succumbed. They deplore their weakness, exercise themselves in humility because of it, and animate themselves with a still greater desire of union with God as a protection against it. They continue to defeat sin in its very successes.

What is true of the saints in this respect is true of ourselves in a more pronounced fashion. Even when we have experienced the Passion of Christ in our limited manner there remains a hostile force within us, and if we cease to combat it we shall not remain at peace with God nor in tranquil possession of our " risen life ". The old evil inclinations, though suppressed, have not been entirely destroyed. The energy of the evil habits has diminished but has not disappeared. Even after long years of inactivity they remain ready to resume their vitality if only the occasions by which they are called into play present themselves. Things which formerly attracted us retain their power of attraction still, in some measure, and will exercise it once more unless we are vigilant and careful in protecting ourselves against their appeal. We must keep ourselves outside the range of their influence. If we, relying on our strength, place ourselves in the circumstances that once were a stumbling block to us, if we make any concession to the ways of acting that were associated with our failures in God's service, if we return to the associations that proved harmful, if there is any resumption of the old conditions of life that witnessed our betrayals of God, then there is grave danger that the smouldering passions will blaze up anew from their ashes.[8]

---

[8] Mgr. Benson's novel. *A Winnowing*, is an interesting psychological study of this " going backwards " through the effect of " old associations."

If we are to preserve our new life intact we must resolutely renounce everything that once proved a temptation to us, and uncompromisingly turn our back on the old ways. We sometimes think that we can safely indulge in an innocent manner an inclination which we formerly indulged in with guilt. This is an error. If we yield in any way to anything evil in ourselves, we shall drift back, little by little, into the channels of sin. To die with Christ and to rise with Him we must push our detachment to the very root of these inclinations in us which if at any time indulged in set us at variance with God.

We must not temporise with the things which make a strong appeal to our sensitive nature. No matter how strong we may feel, we have our strength in weakness. We can never afford to relax in our war with concupiscence. This enemy, in ourselves, cannot be fought without risk, controlled without effort, restrained without anxiety. This strength of our weakness, this energy of what is death-dealing in us should make us humble, vigilant and constantly mortified.

Our conversion must then be wholehearted and must mean the paralysis, if not the death of the tendencies to evil in us. It is our affections that lead us astray by attaching us to what draws us from God. Having once broken these attachments we must on no pretext (and our nature will allege many a specious one) allow them to resume their mastery over us even in a very mild and modified form. Any affection that can draw us away from God or stand between us and God must be combated without truce.

The most successful way to overcome these dangerous

attractions is to set up a counter-attraction. Life is not a negative process. It is positive. The new life must not consist in the mere cessation of loving what is evil; it must express itself in the love of what is good. Newness of life does not consist merely in the efforts to avoid sin—it means the positive endeavour to live for God. We die to sin in order to live to God. The destination of our faculties to the interests of God is the characteristic of that resurrection of the soul that follows on its dying in union with Christ. The aim of the soul that has once been purified (or converted) should be not merely to have an aversion to what is evil, but to conceive a strong love for what is good. Love of God, not mere aversion from sin, should be the controlling motive in its new life. Renovation or Resurrection must mean a new love. When at our being broken on the cross, all the false idols which we worshipped in our hearts tumble into dust before our eyes, we must not allow ourselves to be still and motionless in the tomb of our dead selves. We must, by laying hold on Christ, rise to a new life by setting up God Himself exclusively as a new object of love and worship in our hearts. Devotedness to God and His interests is the exercise of the vitality of the life that comes of the death on the Cross.

It is inevitable that suffering should sooner or later present itself in the life of each individual and mingle its bitter savour with every kind of pleasure, even the purest, that one wishes to extract from existence. It did not enter into God's original plan. It is through man's act that it made its way into human life. Owing its origin to human perversity, it is evident that it is an

evil thing. It is a foretaste and a beginning of death.
God's power and goodness is shown in making this
evil thing, this result of man's wrongdoing, an instrument of good. He permits us to suffer. He does not
choose to destroy the consequences of the use of our
free wills. He prefers to repair these evil consequences.
It does not become Him to undo what He has once
done—it would be on His part a confession of miscalculation, error, want of prevision. He created, foreseeing
the entry into the world of sin and suffering in the train,
and as the logical issue of sin, and He takes that evil
thing and makes it productive of good. He permits us
to suffer, not because He takes pleasure in our suffering,
but because He sees that as things now are it is only by
suffering that are burned away in our souls the obstacles
to the free operations of grace. He does not take away
sufferings, but He gives us the power and the means to
turn our sufferings to good account. He makes that
which is the fruit of sin itself effect the destruction of
sin in our souls. He shows us His Divine Son suffering
and He invites us to endure our sufferings with the like
dispositions, promising us that if we be like Him in His
death, we shall be like Him in His Resurrection from
death. God exhibited to us in the risen life of the
Saviour the type and example of what our life on earth
shall be, if we willingly undergo the trials and hardships
that are its condition and its preparation. Not all
sufferings are salutary : it is only those that are endured
in union with Christ. Suffer we must whatever be the
spirit in which we endure suffering. If we look upon
the pains of this life as an evil thing only and, therefore,
as something which we must struggle against desperately,

we shall not assuage but intensify the bitterness of life. If, on the other hand, we look upon sufferings as the necessary instrument in the purification of our souls, if we accept them from the Hands of God as such, and if we draw from Christ's passion the strength to bear them in humble submission to God's providence, we, through them, free our souls from the contagion of mortality, and heal in our souls the wounds inflicted on them by sin. Through sufferings endured in conformity with Christ we work our way steadily back towards the condition of original justice in which sense was perfectly subject to the spirit, and the spirit to God. Through sufferings, endured supernaturally, we clothe ourselves with the justice of Christ, the new Adam. When nature is dead in us and its rebellious stirrings are quieted we walk in newness of life and in the peace of the Resurrection. If we consent to die with Christ, then also we shall rise from the tomb of our dead selves to live with Christ.

APPENDIX

BEYOND Calvary lies not the next world, but the Garden of Eden, the life of Grace. It is the door, not into the heavenly, but into the earthly Paradise where man is united with God and God communicates His life to man, in Grace, which is the end here below. When, by the Fall, the life of Grace, man's real life on this earth, was lost, the life of the concupiscences—the law of the members—was inaugurated. Christ, by His Crucifixion, which was a death to His Body, made it possible for man to rise from this state of death of soul, and by His Resurrection in which He is freed from the shackles of mortality He symbolises what must characterise our "risen life" in its perfection, namely, freedom from the concupiscences. By Humility, Poverty, Chastity, Sufferings borne in union with Christ in a word, by our Cross, we enter into the dispositions which condition, foster the growth of, and make possible our resurrection to this new life, the life of Grace. This is our earthly Paradise—the Garden of Eden—for us again.

The accompanying diagram illustrates the ideas set forth in this chapter and summarises them.

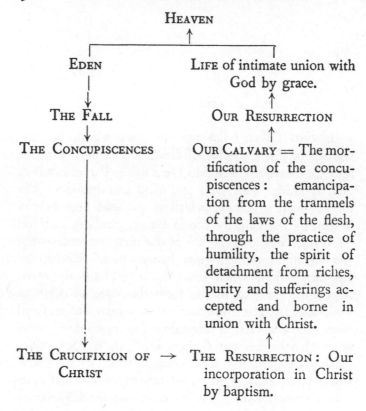

HEAVEN

EDEN

LIFE of intimate union with God by grace.

THE FALL

OUR RESURRECTION

THE CONCUPISCENCES

OUR CALVARY = The mortification of the concupiscences: emancipation from the trammels of the laws of the flesh, through the practice of humility, the spirit of detachment from riches, purity and sufferings accepted and borne in union with Christ.

THE CRUCIFIXION OF → THE RESURRECTION: Our
CHRIST   incorporation in Christ
                          by baptism.

CHAPTER II

THE SENDING OF THE SPIRIT OF JESUS

" I will ask the Father and He shall give you another Paraclete."—
St. John xiv. 16.

THE *decisive* hour in the great enterprise of the
Redemption of fallen man was the Crucifixion—the
perfect holocaust of the sacred Humanity of the God-
Man ; the *crowning event*, that which marked the successful issue of the enterprise of the Redemption, was the
coming of the Holy Ghost, sent by God the Father
and His triumphant Son to redeemed mankind. Jesus
looked onward through the thick dark mists of the
Passion, through its mists of tears and blood, to this
glorious event that was to follow hard on the Crucifixion.
He looked to it as the glorious and perfect fruit of His
earthly career. His thoughts during that memorable
discourse to His apostles at the Last Supper continually
revert to it ; He dwells on it complacently, for He saw
in the sending of the Holy Ghost that which was to
transform for His followers the seeming tragedy of the
Passion into a fertile source of Divine consolation.
" And now I go to Him that sent Me and none of you
asketh Me : whither goest Thou ? " [1] Evidently He
expected that they would rejoice with Him in His going,
and in their interest in His happiness would be all

[1] St. John xvi. 5.

eagerness to know something of that home to which He looked forward with so much longing. " If you loved Me," He said, " you would indeed be glad, because I go to the Father." [2] His words bidding them to rejoice because He was leaving them must have sounded somewhat like a mockery in the ears of the apostles, plunged in grief, as they were, because of the approaching separation. Jesus saw into their hearts ; He read their thoughts and in their thoughts, their incredulity. They never could, they believed, be happy if He left them. The considerations He urged appeared to them like those that men frame to comfort their friends in grief and which they who urge them feel to be hollow and inadequate. Jesus insists, saying : " *I tell you the truth :* it is expedient to you that I go : for if I go not, the Paraclete will not come to you : but if I go I will send Him to you." [3] Strange as it might appear to them, they would not be robbed of His presence by His departure ; His going would make possible His continued presence amongst them in a more marvellous, yet more intimate, manner. Death, His enemy, whom He had fought and conquered, would be persuaded that he was tearing the Christ from His followers. But they would not be orphaned by His death : " I will not leave you orphans," He said to them tenderly, " I will come to you." [4] True, they would be deprived of the presence they were accustomed to, but one more perfect would be substituted for it—" Christ's bodily presence, which was limited to place, being exchanged for the manifold spiritual indwelling in His followers ", limited neither

[2] St. John xiv. 28.
[3] St. John xvi. 7.
[4] St. John xiv. 18.

as to numbers, time or space. He should be present, no longer *with* them, but His spirit would be present *in* them; this is a presence implying a state of closer union. By withdrawing from them, He gave them to understand He would be able to draw much nearer to them than He had been. Their sorrow at His departure from them to the Father was a mistaken sorrow; because the seeming absence from them would bring about a more perfect presence *with* them. If their grief at the loss of His sensible presence, at their not being able any longer to hear the tones of His voice, to walk by His side, to contemplate His features and to listen for His footfall, was to some extent permissible and excusable, the grief would be more than amply counterbalanced by the inward spiritual sight and possession of Him they would enjoy. " Thus Christ's going to the Father is at once a source of sorrow because it involves His absence; and of joy because it involves His presence ".[5] The almost paradoxical words of Christ had their ample fulfilment when Pentecost dawned. On that day the Passion of Christ received its reward: for on that day the virtue of the Passion released the flow of Divine gifts and allowed them to pour in a tumultuous stream on mankind that had been redeemed and " bought at a great price ".[6] Pentecost was the goal on which converged all the redeeming acts of the Incarnate God.

Of course, it may be objected, the Holy Ghost did not await Pentecost to come to men. He had been operative in the world from its commencement. We are told

---

[5] Newman's *P. and P. Sermons*, Vol. VI., p. 121.
[6] 1 Cor. vi. 20.

that in the beginning " the Spirit of God moved over the waters " [7] and at His passage, order, form and beauty sprang out of chaos. It is worth noting *en passant* that this action of the Holy Ghost in the material world is a type and symbol of the action of the same Spirit in the world of souls. At His passage the splendour of the Divine Life replaces the chaos of sin. Later it is mentioned that the men chosen by Moses to do the skilled works pertaining to the construction of the tabernacle were inspired by the Spirit of God " in wisdom and in understanding and in knowledge and in all manner of workmanship ".[8] The Holy Spirit of God worked in the realm of grace as well as in the realm of nature. He instructed Moses, He inspired the prophets and He dwelt in the just. He swayed the souls of Zachary and Elizabeth ; He spoke through the Holy Simeon and the Devout Anna. If things be regarded from the point of view of temporal sequence, the Holy Ghost exercises His function as Sanctifier in the souls of men before the Passion of Christ. But if things be regarded from the point of view of causal sequence, all the activities of the Holy Ghost follow the Passion. The cause must always precede the effect, in the order of reality. The death of Christ was the meritorious cause of the coming of the Holy Ghost to men. Suppress the Passion and there is suppressed with it all the effects of grace preceding it and following it in time. The justice of those who lived before Christ had its source and origin in the sacrifice of Jesus as literally as the justice of those who live in the christian era is derived

[7] Gen. i. 2.
[8] Exod. xxxi. 3, 4.

from the same fountain head. But even if things be regarded temporally, the communication of the Holy Spirit to men is much more abundant since Pentecost—so abundant that relatively, in St. John's eyes, there had been no communication up to then. " As yet," he says, " the Spirit was not given, because Jesus was not yet glorified." [9]

Now the imparting of the Holy Ghost can be considered in regard of the Church taken as a whole or in regard of individual souls.

It helps devotion considerably to differentiate clearly between the *rôle* of God made Man and that of the Holy Ghost (called frequently in Scripture, the Spirit of Jesus) in the work of our redemption. Our Heavenly Father, in His infinite mercy and kindness, commissioned both to this task. The Incarnate God *reconciled* fallen man to his Maker by the destruction in His flesh of the enmities which kept them apart. " For He is our *peace*, Who hath made both one, and breaking down the middle wall of partition, the enmities in His flesh . . . that He might make the two in Himself into one new man, making peace, *and might reconcile both to God* in one body by the Cross, *killing the enmities in Himself*." [10] The Holy Ghost *transformed* that *reconciliation* into a profound mutual sympathy and a strong deep love. Christ merited grace ; the Holy Spirit moulds souls to the graces thus merited. Christ revealed God to His creatures from without ; God the Holy Ghost reveals the same God to His creatures by inward communications. God the Son made Man wrought

St. John vii. 39.
[10] Eph. ii. 14–16.

our salvation by meriting it; God the Holy Ghost
wrought our salvation by accomplishing it. God the
Son saved us, God the Holy Ghost sanctifies us. To
the Third Person of the Blessed Trinity are therefore
appropriated all the activities that bear on the sanctification of souls. By appropriation in theology is meant the
assigning to each Person of the Blessed Trinity such
works as have an affinity with the personal characteristic or properties of that Person even though the
operation of such works belongs to the whole Trinity
in common. The Holy Ghost proceeds from the Father
and Son as the expression of their essential love. He is
the substantial love of God, that is, the love of God
personified. He is Divine Love existing as a Person,
Whose whole personality is, so to speak, made up of
love. Sanctity is nothing else than the love of God.
The Holy Spirit then is sanctity personified. He is,
in virtue of the mode of His procession from the Father
and Son, "Holiness Itself". Being such, He is the
Author and Source of every work of sanctity.

To Him belongs, as peculiarly His own, the function
of uniting the Sacred Humanity to the Divinity in the
unity of one Person. *He is the Divine Artisan of the
Incarnation.* Scripture tells us that it is He that formed
the humanity of Jesus in the womb of the Virgin Mary.
The Angel Gabriel said to her: " *The Holy Ghost
shall come upon thee* and the power of the Most High
shall overshadow thee. *And therefore* also the Holy
which shall be born of thee shall be *called the Son of
God.*" [11] " By the operation of the Holy Spirit not
only was the conception of Christ accomplished, but

[11] St. Luke i. 35.

also the sanctification of His soul "—as had been foretold by Isaias. " And there shall come forth a rod out of the root of Jesse ; and a flower shall rise up out of his root. And the Spirit of the Lord shall rest upon him : the Spirit of wisdom and understanding, the spirit of counsel and of fortitude, the Spirit of knowledge and of godliness. And he shall be filled with the spirit of the fear of the Lord." [12] All His actions were " performed in the Holy Ghost ". Christ, through the Holy Ghost, offered Himself " without spot to God ".[13]

The functions that the Holy Spirit fulfilled in regard to the individual humanity of Christ He continues to fulfil in respect of His Mystical Body. He it is that inspired the Evangelists to leave us a history of the events of the earthly career of Jesus. He taught the inspired writers what sayings and doings they were to select and in what way they were to express them. He guided their narration in all its details. In the Apostolic Epistles He moves St. Paul and the others to take up that same theme of the life of Christ and deal with it from another angle. He teaches them to draw forth for the instruction of the faithful the doctrinal truths and teachings contained implicitly in the narrative of the Evangelists. He inspired them to " *transform history into doctrine* ". The Holy Spirit labours through these inspired writers at the task of glorifying and making known Christ and the Father Who had sent Him. Jesus, before His death, had revealed the Holy Spirit at this work. " But the Paraclete, the Holy Ghost, Whom the Father will send in My Name, *He will teach you all things, and bring all*

[12] Isaias xi. 1 and 2.
[13] Heb. ix. 14.

things to your mind, whatsoever I shall have said to you." [14]
And again : " But when He, the Spirit of Truth is
come, *He will teach you all truth.*" [15]   What can be the
meaning of these texts ? Did not Christ teach all truth ?
How can it be left to the Holy Ghost to do the same
thing ? Why cannot Christ do it of Himself ? All these
questions arise spontaneously in the mind as one ponders
on the words of the Saviour. The explanation is this.
Christ is the Word of God. He is the Godhead expressed
divinely and humanly.   Christ is the *Book of God*—in
itself perfectly revealing God, but hard to be deciphered
by human souls. The Holy Ghost is the great Teacher
Who by His secret and inward illuminations takes up
this Book and expounds it to us. It is only by Him
that we can grasp the meaning and the significance of
Christ and His life. " Without Me ", says Jesus,
" you can do nothing ".   " Without Me ", the Holy
Ghost might say, " you can understand nothing. Christ
the Word of God, would be, without Me, a hidden
word, a sealed Book to you ".   It is then under the
guidance and instruction of the Holy Spirit that the
whole doctrinal implications of the life of Christ have
been built up into that vast scheme of ordered knowledge
which constitutes the teaching of the Catholic Church :
under His inspiration likewise has grown up that wondrous unity and hierarchical diversity in government
which rules and guides infallibly and securely the
Church of Christ. The Holy Spirit has been called the
" Soul of the Church ".   He is its vivifying and vitalising
principle and shall continue to permeate all its parts

[14] St. John xiv. 26.
[15] St. John xvi. 13.

with vigour and vitality to the end of time. "I will ask the Father and He shall give you another Paraclete, *that He may abide with you forever.*" [16]

Still more marvellous and mysterious are the operations of the Holy Ghost in the souls of the just. Theology, following Scripture,[17] speaks of a "mission" of the Holy Spirit to the soul in grace, *because of its being in grace.* The question may be asked, if God is everywhere, how can He be said to be sent to a place? St. Thomas explains thus. A person is said to be sent to a place when, not being yet there, he is bidden to direct himself thither or being there already is ordered to take up a new function or ministry in that place. The Holy Ghost as God being omnipresent is already in the soul, even when it is in sin. But when sin has been taken away He becomes present there in an entirely different manner. He becomes to the soul as God's loving ambassador binding closer the bonds of love between creature and Creator. He is there as cementing and making firmer the friendship of the soul with God. For this purpose He labours to *create in the spirit to which He has been sent an affinity to, a taste for, and what the theologians call a connaturalness with the things of God.* He creates in the soul a heavenly mind—a mind like His own. He transforms the soul. He makes it a new creature. "If then, any be in Christ a new creature, the old things are passed away, behold all things are made new." [18] The Holy Spirit causes the earthly tastes and tendencies to be replaced by heavenly ones. "He impresses on us our Heavenly Father's image

[16] St. John xiv. 16.
[17] St. John xiv. 16.
[18] 2 Cor. v. 17.

. . . and disposes us to seek His presence by the very instinct of our new nature. He unites us to all holy things as before we had relationship with evil." He gives us the spirit of adoption by which we instinctively and readily address God as " Father ". " But you have received the spirit of adoption of sons whereby we cry ' Abba ' (Father). For *the Spirit Himself* giveth testimony to our spirit that we are the sons of God."[19] It is comprehensible that in the soul thus transformed to His image by the love of God, the Holy Spirit should take great complacency. Under His action as Divine Charity Subsistent, diffusing charity in the soul, that soul becomes a dwelling where He abides with delight. " If any man will love Me," says Christ, " he will keep My word and My Father will love him and We will come to him *and will make Our abode with him.*"[20] In these words, the love for the God-Man is stated to be that which adapts the soul to be the dwelling or the home of the Blessed Trinity. A little earlier in the same chapter, that indwelling is appropriated to the Holy Ghost. " I will ask the Father, and He shall give you another Paraclete . . . and you shall know Him, because *He shall abide with you and shall be in you.*"[21] It is love that sets up those conditions in the soul that make of it a dwelling-place pleasing to God. It is the Holy Ghost, Who is Love Itself Personified, that generates divine love in the created spirit. Hence it is that to Him is appropriated that divine indwelling in the soul which is shared by all the three Divine Persons. The indwelling is an effect of love. It is to Him, then,

[19] Rom. viii. 16.
[20] St. John xiv. 23.
[21] St. John xiv. 16–17.

the Third Person of the Most Holy Trinity, that it belongs, as it were by right, whilst to the others the indwelling is assigned by concomitance. " Because the charity of God is poured forth in our hearts by the Holy Ghost Who is given to us." [22] The Holy Ghost dwells gladly in the justified soul as in the veritable house of God, where He receives a meed of worship and love from the created spirit which enfolds Him. The material temple of God does not worship the God in Whose honour it is built ; the spiritual temple can and does. It is its prerogative to do so. Wherever there is divine faith and divine love in a soul, this invisible spiritual temple of God is found and God the Holy Ghost resides therein complacently. It has been a structure of His own fashioning and His own adorning. It is to be noted that there is no question here of a mere metaphorical or figurative presence. It is one which is real and true and substantial. The Holy Ghost is present in the soul in grace in a manner which bears an analogy to, but is much superior to, that in which the Incarnate God is present under the sacred species. This is the central and most consoling truth of our Faith. It was to make this wonder possible for us that Jesus lived, laboured, suffered and died. This intimate and substantial presence of the Spirit of Jesus in the soul is the ripe and perfect fruit of the redemption. If the soul in grace cultivates a close attention to God within it and labours to draw ever closer to Him, by perfecting its worship of love and service, it gradually undergoes a transforming process. It becomes more and more like to the God it loves, and becoming like Him, begins

[22] Rom. v. 5.

to have a foretaste of that bliss enjoyed by God Himself and those to whom He stands revealed in the Beatific Vision. The soul contemplates, in some measure, the happiness to which St. John directed the minds of his disciples : " Dearly beloved, we are now the sons of God ; and it hath not yet appeared what we shall be. We know that when He shall appear, we shall be like Him : because we shall see Him as He is." [23]

" These sublime truths which so clearly show forth the infinite goodness of the Holy Ghost towards us, certainly demand that we should direct towards Him the highest homage of our love and devotion. Christians may do this most effectively if they will daily strive to know Him, to love Him, and to implore Him more earnestly. . . . The Holy Spirit is to be loved because He is the Substantial, Eternal, Primal love and nothing is more lovable than love. And this all the more because He has overwhelmed us with the greatest benefits, which both testify to the benevolence of the giver and claim the gratitude of the receiver." [24]

[23] 1 St. John iii. 2.
[24] Encycl.: *Divinum illud Munus*, Leo XIII.

CHAPTER III

THE SECRET OF LIFE

" Labour not for the meat which perisheth but for that which endureth unto life everlasting."—St. JOHN vi. 27.

IT is a strange thing, that of all those who are born to the supernatural life—and every baptised soul stirs with its first pulsations—so few attain to any degree of development in this life or any degree of strength in its exercise. In the realms of nature growth and increase seem to be the normal condition of every living thing : in the supernatural order examples of arrested development and stunted growth are almost universal. Apart from the saints, how few there are, even among the multitudes who are called to a life of perfection, that give evidence in their ordinary activities of the possession of a healthy, forceful and energetic spiritual life ! This is true of them not only in the early beginnings of the spiritual career, but even after the lapse of many years spent in circumstances which of themselves constitute the favourable conditions for progress in perfection. Whilst the natural life is attaining to its maturity and to its fullest expansion there is no corresponding progress observable in the divine life of grace in the soul. To very few are applicable the words that St. Luke uses in reference to Our Divine Lord—that He advanced in wisdom and grace as He advanced in age : " And

Jesus advanced in wisdom and age and grace with God and man." [1]

With the majority of us it is but occasionally and somewhat fitfully that the supernatural life in our souls, by its faint stirrings and its feeble pulsations, reveals its presence. These slight movements of grace show that the divine life in us is not utterly paralysed but has become extremely enfeebled through want of exercise. The supernatural potentiality is not brought into play when the forces that the soul has at its command are being employed in the functioning of the life of mere impulse, imagination and earthly limited reasonings. And how large a portion of the existence of even an average christian is consumed in activities which have their source in sheer impulse, or, at best, merely natural reason ! Even in the execution of these projects which concern God's glory, we almost take it for granted that both ourselves and those with whom we are brought into contact will be inspired frequently in the activities of mind and will by human motives and human passions. We do not look for the power of grace entering into, energising, transforming and lifting above the earth the activities called forth by the daily tasks of life ; this is because we do not expect to find, and should think it exceptional to find, that the divine life given in baptism should have grown in intensity and vigour with the years and finally subdued to itself every pulsation of the soul's vitality. One is confronted everywhere in the spiritual world with the phenomenon of arrested growth. Now what happens frequently or regularly comes to be regarded as inevitable and necessary ; we consider what

[1] St. Luke ii. 52.

we observe to be the manifestation of some hidden law. So common is it to find souls for whom the years have passed without bringing any supernatural development, that we come to regard this, which is in itself an extraordinary and perplexing fact, as being a normal and comprehensible one. We come to look upon the presence of ordinary sanctity as being something exceptional, and the absence of it as being the rule in ordinary christians and even in religious.

And yet that there should be life without growth and development is surely abnormal, and the frequency of the instances of it should not blind us to this abnormality or dispense us from the effort to explore its causes as well in others as in ourselves. Our faith teaches us that a life with immense latent energies and with almost limitless capacity for expansion has been given to us in baptism, and yet we know as the years pass that these possibilities have not been realised and these capacities have not been evolved. Our souls, when they have not become utterly lifeless through sin, are languishing and weak and atrophied. There is no divine vigour in them : the supernatural life is cramped, confined and deprived of power of expansion in our interior being. Grace is not the dominating and controlling factor in the human activities through which our life on earth unfolds itself. Divine charity remains in our hearts, a tiny spark hidden beneath the ashes of actions which are vitiated through the action of self-love ; whereas the life of our soul should be expanding into a glowing fire, gathering fresh force and brightness through being nourished constantly by activities having their source in divine grace. In other words, in baptism we become children in the supernatural order, and the vast majority of us remain stunted and undeveloped spiritually up to the very end of our earthly pilgrimage. We live and die infants, as far as our spiritual life is concerned.

St. Thomas shows that supernatural life in its origin and in its growth follows closely the analogy of natural life. In all living things, life is increased by the exercise of vital activity proportionate to the strength of the living principle that puts it forth. Our bodies grow in vigour as long as they are capable of energetic actions commensurate with the force of which they are possessed. Our wills gain firmness and power by being used to command acts of fortitude, temperance and justice. Every strong determination, every right decision gives the will added strength. Our intelligence gains range and mastery by being applied to the task of grappling with more and more difficult questions of science, if such questions task fully and yet do not prove too great for our intellectual powers. It is a law that every exercise of vital activity that bears the full impress of the vigour of the vital principle from which it springs increases the life of the being who exercises this activity. The same law holds in the supernatural order. Charity or the love of God is the essence of that participation of Divine Life which we receive by sanctifying grace. Every act we elicit which is animated by the degree of charity of which our souls are possessed (and which is in direct proportion to the measure of sanctifying grace imparted to us) increases and strengthens that charity. Charity is the life of the soul and every act that is animated by the full vigour of the charity actually in the soul causes a growth and development in supernatural life and supernatural love.[2] Divine Charity, or love of God, does not involve, unless accidentally, elements of feeling and sensible emotion. It is a thing of the will and of the will as energised by a very secret divine force. This divine energy imparted to the will, by which this latter is invigorated and emboldened to extend to its God the pure love of friendship, is not felt or experienced in its movements nor in its exercise. Of itself it does not descend into the natural consciousness, and, ordinarily speaking, is, in consequence, unattended by any emotion. Yet it can, in spite of that, be very deep, strong and tender. The ordinary mark of true love is that the lover espouses the interests of the beloved. These interests he makes his own. What is an object of desire to the beloved becomes such to the lover. The latter seeks it as ardently as if it were an object of longing for himself— though it is with a view to placing it within reach of the beloved. The happiness of the beloved becomes the object of the lover, so that he pursues, with ardour, all that makes for or contributes to that happiness ; what the beloved wills that, too, the lover wills. So it is between God and the soul. The soul loves God when it wills what God wills and pursues the objects of that Divine will. God, in regard to His creature, desires and wills that creature's happiness and the perfection which

---

[2] This is true only when the act has in it the impress of the full energy of the habit. If the act is not in proportion to the intensity of the habit, things are otherwise. St. Thomas writes : " The exercise of the virtues (*i.e.*, good habits) is in the power of our will. Now, just as a man may have a habit without making use of it, so also may he use it in acts that do not correspond with its intensity. If the act corresponds in intensity to the habit, or surpasses it, the way is prepared for a development and increase of the habit. . . . But, on the other hand, if the intensity of the act falls short of the intensity of the habit, such an act does not prepare the way for an increase, but, on the contrary, for a decrease of the habit."—*S. Th.* I., II., Q. 52, A. 3.

is a means to that happiness. In this is involved the willing of all that makes for the creature's perfection. The perfection of the soul is proportioned to its likeness to God. Hence, *when the soul is so disposed towards God that it shows itself prompt to embrace what the divine will determines in its regard, it loves God.* In this promptitude it manifests the sign of pure love which, for the lover, consists in making the object of the will of the beloved the object of his own will. Love of God lies in making God's interests and objective the soul's own interests and objective. It is an identification of the soul's desires with the desires of God. It is making God another self. To seek the object of God's will is in final resort and ultimate analysis to seek God Himself, since God cannot seek but Himself. Hence great promptitude in embracing and fulfilling God's will is the indication of a great love of God. To act for the sole motive of contenting God by our actions is to act in the spirit of love of God. This love of God is not dependent on feeling or emotion but on the firmness of the act of the will and its freedom from admixture of any other motives but the motive of the fulfilment of God's will. It is true, of course, that this right-motived activity itself does not effect an increase in divine life. Increase in the divine life of grace can be produced by God alone through a further infusion of grace, but this pouring forth of grace follows infallibly on every good act that fulfils the condition stated.[3]   Every deliberate use,

---

[3] Supernatural life and supernatural love are increased by the sacraments also ; the actual increase depending on our disposition. If we approach the sacraments with the charity outlined in the text, the grace received will, by God's generosity, be most precious. For the relatively poor effect of the sacraments when not accompanied by the active charity spoken of in this context, see Ven. Libermann : *Ecrits Spirituels,* p. 65 and following pages.

therefore, of free will that has its origin in grace and is informed by the full measure of grace in the soul causes the soul to grow in stature and to attain to a higher degree of life. And this progress can be continued indefinitely as long as life lasts. Every day on earth will furnish us with as many opportunities as there are moments for the soul's acting from the principle of charity, and, therefore, every day can mark a stride forward in supernatural strength and vigour. If, therefore, the charity that is in us would find expression in the good acts we are continually doing, our souls would constantly grow in supernatural life and vigour. Development would cease only with death, which is the term of trial and merit. Unlike the natural life, this divine life of the soul is not, of itself, susceptible of decay or diminution. Its nature is to expand incessantly and to know no vicissitudes of weakness or death. No matter how strong or vigorous our bodily frame may be, a day will come when its energies will no longer be able to repair the losses it sustains in the effort of living, and the process of dissolution and disruption will begin. No matter how keen and powerful our intellect may have become, it, in its turn, will, with the weakening of the brain tissues that condition its activity, show signs of feebleness and eclipse. But no such fate can befall the life with which God endows our souls at our spiritual birth. As long as that life is allowed to function it will flourish. If, then, as so frequently happens, it shows no sign of increased strength, no signs of development, no signs of an inner reserve of power capable of high achievement for God, there can be no other cause than this, namely, that the greater part of the acts we do, from the time we begin to act deliberately, are not at all the outward expression of the infused virtue of charity—they are not the exercise of the life of grace within us. Not being so, they have no power to increase the soul's life. They spring from impulse, from natural inclination, or, at the most, from reason, even though externally they bear the appearance of goodness and rectitude. And even when grace, to some extent, enters into them, its action is so feeble and its influence so slight, when contrasted with the influence exerted by self-love, that the resultant movement of the soul is not of a degree of supernatural vigour proportionate to the actual life of the soul, and, hence, no development of life is attained. And when this condition of things becomes habitual, all the symptoms of spiritual atrophy speedily make their appearance. This is the lot of a great number of souls who are really animated by the good will to serve God, and who are moved by the sincere desire to possess at least that measure of righteousness which consists in the avoidance of evil.

God never meant that this spiritual dwarfdom should be the fate of His children. He does all that is necessary to prevent it, so much so that if we, on our part, continued to act as was our instinct to act when, at the dawn of life we were so readily docile to the promptings of grace, we should have escaped spiritual failure. In order to save us from making the mistake which renders our life on earth so barren of divine fruit and in order to instruct us in the art of living in such a way that our life should follow its normal development, the Lord has, within recent times, raised up a number of young saints, who, without *apparent* effort, have attained to a high degree of sanctity. Their lives as a rule present nothing remarkable in the way of external achievement. Many of us when comparing our lives with theirs may easily find, perhaps, that we are called upon to face greater trials, accomplish harder work, and make as painful decisions in the service of God as they. Their lives were outwardly very ordinary, frequently much more ordinary than our own. And yet, when we read the stories of these saints, we realise, with a certain sinking of the heart and with a sense of indefinable sadness, that they are different from what we are, and that they move in a world seemingly inaccessible to us. To assuage the pain we experience at the contemplation of the futility and emptiness of our lives, as contrasted with the fullness and the reality of the lives of God's servants, we persuade ourselves that these instances of sanctity are meant to be exceptional and are something more than the normal consequence of fidelity to ordinary graces.

This is the vain subterfuge of our self-love. We know instinctively that, if we probe deep enough into our hearts and examine with frankness the relations of our soul with God, we should have to confess that it is possible for us to eliminate from ourselves, aided as we would be by God's grace, that which constitutes the difference between these saints and ourselves. What sets them apart from the ordinary throng of good souls is that *from the beginning they made God the pivot on which they made their whole existence on earth to revolve,* and that they abided constantly in this disposition. They unrolled their whole life's activity under the eye, and in the presence of God. They referred to Him in

all things. They never identified themselves with their
own life or their own life's tasks. They habitually
asked themselves : " What will God say ? " They
looked upon each call on their human activity as coming,
at the very moment of its happening, straight from the
lips of God ; they did not regard it as something springing from the condition of things. They lived, as it
were, in God's house and not in their own. Life's
tasks became household duties which they accomplished
in such a way as to please the Master, but the tasks
were His, not theirs. The value of these tasks for them
lay in the fact that they were God's appointment, and
not in that they were materials out of which to fashion
for themselves a life and existence accommodated to
egoistic ideals. The revenue of their works went to
God and not to themselves, for they were not their works,
but His. They looked to Him in all things ; *His
pleasure was the sole determinant of their activity*. Love
for Him, the desire to do His will out of love, was what
made them do each thing, each day and at every moment
of the day. They did merely the things we do, but they
did them differently from us in this sense. They did
them for God ; we do them because they are *ours* to
do, and because in the doing of them we evolve and
build up *our* lives. They regarded their lives from God's
angle of vision, not from their own. We wish, for
instance, to indulge our own grief, undistracted by the
thought of an Absolute Power which may enquire as
to how we are bearing it. We will bear it properly and
well, but as becomes us. We wish to savour our own
joys—in isolation. We wish to get along by ourselves,
to hug our own joys, our own sorrows, without the

harassing preoccupying thought of God. The five talents and the two are used by God's saints in the interests of God : we put the one *talent* of our life in a napkin for ourselves—to possess it all to ourselves ; not to waste, to use or abuse ; but only to possess— and behold, we are condemned. The saints were obedient to their parents because God desired such obedience ; they saw God's order in it, just as they saw God's displeasure in their disobedience, before they adverted to the displeasure of their parents. It was the thought of God that flung them repentant, after their faults, into their own mothers' arms. They played with zest as we do, because God ordained that children should play, and they repented of their ill-humour, their temper or their other faults at play, because such things did not please God—He did not will that children should play so. They, when the time came for it, studied hard, not to make themselves learned, but because God exacted such application of them and was pleased that they should aspire after mental formation and the acquisition of knowledge. And so it was for everything else. *They did not live for themselves, they brought God into everything.* Love of Him was the source from which each act sprang—*desire to please Him was the sole objective* towards which it was directed. They were far more intent on the inner motive than on outward effect. They looked through their parents, they looked through the events of their life—to God. In this way every movement of the soul brought with it an increase of supernatural life and strength, and promoted the soul's growth.

In this we fail. We make the mistake of substituting

God's work for God, of thinking we are tending towards God, when we are making the accomplishment of His work the object towards which we are striving. We think we are promoting our soul's growth, when we are merely bringing into play the natural forces of body and mind. At the dawn of our christian life, when the virtues infused into our souls at baptism begin to stir into activity, we easily act under the influence of charity. God's thoughts and God's views govern our life. What He thinks about us and our doings is what influences us. Christian children brought up in a truly Catholic home naturally look to God as the Master of their existence and make the value of anything depend on His approval. In their own simple way they are prompt to consider bad and worthless what He disapproves of. In all things they naturally ask themselves : " What does God think ? " If they do wrong they repent, not because of the intrinsic disagreeable consequences of what they have done, but because it has displeased God. They act and reason thus, because in them the virtue of charity, infused at baptism, functions with little or no opposition. The perversion due to original sin has not yet been developed by their own vicious acts and hence their nature puts no great obstacle to the activity of the infused virtues. But as they grow up, egoism begins to assert itself. Gradually they begin to withdraw their life from God, and make it their own, to use for their own ends. If they are good christians, they will carefully avoid offending God, but will no longer act from the sole motive of His love. The thought of Him comes into their lives only at intervals, when circumstances arise in which they are in danger of infringing His laws.

But where this contingency does not exist, they develop
their existence and put forth their activities for reasons
that are not the love of God, and that take little account
of His desires. Taking things at their best, it is the
natural interest of the occupation they are engaged in,
the desire to succeed, or mere necessity, that dictates,
guides and governs the exercise of their faculties. Even
when the higher calling of religious life is followed,
things are modified only to a slight degree. We still
strive to avoid offending God without labouring to
stifle our own egoism or detach ourselves from our own
life. We flatter ourselves we are doing what God
desires of us, if only we fling ourselves with earnestness
and zeal into the accomplishment of the duties that the
state of life we have embraced imposes on us. It would
seem undeniable that in doing what is the work of God,
we are doing God's work—that we are doing what God
wants of us. This, though apparently a truism, is not
so. To use a scholastic phrase, we may be doing God's
work materially, without doing it formally. What God
views in our life is the *mode in which our activity issued
from us, not the effect in which it terminates.* We persist
in regarding things in the reverse order. We are prone
to consider the external issue of our activity, rather
than the mode of its origin. *Results, rather than origins,
preoccupy us.* We think that once we have done well
God's work in the world, it is well with us. In the
putting forth of our activity we make the *perfection
of the achievement—the perfection of the work—our
object, rather than the perfection of ourselves.* Yet the
purpose of man's struggle is his own spiritual development and its end, his perfection—not the perfection of

something distinct from himself. Man's perfection is wrought through his winning God and possessing Him. It is to attain God that he must aim at in his life's work— not the satisfaction merely of seeing his task well done. We persuade ourselves that in carefully doing God's work we are seeking God. In reality we may be, in a subtle manner, seeking ourselves. We can put forth an excessive amount of energy where self can somehow or other find its part in what we are doing. And self finds its satisfaction in every activity that is called forth from us by impulse, by the mere desire to succeed, by the natural tendency to give free play to our powers, or by the mere interest of the task in which we are engaged.

Even when we are not moved by ambition, by vain-glory, by the desire of praise or by love of success, we still are not free from everything that can tarnish or vitiate our work. We can approach the task set by God in the spirit of the artist—and not in the spirit of the child working in God's house. The artist as such labours dispassionately. He is all intent on the work that is coming into being under his hands. The perfection of that work is the object that determines and dominates every movement of eye and hand and brain. His task is done when some element of beauty or perfection is realised and made evident to the senses in the material that his art employs. *Something splendid has been done—but it has not, necessarily, perfected him as a man, though it may have perfected him as an artist.* So likewise with ourselves. In the tasks of life we are prone to allow ourselves to be governed by the sole motive of the perfect accomplishment of what is set us to do. We foolishly think that God is concerned with the perfection of the works that come from our hands. Hence it comes that there are many who, to the eyes of men, have rendered great services to God, have accomplished great labours in His cause, and yet who, in His eyes, have done nothing. *Doing* issues in *effects—action terminates in perfection.* God is indifferent to *effects.* He is attentive to *actions* because He is interested in perfection. Action has its term in the agent—immanent in him, producing perfection in him. *Mere doing* terminates in effects and all its value is found in the effect—the thing effected. His own life in our souls and the growth of that life is the only concern of God. Whatever activity of ours does not foster that life has no value in His eyes. It is *action* not *making; living not mere effecting, that God looks to in us.* The perfection in a thing which is due to the spirit of the artist as such is all in the work, and not, to any extent, in the worker. God considers nothing as living action except the movement of our soul and its faculties which has its origin in charity and is directed towards charity as its final end. Nothing else has any reality in it for God. What we do has reality in it for Him only to the extent that it is informed by charity independently of any external effect achieved. God is life itself—God can be drawn only towards life—He can be attracted to such actions as have true life in them, and this real life belongs only to those acts that are animated by divine charity. All other movement, no matter how forcibly it may strike the senses, no matter how potent it may appear to reason, is to Him as death. The saints understood this well; hence it was their great concern to bring every pulsation of their deliberate existence under the dominant influence of grace. The love of God, that is the good pleasure of God, was made the sole moving principle of their life on earth and they in consequence grew in spiritual stature by the accomplishment of the most ordinary and trivial duties of the day. "Those who are not saints are all absorbed in the doing of things, and allow their life to pour itself out uselessly in the matter of external activities—like water over a thirsty soil." They allow themselves to ignore that the real activity of life is within us and consists in using our powers to give us what is wanting to us as men, and to introduce into our souls the perfection which they need—namely, the life of God and with it God Himself.

This does not imply, of course, that the person aiming at a supernatural life is to take refuge in immobility through fear lest self-love may insinuate itself into his external activity. A strong inner life is not equivalent to an inactive or indolent life. Quite the contrary. There is no inner life without Charity. A man has Charity, that is, he loves God, when he pursues the interests of God with the same eagerness as the self-lover, that is the egoist, pursues his own. One cannot love God with any intensity without being driven by that love to make God's purposes on earth to be realised. God is charity. His purpose is to achieve the welfare, the peace and the happiness of mankind. God is the doer of good to His creatures. He is ever working at this object. To the Jews Jesus said: "My Father worketh until now; and I work." [4] God is ever actively

4 St. John v. 17.

beneficent. It is impossible to become intimate with Him—and intimacy is the fruit of all real prayer—without catching His spirit. The truly interior soul is always energetic with the energy of God. The saints are always " doers ". Efficiency stamps their work. They have been the great benefactors of mankind. Enduring works of charity mark their passage on earth. They too pass, doing good.[5] Without seeking success in the sense of making it a motive of action, none have been so successful as they. Charity is essentially energetic. The love of God necessarily expresses itself in devotedness to one's fellow man. To love is not to have a mere pious aspiration for another's good but to procure that good actively by every means in one's power. " My little children ", says St. John, " let us not love in word, nor in tongue, but in *deed* and in truth ".[6] It would be an illusion then to take refuge in inactivity lest activity should be vitiated by self-seeking. There can be a devotedness to prayer which can be a very vicious egoism. It can be a secret—a camouflaged (if the word be permissible in such a connection) refuge for indolence and self-indulgence. There is such a thing as the " luxury of prayer " indulged in by those for whom it can frequently be a clothing for indifference to the welfare and happiness of others. Such prayer is only seeming prayer. It is an illusion. It is not real prayer. The man who prays in spirit and in truth can never be slothful. His life will necessarily be effective of good for others. The soul that aims at perfect charity in its actions must not shrink from action,

[5] Acts x. 38.
[6] St. John iii. 18.

through fear of self-love, but fling itself energetically into action and labour to purify its doings of all self-love and all self-seeking. It is to be noted that what is imperfect is not bad—it is simply not perfect. A taint of egoism may creep into good works and yet leave these works *substantially* sound and supernatural. But in all things it is well to have clearly before one's mind the cardinal principle that what a man does or achieves must forge himself to a better form even though it may not result in a better form being wrought in something outside himself.[7] The sculptor's work must, whilst evolving a form of beauty out of marble, tend towards the development of a higher moral life and a better form of spiritual beauty in his own soul. His " doing " must be an action, that is something that not merely issues in a perfection in the work but also a perfection in the worker.

To live rightly, that is to live in such a way as to promote life by the act of living, one must not only do right things but one must do them in the right way. *There is only one right way for us Christians to act, and that is, to do all things for God and because of Him.* The more directly the thought of Him bears on that movement of our will which issues in the effecting of something, the more perfect and the more life-giving is our activity. If we consider something else than God, there is danger of the effective influence of charity being diminished. If we make the intrinsic result of our acts the object we aim at, and still will it as a means towards

---

[7] A man can be wrought, by his activities (when inspired by charity) to an ever higher state of spiritual beauty and perfection, even though his efforts, as far as practical results in the world are concerned, may issue in failure. Man's idea of success differs much from that of God.

serving God, our action is in order and meritorious as
well as good ; but it is not as perfect as when directed
towards God Himself. Besides, there is always the
danger for us of making an end of what is a mere means,
if the attention of our soul is too closely directed to the
execution of those tasks that Providence places in our
way. Gradually the interest in the work itself, the
natural desire to do well, that on which we are engaged,
will occupy the place of God, as the motive (or final
cause) of our actions. To escape this danger, it does not
suffice to formulate a right intention from time to time.
Unless the motive of the love of God, or the desire to
fulfil His good pleasure, really influences the act of our
will that we are at the moment eliciting, this act will
not have the supernatural vitality that it ought to have.
The act is vital only if it springs from charity—if it does
not do so, it has no vitality as far as the supernatural life
is concerned. It is not the outcome of life and it cannot
minister to life. No previous mechanical formulation
of a right intention can rectify this. To secure ourselves
against the continual wastage of our existence on earth
we must bring the thought of God to bear on the details
of our life as they develop themselves hour by hour.
This ideal is not beyond us by God's grace. To live
so that every act of ours is done under the influence of
Charity it is not needed that the thought of God be
always actually before us. It suffices that we have
developed the spirit in which all our life is suspended
to the Divine Will. This attitude abides in its effect
even when we are not consciously adverting to God.
We must then cultivate a spirit of aloofness from he
things we effect outside of ourselves, concentrate upon

the effort of making our acts proceed interiorly from a principle of grace and learn to look upon the external conditions of our life and the activities that they call forth from us as simply occasions provided for us by God to elicit from our souls effective acts of love of Him and of obedience to His will.

NOTE.—Life is not measured by the amount of external activity, but by the closeness of the union of our soul with the spirit of God and by the extent of the *subordination* of the inner beginnings of our actions to the influence of the Holy Ghost, to the influence of His grace.

We are living in Christ in proportion to the degree of sanctifying grace that is in our souls. A great measure of sanctifying grace means a high state of vitality; a small measure, low vitality.

CHAPTER IV

THE WAY OF PEACE

" He that shall lose his life for My sake shall save it."—St.
Luke ix. 24.

We are all consumed by an insatiable desire for
happiness, and though this yearning after beatitude is
not in itself a torment, for it is the essential aspiration
of our whole being, it becomes, in fact, a torment,
because our efforts after it are being constantly thwarted,
and our attempts to grasp it are being perpetually
frustrated. The pains of all kinds, internal and external,
affecting us directly in ourselves, or affecting us indirectly
in the sorrows we endure because of others, never allow
us to be at peace, never permit us to enjoy for long a
state of contentment. When the woes of life press on
us we are keenly sensitive to the pain they cause, our
attention is wholly absorbed by this pain and we are
conscious of no other desire in our being save that of
escaping the sufferings we are enduring. It is our belief
when we are a prey to grief, or sorrow or pain, that the
trial or trials we are actually enduring are the sole
obstacle to our well-being. We fondly believe that were
these trials to end, we should possess the happiness that
we are ever yearning after. This is a delusive hope.
Even if we were to enjoy perfect health of body and
were to escape the sorrows caused by separation and

death; even were we to be exempt from the grief provoked by the sufferings of those dear to us; were we to live in that happy condition of things which should give us free scope to enjoy the pleasures of intellect and imagination—in a word, even were we to know no sorrow or pain or loss, and were we at the same time to be provided with all things which can minister to our physical and mental well-being, we should still be a prey to restless longings and unsatisfied cravings. *All those things that a man can possess may become his, but they cannot become himself;* they are of man but they cannot be man. No matter how perfectly they may be possessed they remain external to him, and therefore cannot perfect him in himself. *And it is his own perfection that man is instinctively reaching out after in all his restless strivings,* or rather it is God, Who alone can complete and perfect man. We are unhappy because we are not perfect, and we are not perfect because we have not that plenitude of existence for which we crave and for which we have the capacity. Perfection means fullness of life, and fullness of life means complete happiness.

Of ourselves we have not life (as the Saviour understands that term), but merely an immense capacity for life. Every natural thing reaches out after the possession and enjoyment of the fullest measure of existence of which it is capable. We, by our baptism, are made participant in a higher than created nature. We, in a mysterious manner, are made sharers in a divine form of existence. Emerging from the waters of regeneration we possess it only in its beginnings. It is in us, but in an inchoate form. As is the case with the natural life

we receive at our birth, this inchoate divine existence
participated in reaches out after fullness and completion
in us. Of itself it tends towards expansion and development as must all forms of life. All the restless, feverish
strivings after something we know not what, that we
experience constantly within ourselves, are provoked
by the deep-seated fundamental realisation of the
emptiness of our being, its profound limitations, its
finiteness, its abysmal unfilled capacities, and its own
utter insufficiency to itself.

The light shed by Faith on our origin and our destiny
makes us see more clearly still our utter nothingness in
the supernatural order. The gifts of God given us in
Baptism, great as they are, do not take away this sense
of incompleteness ; they rather intensify it. Outside
the order of grace our yearnings would be satisfied
when we should have attained that measure of being
which should consist in the assimilation to our minds
of every created object of thought. The mind, as it
were, becomes what it knows ; it draws its object to
an ideal form of existence within itself : it enters into
possession of and makes it its own, in an immaterial
or spiritual manner. When the spirit should have thus
taken to itself, and made one with itself all objects of
thought, its strivings would have attained to the supreme
height of being and nature's desires would be satisfied.[1]
But once the created spirit enters into the order of
grace, its horizons become wider, its aspirations higher,
and its capacities deeper. Its needs and its wants become
infinite, and transcend all created limits. Grace has made

[1] Aristotle says : " The mind becomes in a certain manner all things "
(i.e., when it knows all things).

the soul a gaping void which can be filled up with nothing less than God ; it has made what was a finite capacity, infinite. This is the secret of the restlessness that tortures humanity, and affects both bad and good alike. In the present order of things all, whether they advert to it or not, are created for the same destiny ; believers and unbelievers, Christians and infidels, faithful and faithless, have as their final end to possess God by vision and in that possession to hold and to own infinite life. " A species of communion is at the origin of the supernatural order. Grace makes us participate in the Divine nature by endowing us with a power of tending towards God in Himself. It is, as it were, a ray of the Divine intellectuality penetrating our soul and raising it up to embrace God as an object specifying the soul's acts of knowledge and love. Henceforth He becomes, Himself alone, our food, the food of our spirit. We are not actually in exercise of our supernatural life, save in associating ourselves with His eternal act, by movements of faith and love, called into play at the moment." [2]   Our being, therefore, once it has received the first touch of Sanctifying Grace, is submitted to the pressure of a mighty inward force.[3]   The element of life in us struggles against its limitations and strives after expansion. It reaches up to God Himself, to bring Him more and more into the soul.

All men are urged onward by this consuming desire for life. As things are, there is no life for us except that of God. The divine source of that life abides in the

---

[2] *La Vie Spirituelle*, Vol. XVI., p. 357, June, 1927.
[3] This inward pressure set up by the strivings of supernatural life is not, *per se*, a part of consciousness. It is of an ontological, not a psychological character.

soul that is in the state of sanctifying grace. As water from the spring, so life tends to well up from that source and communicate itself to the soul. Every other form of life but this has in it the elements of mortality and decay. Our consciousness tells us that the existence which moment by moment is passing from us is but a form of death. We cannot lay hold of it ; we cannot retain it : it slips from our grasp and leaves nothing with us as it goes. The before and the after are not in our power, and even the present glides away from us as we seize it. Were we to have all power, all know-ledge, all possessions, they would not give us even the illusion that we had thereby secured the perfection of existence—for being finite, limited, transient, they would leave us still dissatisfied. Death in itself cannot be an object of desire for us—and everything that is transient, passing, that knows succession, is touched with death. Men, realising that the existence they have consciousness of, no matter how perfect it is or might be, is still one that is made up of succeeding moments, turn from it, as from death, and grope blindly after what will not pass. *Life, to be perfect, must be possessed altogether :* there must be no past which is gone, no present which is going, no future which is to come. *It must be permanent, abiding, full and without succession.* Life which would be past is lost life ; that which is to come would not be life possessed, and that which is passing would be life in decay. *God alone, as He is in Himself, realises the full conditions of perfect life. He alone can impart it by giving Himself.* Men, in their feverish, passionate, almost agonised struggles to seize, from out the perpetual flux in which they find themselves involved, some abiding, permanent, assured existence knowing no vicissitude of change or decay, are really groping after God—and after God as He designs to give Himself to men in the supernatural order. These restless strivings are very pronounced in the case of those who have received the vocation to be the adopted children of God. Though the stirrings of grace and its reaching out after God are not a fact of consciousness, yet the profound dissatisfaction and restlessness and indefinable cravings which probably every christian soul, at times, experiences are due to this—that outside the realm of consciousness a thirst after God to be loved and possessed has been generated by grace. Though that thirst does not itself penetrate into consciousness, yet the restlessness which is felt may be traced to it as its ultimate cause. To have the life which we are driven to seek by the forces created in us by grace, we must have God; we must bring Him into our souls. As long as we are not in possession of life we shall be tortured by the insatiable desire for it, and know no peace. There is no tranquillity possible for us unless we possess God.[4]

As has been said then, life is always seeking its fullest expansion, and uses its innate forces to make the elements, which it takes to itself, minister to its nutrition and growth. The germ of supernatural life deposited in our souls by Baptism is submitted to the same law of expan-

---

[4] Cf. " The Nostalgia for the supernatural is as it were the urge that drives the whole christian world, and it seems at the root of all christian movements, even of heresies . . . the trouble with the post-Christian is that he is quite unable to narrow himself down again to the little world (from the spiritual point of view) which the pagan lived in. He still preserves the christian nostalgia, without the christian belief."—*Colosseum*, December, 1934, p. 56.

sion. It, too, like nature, is driven by an inward necessity to evolve itself to the utmost. From the first
moment of self-determined existence there are stirred
up in the soul cravings which cannot be stilled, as the
tiny germ of the life of grace begins to reach out after
its complete evolution. The soul cannot know contentment unless it is providing that nourishment by which
its supernatural life is nurtured ; it will never know final
repose until grace has attained its fullest measure in the
Beatific Vision.

*Now, it is only from God alone, dwelling in a super-
natural manner in the soul, that the latter can draw draughts
of life.* To grow and expand it must, as it were, drink
of God. " But the water that I shall give him shall
become in him a fountain of water springing up into
life everlasting." [5] The source of living water in the
depths of the created spirit is the Divinity Itself. The
soul, by grace, is empowered to possess within it that
Fountain of Life. It can envelop the divinity within
it in acts of divine faith and divine love. These acts
of faith and love not only place the soul by the fountain
but cause the fountain to gush forth more abundantly.
It is Faith that points out to the soul that from which
its life may draw nutrition : but it is charity, or love of
God, that brings about the union of the soul with the
source of life. It is love that brings us in contact with
God—and with every aspiration of love God is, as it
were, drawn into the soul, as the atmosphere is, in
breathing, drawn into the lungs. Nothing further is
needed to give the life of grace the nourishment it
requires, and give it that expansion towards which it

[5] St John iv. 14.

tends. The virtue of Charity unites the soul with God, and every act of the virtue enables the soul to draw its Creator more and more into itself. It is in vain that it would fling every object short of God on the fire that burns within it. The flames would find in these objects nothing with which to feed themselves, and would gradually sink down into ashes. This fire that has been created in us by God can be nourished and maintained only by the Divinity Itself.

Peace cannot come to us except through perfection. Advancement in perfection is progress in life, which for us, children of God, means progress in the Divine Life given us by grace. And since this development is reached through the soul's drawing God into itself by acts of love, it is evident that the constant aim of our earthly activities ought to be the acquisition in ever greater measure of Divine charity. " And now there remain Faith, Hope and Charity, these three : *but the greatest of these is charity : follow after* charity, be zealous for spiritual gifts," [6] says St. Paul : and again he repeats to the Colossians : " But *above all* these things have charity, which is the bond of perfection." [7] The phrase, " All these things ", to which the apostle counsels the Christians to prefer Charity, refers to a series of moral precepts, the practice of which would imply the possession of high moral rectitude. And yet the apostle tells the Colossians to lift their aspirations higher and aim directly at the intimate friendship and love of God Himself, as He is in Himself ; for it is this love, and not the mere morality which it includes and transcends,

[6] 1 Cor. xiii. 13–14.
[7] Coloss i. 3.

that will give that fullness of Being that our nature,
supernaturalised, reaches out after with insatiable longing.

If, then, we were to use our life and what it brings
us in the way of doing and suffering *as supernatural
prudence dictates, we should use it as something
whose function is to yield us Divine Charity and
nothing that conflicts with Divine Charity.* As the bee
distils honey from the flowers, so should we distil
Divine Love from every activity which is called forth
from us through the circumstances of our existence on
earth. Unless our acts are informed by Divine Love,
and our intentions are directed by it and towards it,
the use of our free will will not have that form which
it ought to have if it is to be of that perfection demanded
by our condition as children of God. If in our acts we
aim at mere righteousness of conduct, even though the
motive be supernatural, God is not perfectly attained,
and there is, therefore, not so great an increase in supernatural vigour as if we made charity our final object.

Many, in pursuit of the final end of the christian life,
prefer to devote their attention to acquiring perfection
of conduct rather than to cultivating the love of God,
and find, as the result of their efforts, that they are as
far off from one as from the other. To seek to avoid
offending God, by watching over our conduct, rather
than by inciting ourselves to an affection for Him,
Whom we wish not to displease, is an endeavour that
meets with scant success. Eagerness to possess moral
rectitude and shrinking from the ugliness of moral
imperfection is not quite the same thing as actually
seeking intimacy with God. Many there are who are
more moved by the ideal of their own freedom from

moral flaw than by the ideal of loving God with the love of friendship or with the affection of children.   In this lies the explanation of the poor quality of the lives of so many Christians.   They have not resolutely set before them *God to love with all their hearts, and to love with an ever-increasing love every day, as the object towards which to direct all the energies of their souls.*   They have set their eyes on a lower ideal—to work out their existence on earth in a righteous way, but according to their own tastes.   They determine not to offend God, but they have no intention of suspending every moment, every act, every thought, every desire, every feeling, every aspiration to His good Will and Pleasure.   They do not seek to misuse their lives, they desire only to use them according to their own good will and pleasure.   Like the prodigal, they ask the substance of their term of earthly existence from their Heavenly Father in order that they may dispose of it freely.   Their intention is not bad ; they have the desire to regulate each action by the standard of moral rectitude.   They merely do not aspire to have their every act regulated by the dictates of paternal love.   They do not desire actually to squander their existence ; they merely intend to use it for human and personal ends.   Whilst doing all this they have no wish to be estranged from God their Father ; on the contrary, they are ever tortured by the fear of His displeasure.   They make continual efforts to maintain good relations with Him.   They will do anything to succeed in this, short of the one thing necessary, the surrender of their lives to His controlling love.   Finding themselves in spite of all their efforts to keep within the limits of the moral law, sometimes through frailty, surprise, weakness or passion, betrayed into thoughts or acts which do not conform to the christian code, they, at fixed intervals, institute a strict examination of conscience and cleanse their souls in the Sacrament of Penance. After each reconciliation they are firmly resolved to avoid all sin and are persuaded that the uneasiness they have felt, when oppressed by the sense of guilt, will act as a sufficient deterrent against sin for the future. But the impressions created during the time of repentance gradually fade and the faults recommence. Many strive to secure themselves against these lapses by exercises of mortification or by practices of devotion. But again, utilising these things for the sole purpose of being able to keep their conscience free from guilt, and so to escape the serious consequences of God's displeasure, they do not find in their practices of religion what they hoped for. They have not the peace of soul that comes of the abiding sense of God's presence and God's love, and the uneasiness caused by their habitual uncertainty as to their spiritual state poisons the pleasure they hoped to extract from their existence, rationally enjoyed. Their endeavour to control their life's activities solely by the requirements of the moral code leaves the currents of their thoughts, their feelings, and their emotions, open to a multitude of conflicting natural influences, which produce a continual restlessness and agitation. This agitation, restlessness and inconstancy is due to the fact that there is present no unifying force to bring to bear on the multitudinous activities of the inner life, and make them all converge on one object.

To secure peace of soul and to dispel all troubles of conscience there is only one course to pursue—it is to aim

at nothing lower than God in the exercise of our free will.
Our will is the faculty that commands all our powers.
To act (that is, to put forth a human act) is to use our
powers in such a way as to give us what is wanting to
us as men—to complete and perfect us. It is only the
life of God poured into our souls by God Himself
through vital contact with them that can give us that
perfection. It is charity that brings about union and,
therefore, vital contact between the soul and God.
The Divinity, being Life itself, must necessarily vivify
that with which it is in vital union. The union between
spirit and spirit is vital when it is brought about by the
spiritual activities of the faculties of will and intellect.
We must " act ", then, to give ourselves the possession
of God—ever more and more. *Happiness is, then, for
us, and peace lies in making God the term of our " actions ".*
This, and not mere righteousness, is what we must seek ;
our very observation of the commandments must be
an expression of filial love and regard ; what is more, it
is only love for God that can secure us effectively against
failure in perfect observance. *To keep the Commandments
without the love of God is impossible, to love God without
keeping the Commandments is equally impossible.* Hence
it was that Our Lord identified the whole law with the
love of God and the love of one's neighbour, explaining
that the latter was included in the former when rightly
understood. This is the greatest and the first commandment : " Thou shalt love the Lord Thy God with
thy whole heart, and with thy whole soul, and with
thy whole mind." . . . And the second is like to this :
" Thou shalt love thy neighbour as thyself." On these
two commandments dependeth the whole law and the

prophets.[8] The election of God as the unique object of its love will alone set up unity and harmony in the soul's activities and establish therein the reign of perfect peace.

This is not an impracticable ideal : God never asks the impossible. Of course man must live. Life expresses itself in action. The multiple relations which bind a man to his family, to his city, to his country and to his God, make incessant calls on his activities. He must endeavour to respond to all in a spirit of fortitude, kindness, forbearance, devotedness, prudence and justice. He must in all things strive to be " good ". But he must aim at this goodness not for the sake of being good but because God would have him so. He must shun what is unkindly, base, selfish and unbecoming, because as the adopted child of God he incurs God's displeasure in succumbing to any of these failings in his handling of life's tasks and duties.

Making the love of God the sole object of the christian endeavour, we should have *as the matter of our examen of conscience our real attitude or disposition of soul with regard to the demands of Divine Charity.*[9] *Our vigilance over ourselves should be directed towards eliminating from our actions all the elements that tend to supplant, to corrupt, or to diminish the charity in them.* When seeking to purify our conscience, we should ask ourselves if our manner of living our life responds to the essential requirements of a real undivided love for God. Our watchfulness over our interior, over our dispositions, our decisions, our judgments, should have as its aim

[8] St. Matt. xxii. 37–40.
[9] Cf. *supra.*, p. 329.

not merely the flight from sin and its occasions—the obstacles to sanctify—but rather the direction of all our energies towards the development of the love of God in our souls. We ought to examine ourselves not only on our faults, but on our advancement in charity, questioning ourselves repeatedly as to whether our affective faculties are rightly disposed in relation to the end of the life of grace, that is, God to see and love. Charity rectifies our will with respect to the final end, and, therefore, from it flows rectitude of heart with regard to the means.

The real reason why we find it difficult to concentrate all our efforts on regulating our life according to the exigencies of divine love is that we instinctively feel that this demands the complete surrender of our lives to God. *To possess life in its fullness, that is, to submit ourselves in all things to the law of charity, is to lose our life utterly.* " For whosoever shall seek to save his life, shall lose it : and whosoever shall lose it, shall preserve it." [10] All men of good will are ready to carry their renouncement to the limits prescribed by the moral law ; that is as far as foregoing every satisfaction condemned by reason. Many would find it relatively easy to face physical death in the service of Christ. But the life that the Master calls on us to sacrifice is something more dear to us still than that which comes of the union of soul with body. There is nothing so intimate to us, so closely knit to the very elements of our being, as our free activity. It is more one with us than the child is with the mother whose life it shares. It is the fruit of our life and part of our being. There

[10] St. Luke xvii. 33 ; ix. 24.

is a deep satisfaction in the very function of life, especially
of rational life, unfolding itself in the exercise of the
faculties of will and intelligence on objects proportionate
to them.   Now to renounce, as it were, our dominion
over all this, to make a complete abandonment of it
into the hands of God, that is a rude sacrifice.   To withhold all self-gravitating interest in what we do, and
have no other motive for acting than to please God,
demands a detachment which few have the courage to
aim at.   And yet, the attaining of this detachment
wonderfully simplifies one's life on earth.   The christian
who esteems human things only according to the
measure in which they can contribute to the development
of charity in his soul acquires a perfect freedom of spirit
with regard to all created objects.   In the words of St.
Paul he becomes as they " that use the world as if they
used it not ".   There is no danger that this attitude will
lead to apathy or inefficiency in work.   The order of
Divine Charity demands that the powers of God's
servants be employed with all the energy and attention
that the perfect acquittal of their tasks calls for.   Care-
lessness, indolence or slovenliness in work cannot
dispose the soul for, or merit an increase of divine love.
If our activity is to merit for us an increase of grace and
love, it must contain the full perfection that we are
capable of giving it.   But it must neither be the pleasure
of " doing ", nor the natural attraction of perfection
to achieve in what we are doing, that supplies the
motive that inspires our work.   *We should forego all
that, and adhere to the unique motive of the love of God.*
In acting in this manner our gaze is, as it were, turned
away from our life as it develops itself by our activity,

and is fixed on the face of God, to read therein the tokens of His approval. In this we lose all interest in life for its own sake and come to esteem it only as a means to charity. The nature of the task on which we are engaged becomes a matter of indifference to us. Whether it be congenial or uncongenial we can make it minister to the growth of divine love. And as each thing can serve equally well for that purpose we can pass from one thing to another with perfect freedom and ease ; our activity is regulated, not according to the intrinsic good that is to issue from what we are engaged in, but according to the measure of love of God that can be infused into the doing of and the degree of grace that can be extracted from it. One might fear that in reason of this our work would lack that effectivity which comes to it from giving it the impress of what is called " personality ". That is, perhaps, true, but the work gains a higher effectivity through bearing the impress of a higher personality. The less our work bears the stamp of ourselves, by this substitution of the motive of Divine Love, the more it will bear the mark of the personality of Our Divine Lord. The quest of unalloyed charity in our acts secures that in the doing of them we reproduce, in some little measure, the image of Jesus in ourselves. The least of our operations done in this spirit reflects something of the ethical beauty of the Saviour.

Another important advantage flows from the same source. The deep-seated cause of the anxiety that constantly gnaws at the heart is our uncertainty with regard to the state of our soul. The agonising doubt as to whether we are in God's friendship tortures us continually and makes us shrink from the certainty that comes with death. Our fear of dissolution is traceable to this source. Now Charity, Scripture tells us, drives out fear. Having renounced in the pursuit of Charity the absorbing interest that our own life has for each of us, there is substituted, for the interest we have abandoned, an interest in God and Divine things. As the taste for life lived according to our own will disappears, the taste for God grows. The conviction that nothing is of value, except Divine Grace, deepens. Detachment from the earth becomes easy, as a consequence. Nothing can attract us except what has value and worth in our eyes and, nothing but God holding our esteem, we embrace what leads to Him and find little difficulty in renouncing what holds us back from Him. Making the demands of Divine love, rather than the mere freedom from fault, the theme of our examinations of conscience, we are unable to bear the consciousness, not only of sin, but even of what diminishes the love of God in our souls. We achieve freedom not only from deliberate mortal, but even from deliberate venial sins. As a result, it is easy to discover in ourselves these three signs which St. Thomas regards as giving a moral certainty of being in the state of grace : namely—inability to discover in ourselves sins unrepented of, an aloofness from the things of this earth, and the faculty of taking delight only in God and the things that appertain to Him. Having lost taste for created things as such, we acquire a taste for God alone. And when one has arrived at this state of esteeming nothing of any worth except Divine Grace and Divine Charity, one has found " *The Way of Peace* ".